Outdoor Life's
DEER
HUNTING
BOOK

AN OUTDOOR LIFE BOOK

Outdoor Life's
DEER HUNTING BOOK

Foreword by
CHET FISH
Editor-in-Chief, *Outdoor Life*

OUTDOOR LIFE / **HARPER & ROW**

New York, Evanston, San Francisco, London

Library of Congress Catalog Card Number: 74-83593
SBN: 06-013267-1

Designed by Howard S. Leiderman

Manufactured in the United States of America

Contents

Continued

Foreword

One sort of letter I get from time to time says something like this: "You've got a pretty good magazine, but why don't you run more stories on deer hunting?"

Well, in *Outdoor Life* we run a lot of stories about deer hunting. The popularity of information about our Number 1 big-game animal is hard to exaggerate. And yet in a magazine that aims to cover the wide-ranging interests of active hunters and fishermen and their families, no single issue can come anywhere near telling a reader everything he'd like to know about deer hunting. A book can come a lot closer.

I once heard an editor (not an *Outdoor Life* editor) say, "If you've read one deer story, you've read them all."

I felt sorry for the guy, because he didn't know how wrong he was. And now he's doing something else for a living. Some observers might even think that if you've read one deer book, you've read them all. This book you've just opened shows how far wrong that opinion is.

My feelings about *Outdoor Life's Deer Hunting Book* are hard to describe. Whichever chapter I look at makes me feel as though I'm meeting a friend I haven't seen for a while. Most of these chapters appeared as stories in the magazine under the editorship of Bill Rae, my predecessor. But I had a hand one way or another in getting most of them into print, so I feel a closeness to the words and to the writers.

I feel especially close to the two pieces that appeared since I became editor of the magazine — "Small Drives for Big Bucks" and "Butchering the Easy Way." How many stories have you read about driving deer? How many have you read about butchering? Probably plenty of both. You might think nothing is left to say on either subject. Yet Norm Nelson has a good many little-known tips to pass on to you about driving deer — ideas that increase your chances for getting your venison. And Bob Davidson reports on a new way to approach deer butchering that doesn't require you to be a veteran deer hunter or professional butcher to get gratifying results. In these days of ever-higher meat prices, this chapter alone can be worth far more to you than the price of the book.

Every chapter in this book is helpful on its own. And in combination, the thirty of them form a unique information bank for deer hunters all across the nation. I'm not saying that reading this book is a guarantee you'll shoot your deer this year or any other year. But it will sure help you avoid a lot of mistakes you might otherwise make.

Neither am I saying that this is the very last word in books on deer hunting. But this one, packed with lore from Jack O'Connor, Erwin A. Bauer, Byron Dalrymple, Clyde Ormond, Charlie Elliott, Ben East, and all the rest, just might be the best book on deer hunting to come along so far.

Chet Fish
Editor-in-Chief
Outdoor Life Magazine

Outdoor Life's
DEER HUNTING BOOK

Bauer and others regard the whitetail as the world's smartest big-game animal. Here, with tail flagged high in alarm, a good buck explodes away.

The Whitetail

Erwin A. Bauer

Last fall Lew Baker blew his finest opportunity in forty years of big-game hunting. Lew is a bachelor and retired farmer who has done more than his share of seeking trophies around the world. With all that experience behind him, he doesn't make too many mistakes in the field.

Despite Lew's wandering, far from home base in Ohio, his favorite quarry is the whitetail deer, and he wouldn't miss the deer season for any reason. He usually buys several nonresident licenses so that he can hunt deer in as many states as possible. Late last fall, he hunted in northern Wisconsin, and that's where this incident occurred.

It was not one of Wisconsin's best seasons. Lew, in several days of watching and waiting, had seen only a few nervous does. But one

This chapter originally appeared in the July 1972 issue of *Outdoor Life* under the title "Whitetails, Hit or Miss."

bitterly cold morning, he found a set of very large tracks that virtually shouted big buck. The tracks were fresh.

"I decided," Lew told me later, "that my best bet was to follow
that animal no matter where or how far it went."

By noon, my friend had gotten no glimpse of the animal — but the
unhurried hoofprints continued across a thin blanket of snow. The
deer seemed to be wandering aimlessly, but then the tracks led Lew
to a highway. Instead of crossing, the buck had turned sharply west,
directly into a wind that seemed to grow stronger by the minute.
Lew was thoroughly chilled but kept pushing ahead, knowing that
the odds had suddenly changed in his favor. The deer would be
unable to scent his approach, and the howling wind would blot out
the crunch of his boot pacs on the snow. Even the buck's vision
would be impaired because the cruel wind was now laced with
driven snow.

Lew followed the deer tracks down a thicket-covered slope to a
small boggy stream at the bottom. In the soft earth, not yet frozen, he
noticed how deep the hoofprints were. He could be sure that the
buck was a very heavy deer.

Next the tracks led around a hillside toward a balsam swamp
where Lew had bagged venison in the past. Maybe the buck would
bed down there. Instinctively, Lew checked the safety on his .30/06
Remington Model 760. He felt a fresh surge of excitement — or call
it what it really was — buck fever. Lew slowed his slow pace still
more so that he'd be ready for anything.

Suddenly the snow erupted not twenty feet in front of him, and
the giant buck jumped up from a perfectly concealed bed.

For a second or maybe longer, the hunter and the deer stood still.
Then the buck broke, and Lew swung his Remington.

"The buck was so close," Lew told me, "that I just couldn't find
buckskin in the scope. By the time I did, the deer was well into
heavy cover only twenty-five or thirty yards away. My only shot
slammed into a sapling, and that was that."

"Never," Lew continued, "have I seen a whitetail to match that
one. Boone and Crockett was written all over him."

It is true that hunters often exaggerate when they describe deer,
particularly those that get away. But Lew is reliable, and I believe
him. My reason for telling about his misfortune is that it is so typical.

Missed shots at vanishing whitetails are as common as red wool
shirts during the deer season. If shirttails actually were cut off every
time somebody blew a shot at a buck, America's shirtmakers
wouldn't be able to keep up with the demand.

No statistics exist to prove it, but I'm sure that the number of
shots fired for each animal bagged is greater with whitetail bucks

Bauer classes this seasoned monarch as the greatest single trophy animal he has ever photographed — or seen.

than it is with any other big-game animal. That claim is certainly true in my own experience, and every other veteran big-game hunter with whom I discussed the matter says the same thing. Missing shots at whitetails even happens quite often when you hunt with a camera, which I do professionally all year. But why are so many whitetails missed, and what can you do to improve your score?

First, let's consider the quarry. The mature whitetail buck is an extraordinary animal. He is as tough and tenacious of life as he is handsome. A buck that has survived several hunting seasons and the brutal northern winters has been honed sharp by danger and hardship. He is not the fastest animal on four feet, but I believe he can reach his top speed more quickly than any other animal of similar size.

The whitetail's vision, excellent hearing, and superb scenting ability have been thoroughly described in hunting literature, and the wise whitetail takes full advantage of the environment in which he lives. The forests of mixed hardwood and evergreen, the swamps and second-growth thickets, the laurel and honeysuckle tangles

are perfect for the deer, but not for the modern deer hunter. When
you consider the habitat and the whitetail's ability to race through it
at high speed or seemingly vanish in the cover, you know you are
hunting an animal that was made to be missed.

Of course most deer hunters add to their troubles because they
only dust off the old shooting iron once a year. Misses are to be
expected if you don't shoot much, but even very experienced
hunters and marksmen miss whitetails too. Few men can honestly
say that they always connect. In his excellent book *The Hunting
Rifle*, Jack O'Connor admits that he has missed more deer in the
brush than anywhere else.

Too many deer hunters do not use the best firearm for the purpose.
There are two types of deer rifle—one for short-range use in brush
or forest, the other for shooting in open or hilly country. The long-
range rifle is used mostly for hunting mule deer out West. The
ideal brush rifle for whitetails should be light, should be fast to

*Many a hunter would trade his car for this shot. But the buck's upraised tail
indicates alarm and the hunter's need for decisive action.*

operate, and should have a short barrel chambered for a cartridge with a fairly heavy bullet traveling at moderate velocity.

It's obvious that the whitetail hunter must be able to get on target fast, not unlike a scattergunner swinging on a flushed bird. With whitetails, you seldom have time to squeeze off a shot at a stationary target from a rest. When spotted, two out of three bucks are already in motion, and the third soon will be.

Another reason for using a brush rifle and heavy bullets is the matter of getting through brush to reach the target. Any bullet can be deflected by brush, but the deflection is far greater with light, high-velocity, sharp-pointed bullets. I have killed two whitetails with 180-grain bullets from a .30/06 that both cut off twigs and a sapling on the way. Lever-action, pump-action, and semiautomatic rifles are popular for whitetail hunting because they are considerably faster to use than a bolt-action rifle. In the brush, a second, or sometimes even a third shot can be very useful, but you must get them off before the deer vanishes.

A list of good, fast whitetail rifles would have to include the Browning Automatic Rifle in .30/06, the Marlin Model 336 lever in .35 Remington, the Marlin Model 444 lever-action Sporter, the Garcia-Sako Finnwolf Sporter (lever) in .308 Winchester, the Savage Model 99 (lever) in .308 Winchester, the Remington Model 760 (pump) in .30/06, the Remington Model 742 (auto) in .30/06, the Ruger 44 autoloading carbine, and the Winchester Model 100 (auto) in .308.

In a number of Midwestern and Eastern states, deer hunters are required by law to use smoothbores and rifled slugs instead of rifles because rifles carry too far for use in densely populated areas. When used at close ranges in brush, the 12 gauge shotgun slug is extremely effective. It is practical to mount a peep sight or a scope on most shotguns. For many years I have used a Remington Model 870 Brushmaster pump with a 20-inch improved-cylinder barrel, designed especially for rifled slugs. On it is mounted a 2½X Weaver scope. The gun has accounted for lots of deer.

Rifle sights for brush hunting cause many arguments among deer hunters. Open iron sights may be best for a hunter who remains fairly calm when he gets a shot, but an excitable hunter has a tendency to hold high and shoot over the target when he's using a notch rear sight. Peep sights suit some shooters very well, and with them, there's no built-in tendency to shoot high. For the average whitetail hunter, however, a low-power scope, say 1X to 2½X, is the best possible sight for whitetails in the woods. Low-power scopes have a wide field of view, which makes it possible to pick up the target quickly. A magnifying sight also makes it easier to pick out detail—to dis-

First snow brings better tracking and makes bedded deer easier to spot.

tinguish deerhide against a brushy background and spot antlers.

On the other hand, rain or snow can be a severe handicap to the man who uses a scope to hunt whitetail. Rain or snow can block vision through a scope, and no scope cover or protector has yet been designed that can be removed fast enough to permit a shot at an alert buck through a Northern forest. My own feeling is that quick-detachable and swing-off scope mounts aren't much help. If you suddenly get a shot and find that your scope is fogged or clogged, it takes too much time to get the scope out of the way, and sometimes these mounts freeze up. Some hunters, however, manage very well with them.

To complicate things still more, most shots at whitetails come very early and very late in the day, when the light is poorest. Long shadows and dim light give the deer one more advantage.

Using the best possible rifle will not guarantee venison in the freezer. The hunter must know how to shoot it accurately and quickly, and that takes a lot of practice. The hunter must also learn to aim at a particular part of the deer—not the whole deer. The best aiming point is the heart-lung area just behind the front legs. A hit anywhere in that area will eventually drop any deer if it does not do so instantaneously. If the animal is not standing or running broadside, the shot should still be aimed to reach the forepart of the rib cage by quartering into it from the rear or driving forward between the hams.

6

There is still another and very important matter that causes hunters to miss whitetails. It is a combination of unfamiliarity and surprise.

During the past few falls I've spent much time photographing a certain deer herd on a military reservation. Public hunting isn't permitted, but the deer are harvested regularly to keep the population within bounds, and the deer are wild and wary.

When I first began photographing the deer with a telephoto lens, my success was poor. I missed many "shots." Only a small fraction of my exposures were worth keeping. But I gradually became able to anticipate what the deer would do. Surprise on my part became less important. I began to make more and more camera kills and even connected on some of the tough running shots that accompany this chapter. The lesson was plain. The outdoorsman who goes out in the deer woods as much as possible all year long is tilting the odds in his own favor. He learns much about the land and whitetail behavior.

Bucks are typically more cautious than does and make better use of cover.

Most hunters are not at all aware of how many deer they move during a typical day's hunting. Many men flush whitetails without knowing it. In addition, a good many animals hold tight in the cover and are never seen by the hunter. It is possible to spend an entire hunting trip in a region where whitetails are plentiful, and yet conclude that deer are very scarce. You have to learn to use your eyes.

Several seasons ago, Lew Baker and I hunted with Lew's young nephew Tom in the Daniel Boone National Forest of eastern Kentucky. State game biologists had established that the deer there were fairly numerous, and these men predicted good hunting success. But in six days of serious hunting, Tom did not get one fleeting glimpse of a whitetail. That night in camp, he recited the familiar deer-hunter's lament: "The biologists," he declared, "are giving us bad dope. I think all the deer have been shot out."

Tom went hunting with that glum attitude on the final day of the trip.

Shortly after daybreak, he was still-hunting through a brushy draw, but his heart wasn't in it. His thoughts wandered. He carried his rifle, he admitted later, first over one shoulder and then over the other, never really ready. So when Tom bounced a pair of bucks out of their beds not twenty yards away, he was so unprepared that he couldn't shoot.

This big fellow appears eager to engage in some heavy hooking.

The escape of those two deer isn't surprising. Whitetails can clear a seven-foot barrier from a standing start, and bounds 25 to 30 feet in length are common. Few animals can vanish so suddenly. No matter how fast a whitetail is running, the animal can brake to an instantaneous halt and take off immediately in another direction. You'd think that the maneuver would break the animal's seemingly frail legs. That sudden switch in direction has caused many hunters to miss.

A few years ago, Michigan conservation officials conducted an unusual experiment that showed dramatically how whitetails make fools of hunters. Thirty-nine deer, nine of which were bucks, were released in an escape-proof enclosure of one square mile at the Cusino Wildlife Experiment Station. It was typical Michigan white-tail cover—hardwoods and pines laced with wetlands. In good weather and with a tracking snow, six experienced hunters went after the deer inside the enclosure.

Who couldn't bag a buck in such a confined area? Some local observers sneered at the idea. They said it provided a license for unsportsmanlike behavior. But four full days passed before any of the six hunters so much as saw antlers. In fact, it was difficult for them to glimpse any deer at all. And fifty-one total hours of pursuit were required before one hunter finally connected with a killing

A bounding buck presents a tough shot for the best of marksmen.

shot, even though the deer were confined within one-square-mile area from which there was no escape.

Another experiment, this one in South Dakota, is also worth describing. A radio transmitter and long orange ear streamers were attached to a mature buck that was then released in a public hunting area during the open season. The researchers were able to keep track of the animal's wanderings and whereabouts by radio. They were confident that some hunter would soon collect the buck.

A week passed, and the marked deer was never seen by hunters. Some of them complained at an official checking station that the area was devoid of deer. Some of these same hunters were known to have passed within 40 or 50 yards of the buck, but they didn't see the animal despite its conspicuous ear streamers.

During the second week of the experiment, a team of veteran deer hunters was dispatched to the exact area where the whitetail was known to be. A careful search of all likely cover, which was not particularly heavy there, revealed absolutely nothing. Finally, by accident, one hunter practically stepped on the deer where the buck had been holding tight in a thicket. And yet, the animal raced away unhurt. The nearest hunter was so surprised that he missed as easy a shot as he will probably ever have at a whitetail buck. The deer is probably alive and well and living in that same patch of woods.

The moral of this story is very simple. When you go whitetail hunting this fall and miss your big opportunity, do not despair. You have just joined the largest club in all the great outdoors. Shake the hand of a charter member—me.

The Desert Mule Deer

Jack O'Connor

In my trophy room I have the mounted heads of two very good mule deer. At a quick glance they look much alike, almost identical, but a closer examination shows that they are in some respects rather different.

Both are magnificent specimens—big bucks a little past their prime and at the stage when they grow the most interesting antlers. One head would have been perfect and symmetrical with six points to a side except for one odd point. The other has a wider spread, is somewhat less symmetrical, and has six points on one side, eight on the other.

The coloration of these two bucks is quite different. The buck with the wide spread has a bright, contrasty scalp. The brown triangle on his forehead is so dark that you might call it black. The

This chapter originally appeared in the December 1970 issue of *Outdoor Life*.

Heads in O'Connor's trophy room reveal differences between Rocky Mountain mule deer, left, and the desert variety.

light patch on the front of his neck below his chin is white. The dark spots on either side of his lower jaw are black and conspicuous, and the hair on his brisket is black. His coat is a brownish gray.

The cape of the other buck is much less vivid. The triangular patch on the forehead is definitely brown. The light-colored neck patch is yellowish white. The dark spots on either side of the lower jaw are brown and so small that they are inconspicuous. Incidentally, the farther north the mule deer is found, the larger and more conspicuous this jaw patch is. At the northern limit of the mule-deer range, in Alberta and British Columbia, the patch is coal black and almost encircles the lower jaw. At the lower limit of the range, in the deserts of the Southwest and Sonora, the patch is barely noticeable.

The hair on the brisket of my lighter-colored buck is brown, and the dark area is less extensive than that on the other buck. And the light buck's coat, instead of being a brownish gray, is definitely a grayish brown.

Both animals are mule deer with the characteristic large ears and evenly branched antlers of the species; but the buck with the contrasty scalp is a Rocky Mountain mule deer that was shot on the Salmon River in Idaho a few years ago. The lighter-colored buck is a

O'Connor poses in Sonora with his best desert mule deer, shown mounted on the opposite page.

desert mule deer, the best I have ever taken. He was shot on either December 30 or 31 in 1941 on the Sonora desert of northern Mexico.

At that time of year the Rocky Mountain mule deer have pretty well finished the annual rut, but this old desert buck had just started getting interested in the does. His neck, as I remember, had not yet begun to swell. He did not have the odor of a rutting buck, and his meat was tender, juicy, and tasty. He was a very heavy buck. Several days later when I delivered his four quarters to a meat locker in Tucson to be cut up, packaged, and stored they weighed 175 pounds.

American zoologists are great classifiers and dividers. Consequently they have listed many subspecies of mule deer in North America. I grew up on the Arizona desert and hunted desert mule deer in Arizona and Sonora for many years. I always thought that Arizona had only two subspecies of mule deer — the Rocky Mountain mule deer and the desert mule deer. I presumed that the deer found in the high country north of the great fault called the Mogollon Rim were Rocky Mountain mule deer and that those south of the rim in lower and hotter country were desert mule deer, or burro deer.

However, the last time I was in Arizona I was told that biologists had decided that the deer north of the Grand Canyon of the Colorado were Rocky Mountain mule deer, those south of the Mogollon Rim were desert mule deer, and those between were some sort of an intermediate subspecies. Just what they have decided to call it I cannot say.

When I was growing up in Arizona these desert mule deer were almost always called blacktails. Actually, like all mule deer, they have light-colored rump patches and little dinky off-white tails with black tips. The true blacktail deer of the Pacific Coast has a much larger tail that is black on top. He extends his tail to a horizontal position when he runs—or so I have read. (I have never shot a Columbian blacktail.) He never lifts it high and waves it around the way a frightened whitetail does. All I have ever seen a mule deer do with his tail is to wiggle it.

The Mexicans, too, sometimes call the desert mule deer a blacktail (*venado cola negra*); but the ordinary backcountry Sonora Mexican simply calls him a *bura*, while he calls the whitetail *venado*.

Many Arizonans in my youth swore that there were at least two strains of desert mule deer. One, as I remember, was the bench-legged deer. He was supposed to be wide, blocky, and short-legged and to have antlers with a narrow spread. The other deer, the "regular blacktail," was supposed to have longer legs and wide-spread antlers.

Actually, wide-spread and close-pinched antlers are found in all subspecies of mule deer. If there is any important difference between the mule deer of the southwestern Arizona desert and those of the desert country of Sonora, I have failed to see it. The pale-colored big buck I shot in 1941 would plainly be classified as Odocoileus hemionus eremicus, as the type locality for this subspecies is not far from the area where I gathered him in. (The "type locality" is the spot where the "type specimen"—the animal on which the sub-specific classification was made—was collected.)

Mule deer found in various dry areas of the United States are called desert mule deer. Some, such as those found in the dry sage-brush flats and hills of southern Idaho and eastern Oregon, are simply Rocky Mountain mule deer inhabiting arid country.

A desert mule deer is found in southern New Mexico, Chihuahua, and the Big Bend country of Texas. I have hunted these deer. They are a good deal smaller than the burro deer of southern Arizona and northwestern Sonora. From what I have seen, an average mature Big Bend mule-deer buck with four points to a side will field-dress at about 150 to 160 pounds. The largest I have ever seen weighed 175. The antlers tend to be light.

On the other hand, the burro deer of southern Arizona and Sonora are heavy-bodied and heavy-antlered. Bucks field-dressing at 180 to 200 pounds are common, and now and then one is shot that will weigh 225 to 250.

The elk, the moose, the mountain sheep, and the caribou arrived in North America from Asia in times that geologically are fairly recent, but the American deer evolved here from stock that migrated from Asia many millions of years ago. Our desert mule deer has been around for a long, long time. His ancestors were in the Southwest and northern Mexico when the ice sheet came well down into the United States and the deserts were lush and well watered. Excavations in caves that were long inhabited by primitive people have shown that the desert mule deer was hunted for hundreds if not thousands of years before the bighorn sheep was.

There are mule deer on Tiburon Island just off the Sonora coast— but no desert sheep, though the desert bighorn is found on the little range called Tepopa, just across the strait from Tiburon, and on desert mountains along the coast both north and south of these. The explanation is that the deer crossed over to Tiburon during one of the glacial eras of the Pleistocene when the seas were lower than they are now. By the time the bighorns arrived in Sonora the glaciers and ice caps had melted and the rising sea had cut the sheep off from Tiburon.

In Arizona the desert mule deer are found not only out in the rolling hills and wide arroyos in the lowland desert but also in the canyons that break off the high plateau country and part way up the taller and rugged mountains. In the area of transition between the desert vegetation of the Lower Sonoran Zone and the live oaks, manzanita, and mountain mahogany of the Upper Sonoran Zone, the Arizona whitetail takes over.

In the deserts of the Mexican state of Sonora, however, the mule deer is entirely a low-country animal and even the little hills not over 100 feet higher than the desert flats have their complement of the beautiful little whitetails (Coues deer). Often I have seen whitetail tracks in the low country where the deer had come down to feed or to cross from one range of low hills to another; but I cannot remember ever seeing a mule deer or his tracks in the whitetail hills. (The tracks, incidentally, are unmistakable: those of the whitetail are heart-shaped, those of the mule deer narrow and longer.)

How much work biologists have done on the ability of animals to tolerate other species I cannot say. In Africa, zebras and wildebeests habitually run together and it is common to see several species grazing peacefully together on the same plain.

I think American animals are much less tolerant. In desert-sheep ranges in Sonora where there are few if any deer, the sheep habitually come down to feed out on the flats and sometimes even bed down in dry arroyos during the day. In areas where there are a good many deer, the sheep don't come down as often or stay down. On Tiburon Island the mule deer range well up in the rocky cliffs and canyons. The reason, I am sure, is that there are no desert bighorns on Tiburon.

An interesting result of the whitetail's and desert mule deer's ranging in adjacent areas is the occasional cross between the two species. I have never shot such a cross, but I have seen several hides from hybrids. The result looks just about like a Columbian black-tail. The tail is a blacktail's tail, the placement of the metatarsal glands is the same, and so are the markings of the face. For many years a blacktail deer was listed for Arizona. It was called the Crooks's blacktail and was considered to be allied to the coast blacktail but very rare. We know now that it was actually a cross between the mule deer and the whitetail.

For many years Arizona had no open season on the desert mule deer, whereas the whitetails were hunted hard. The big mature buck mule deer did their best to keep the young bucks away from the does. At the same time, many unmated whitetail does were running around, since there were many more whitetail does than bucks and the whitetail is much less promiscuous than the mule deer. Along the edges of the whitetail mountains where the ranges of both species adjoined, an occasional romance occurred between an amorous young buck mule deer and a lonesome and neglected whitetail doe. I know of several hybrids that have been shot in southern Arizona and of two that were killed in Sonora.

The yearly cycles of the burro deer and all other desert big-game animals is quite different from those of their relatives that live in colder climates. In high cool country from Arizona north of the Mogollon Rim clear to central Alberta, the mule deer are generally well into the rut by the middle of November. With their seven months' gestation period their young are born in the spring. The desert mule deer, however, do not begin rutting until late December. The fawns are dropped in late July or August.

As I mentioned before, the big buck I shot at the very end of 1941 had collected himself a herd of does but his neck had not swelled much, if any, and his meat was mild and tender.

My wife and I had a Mexican friend who owned a ranch, and we had arranged to rent a couple of horses from him and to borrow one of his vaqueros to take care of them and to show us around. We had driven up to a little adobe hut by a well in the desert, miles from anywhere, and were making camp when the vaquero rode up with the horses. He suggested that he and I take a turn to see if we could find a deer.

We had turned back toward camp about two hours later when we saw a couple of desert-mule-deer does about 300 yards away, across a wide arroyo. We got off the horses and I was watching the does with binoculars when one of the horses reached up and yanked off a mouthful of ironwood leaves. A branch cracked. The does heard the noise and started to run. As they did we saw a magnificent buck—but only for an instant.

Santiago, the vaquero, took off at a run and motioned for me to follow. I did. How he knew where the deer were going I have no idea; but he knew. We crossed the arroyo and went up the other side. A moment later a doe came by, then another. Then the buck came into sight. My first bullet turned him around and my second put him down. He was so heavy that Santiago and I had to hoist him up into a tree with a riata so that we could put him across Santiago's saddle. We tied him on. Santiago then scrambled up on top of the buck, and in triumph we rode back to camp.

I do not know what the open seasons are in Sonora now, but when I lived in Arizona and hunted often in Mexico the best time to get big trophy Mexican bucks was toward the end of the year when they were getting interested in the does. They have their minds on something more important than self-preservation then, and they move around more in the daytime.

West of the Santa Catalina Mountains, which loom like a wall north of Tucson, there is a stretch of rolling cactus-covered hills, wide arroyos, and flats covered with grass, cholla, and brush. When I lived in Tucson that area always held desert mule deer, and it was not difficult to find does, fawns, and young bucks. But during the hunting season you could hunt hard and carefully for a weekend and rarely even glimpse a big trophy buck, though you would see plenty of big-buck tracks. There was just too much cover and they were just too smart. But in January when the rut was in full swing, big trophy bucks were all over the place.

I used to go out in January and hike back into the low hills to watch the deer. Each big buck would gather a harem of from five to a dozen does. Together they moved restlessly uphill and down. From two to five young bucks always hung around the edge of the herd of does. Now and then a bold youngster would rush in toward a receptive doe. The big herd buck would drive him off, and while the big buck's head was turned another youngster would charge in and cover the doe.

I used to feel sorry for those poor herd bucks. Theirs was a hell of a life. They appeared to be exhausted. I never saw one eating. The love-making I saw performed was all done by the youngsters. The old bucks ran frantically around, overwhelmed by their cares, their mouths open, a wild and desperate look in their eyes. I have had them trot within a few yards of me and ignore me completely.

I have shot some desert mule deer at the beginning of the rut but never after it has got well under way. I would not consider it sporting to hunt in the middle of the rut. The meat is no good then, and I would not value a head taken under those conditions.

The mating season of the desert whitetails is even later than that of the desert mule deer, but just why this should be I have no idea. When I was a professor at the University of Arizona back in the 1930's I used to hunt in Sonora between Christmas and New Year. All that time I shot only one whitetail buck that had begun to get interested in the does. My Mexican friends tell me that the whitetails do not start playing ring-around-a-rosy until late January or early February. Their whole cycle is later. I have seen desert whitetail bucks in April, when I was hunting javelinas, that were still wearing their antlers, and I have seen spotted fawns in November.

When I show friends the mounted head of my big desert-mule-deer buck I tell them that he never had a drink of water in his life. If he did he would have had to take it from a swift and briefly running arroyo after a violent summer storm. There is simply no natural open water in his country, which gets probably no more than from three to five inches of rainfall a year. The soil on the flats is mostly loose large-grained sand from the decomposing granite hills, and it soaks up water like a sponge. Mexican ranchers have dug some wells and installed windmills, but it is rare for a deer to use this water.

Instead, the mule deer and all the other desert big game have learned to make out with the moisture they get from the dew on the leaves of the browse they eat and the water in the fruit of the various cactuses. Near the Gulf of California, the dew is often quite heavy and various plants contain considerable water. From my observations I would guess that the desert mule deer, if suitable vegetation is present, can live and die without tasting open water.

You would think that in this dry environment the flesh of desert game would be strong and dry. Actually, most of the browse is mild and delicately flavored and there is no better meat anywhere than that of a fat desert mule deer or whitetail or a good fat ram taken before the rut — or after the rut when he has had sufficient time to recover his condition.

I have eaten a lot of desert venison in my day, and I have also cooked a lot. One time I arrived at a ranch and told the Mexican rancher that I would like to go deer hunting and would like to borrow a horse and a vaquero. He told me that he too was overcome by a desire to hunt deer and he would go along. His brother likewise felt deery, and so did a cousin who lived on a ranch about fifteen miles away. By the time we got organized our party consisted of about a dozen people. I had someone to make my bed, wash my sweaty shirts, round up and saddle my horse, and skin the deer. But there was no one to cook.

For two weeks I fed the mob on coffee, pancakes, and syrup made of hot water and pinoche (unrefined Mexican sugar) for breakfast;

at night I made biscuits and gravy and fried venison in Dutch ovens. I kept a big pot of frijoles simmering on the ironwood fire twenty-four hours a day. The camp handyman kept the fire going and watched the frijoles to see that they didn't boil dry. He also made a batch of tortillas every day. We took these with us when we rode out, and at noon we would build a little fire, make a tin-canful of coffee, and heat the tortillas by tossing them onto the ashes.

My rancher host had brought along some tasty homemade white cheese, and his brother had contributed a couple of cases of delicious Hermosillo-made beer called High Life. One of the cowboys had foresightedly brought a jug or two of wild Mexican booze called sotol. It tasted like a mixture of hightest gasoline and horse liniment, but I discovered that if I mixed it half and half with pineapple or orange juice it became fairly potable.

My host was a very thrifty hombre who believed that a peso saved is a peso earned. And as fast as he, his brother, his cousin, and I collected deer he had his henchmen cut the meat into long strips and hang them on the bushes to dry into jerky. He was laying in his winter's meat.

I used to come in dog tired. I'd have the boys put the Dutch ovens on to heat. Then I'd take a belt of sotol and pineapple juice and start cooking while my hungry Mexican friends squatted around watching me like starving vultures waiting for a sick steer to die.

It was December, and almost every morning we would awaken to find frost on the ground. My host, his brother, the cousin, and I slept on heavy Mexican cots we had brought in a truck from the ranch. They slept in blankets, I in a sleeping bag. Most of the vaqueros slept on saddle blankets near the fire. The camp boy who watched the beans was a tough little Papago Indian about twelve years old. He simply took off his chaps, rolled them up for a pillow, lay down on the hard, cold ground, and slept like a baby!

Mule deer differ greatly in size from area to area. I have read that the mule deer on Cedros Island off the coast of Lower California are very small. For whatever the reason, animals that live for many generations on small islands tend to become small—and Cedros is a small island. On the other hand, the deer I have seen on Tiburon are large—but Tiburon is a large island.

The antlers of the burro deer compare favorably with the antlers of mule deer anywhere. I remember one magnificent and massive head taken near Caborca, Sonora, that had eight and nine points and a spread of forty-two inches. Clients of the late Charlie Ren, who for a time operated a hunting outfit in northern Sonora, used to get some superb heads down on the deserts around Caborca and Altar. For whatever the reason, I believe I have seen more outstanding heads from Sonora than from Arizona.

The outlook for the desert deer is, alas, not so good. In both Arizona and Sonora he is receiving pressure from every side. In Arizona most of his range is either leased from the state for peanuts by cattle ranchers or is Bureau of Land Management land leased from the federal government. The ranching interests are very powerful in Arizona—so powerful that they have fought off any attempt to regulate the use of state-owned land. As a consequence, most state land in Arizona is fantastically overgrazed and overbrowsed and the desert deer must compete with cattle.

In Sonora the story is about the same. Most of the land is public domain; some of it is privately owned. All is overgrazed and overbrowsed. Most Southwestern ranches, whether in Arizona or Sonora, do not sell beef; they simply sell ambulatory carcasses that can be fattened and made into beef. Desert land is fragile. Growth is slow. Though the annual rainfall is only from one to nine inches a year, rains are often torrential and topsoil that has been laid bare by overgrazing is washed away. The desert was never intended to be cattle country.

For a long time the dryness of the country in remote parts of Sonora protected the desert mule deer and the big-horn sheep from competition. But now Mexican ranchers are developing water. They bring in bulldozers and throw up dams across arroyos to catch the occasional floods. The effect will be that sheep and deer, which have had a rough enough time anyway, will find it even harder to survive.

And in many areas the desert deer can be hunted from four-wheel-drive vehicles. In Arizona there are probably a hundred hunters today where there was one in the 20's and 30's. Country Mexicans have always hunted deer and sheep twelve months out of the year, and now big-game hunting has become fashionable in Mexico and rich Mexicans come from all the large Mexican cities to hunt desert bighorns and trophy mule deer. Some attempt is now being made in Mexico to enforce the game laws, but I understand that enforcement is still pretty sketchy.

In the Southwestern U.S. the desert bighorn has been saved for posterity by the establishment of rigidly patrolled game preserves administered by the federal government. Such a setup could be the salvation of the desert bighorn in Sonora and Lower California, too—and also of the desert mule deer.

I hope he is saved. He is one of the handsomest of the North American deer and he lives in the great Southwestern desert—my first love, the land where I grew up, and one of the most beautiful, unusual, and interesting regions on earth.

A Plantation Hunt to Remember

Archibald Rutledge

There are many standard deer crossings on my South Carolina plantation. These do not differ from those in any other state, regardless of the differences in the topography of the land. Once I asked an old backwoodsman why deer persist in running these same crossings year after year. "That's easy," he answered. "They want to get from here to yon, and they knows the best way."

Wherever a man hunts whitetail deer, I believe he will find that this splendid animal's crossings are of two kinds: crossings used by all deer, and those preferred by bucks. These latter stands are usually secret and in unexpected places, though at one of them a buck may just fool a hunter by coming straight at him. This always makes for a difficult and disconcerting shot. I believe that the two hardest shots at any deer are the head-on shot and the straightaway one.

This chapter originally appeared in the March 1965 issue of *Outdoor Life* under the title "The Buck at the Secret Crossing."

Here, in the mid-1950's, the late Archibald Rutledge was in his seventies. The author's son, Judge Irvine H. Rutledge, recently captioned the snapshot as follows: "My father killed this buck in a drive called Wambaw where he and his driver Prince had gone to hunt. They jumped this buck several times. He was big and full of himself and would stop occasionally to beat off the hounds just for the hell of it."

As a rule, however, a buck circles in a drive, and if he comes out at all, he sidles out. I once had a grand old stag pass me in a wide arc and then skulk around in a dense cornfield. Beyond the field was a road, and beyond that a huge stretch of wildwoods. The buck's natural run would have been straight over the road and then into that dense forest. But he didn't do that. He kept circling back toward me. I thought I knew what that wise old boy had in mind. He was doubling back in order to cross a river nearby. I intercepted him on a typical buck stand. A stander on the road would have been at an obvious crossing, but no wary buck would have done anything so lacking in craft as to have run that way.

Before I tell about the buck that is really the subject of this story, let me say a word about deer and roads. In the shadowy hours of twilight and early dawn, as well as in the dark of night, deer love to loaf along old roads. It has been my experience that deer, and bucks especially, prefer to roam in open places in the darkness. In the case of the buck, perhaps this is because of his horns. Incidentally, I once knew a man who ran down a buck that had been only slightly wounded. The buck carried a tremendous rack, though he had only a medium-size body. The man seemed to think that the weight of the antlers wore the buck down. Such a supposition is by no means unreasonable.

It was in that very same drive that another thing happened. I knew of a secret buck crossing in a wild stretch of country. I doubt if anyone else knew of it, though years ago it was a favorite of one of my sons—a boy I lost in World War II. For reasons you will understand, I had not cared to go there for a long time.

But shortly before Christmas in 1956, I stationed my eldest son on this crossing. He hadn't killed a buck in two years, and I was eager to have him get one. He's an experienced deer hunter, and when I placed him on the crossing, he was skeptical.

"Has a deer ever run here since the Revolution?" he asked.

"Wait and see," I told him.

In my country, which is only about seven miles from the ocean, we have no real hills, but we do have elevations of considerable height. It was at the top of one of these that I posted my son. He looked so dubious about the place that I wasn't sure he would stay there. There were a lot of other crossings covering the head of that drive. He knew them, and I realized he might decide to change his stand.

"Hold this place, son," I said as I turned to leave him. "Try it this once, and see what happens."

Then I went to cover another crossing down in a swamp 300 yards away.

The place where I left my son was at the juncture of an old road and an old dirt bank—both permanent features of the landscape. Every deer hunter should remember that, though deer know the forest better than he does, they usually steer their course by big trees, tar kilns, charcoal hearths, ancient animal trails, and even by huge rocks that have marked certain locations from time immemorial.

I know a famous crossing called Saddle Oak. It's an ancient post oak with a deep crook near the base which resembles the seat of a saddle. To this tree, not to thousands of others around it, countless generations of deer have run. It is on one side of the famous Turkey Roost Drive, and it's one of my favorite buck stands. Over the years, I have killed seven bucks at that crossing. In my long and misspent life I have killed 283 bucks; but it must be remembered that in my early life there were no bag limits, and also that, to this day, my state of South Carolina has no bag limit on deer in some of its counties, and a high five-bucks-a-season limit in the county where I live.

Before my son's stand was a rather steep declivity overgrown with dense bushes that grew taller at the bottom than at the top. In the low thicket, a deer could hardly be seen before he was within gunshot range, but as he mounted the hill toward the old road, he would have to break cover.

This crossing might seem a difficult one to handle, but then, any crossing is if you don't know how. I had advised my son to stand on top of the old bank and to the right of the deer's run. That would give him a left-hand shot, but he shoots equally well from either shoulder. The advantage lay in the rise, since at any crossing anywhere the hunter should be slightly elevated so he can see what's coming his way. A buck is likely to slip by a man who stands in a depression.

It was warm that morning and, fortunately, very still. I say fortunately because stillness is perhaps the greatest advantage a deer hunter can have. On a windy day, game is skittish and hunters are skittish. There are so many noises that deer sounds cannot be detected or distinguished. But if the day is still, the hunter can use his ears as well as his eyes. So far as I'm concerned, I can take cold, rain, and snow while hunting, but wind drives me crazy. I'd rather stay at home.

This particular morning was made for deer hunting. In addition to my eldest son and namesake, I had with me my youngest son, now a lawyer in Maryland, and one of my grandsons, aged twelve. As a rule, I have many friends hunting with me, but for some reason, this particular hunt was a family affair.

The drivers went back almost a mile to the Santee River, faced about, and then came toward us, whooping, yelling, and beating clubs against trees. For half an hour there was nothing in their approach to indicate they had started a deer. Yet they were driving a long-deserted plantation, little hunted, and in perfect deer country.

For some reason, deer hunters who do not live in the South often regard with some scorn our use of the shotgun and the hound. Yet our way of hunting is akin to the ancient English and European custom. It is both safer and more exciting than ordinary stalking.

I have hunted deer with a rifle in the snowy mountains of West Virginia, Maryland, Virginia, and Pennsylvania. Frankly, I didn't like it. Aside from the bitter cold, I didn't care for the multitude of hunters, the constant whine of high-powered rifles, and the way in which everyone — men, women, and children — took to the woods. Nor did I like the way four hunters tried to take from me a buck I had killed. There is an ancient fraternity among woodsmen — almost a kind of sacred bond between brothers — that should forever prevent disgraceful performances of this kind.

Earlier I mentioned an old buck that circled me on a wide arc. Though that buck was far out of sight and hearing, I could tell approximately where he was by the position of my two hounds, Jeff and Southwind. The exact position of a fleeing deer, however, can't be told with certainty since a deer usually runs several hundred yards ahead of the hounds, and sometimes as much as half a mile. For example, the dogs may be heading away from you at full speed, and before they make the turn that will tell you what is happening, the buck, having doubled back, may be right beside you. When I hunt deer with inexperienced hunters, I have the hardest time convincing them that, while it is well to listen to the hounds, the deer is not where the dogs are.

Whether you hunt with hounds or without them, it is astonishing how many bucks slip past watchers on crossings. All of us must pay tribute to a buck for being able to leave his bed, steal along within easy range of a stander, and get by without being seen or heard. On the other hand, I have had a doe or a yearling nearly scare me to death by exploding out of a thicket. Delicacy of maneuver is supposed to be a feminine trait, but when it comes to the whitetail deer, the buck has this quality to a supreme degree.

An hour after my son and I had stationed ourselves at our crossings, I heard Jeff trailing about half a mile away. I may be wrong, but I've always felt that, given the option of trailing a buck or a doe, the hound would always choose the buck. I once had a hound that would never run anything but a buck. The scents of buck and doe, of course, are different. In fact, I believe that every individual deer has its own aura. How else does one particular deer find another particular deer?

If old Jeff should come on the tracks of a brontosaurus, imbedded in mud that turned to rock about 2,000,000 years ago, he will not take the trail. But if an old buck has walked anywhere in the vicinity during the previous eight or ten hours, especially if trailing conditions are good, he'll take notice at once and advance. And as the trail gets warmer, he'll tell the world, and especially me, that an old stag is wandering nearby.

Few things in nature are so amazing and mysterious as the sorcery of the trailing hound. My long observation leads me to believe that no dog of any kind pays any attention to any track. The scent is the whole thing. A whitetail, of course, leaves two scents. One is laid on the ground by the glands between the hoofs, and the other is deposited on bushes by glands inside the back knees. These glands are surrounded by heavy projecting tufts of hair. I have long thought that the purpose of these tufts is to transfer the scent from the glands to bushes which the deer brushes in passing.

It might be thought that a hound will run directly after a deer, literally following his track. But since a deer is often a long way ahead, the hound may run wide of the exact direction the deer has taken. The dog picks up the scent in the wind, and by the time he reaches a certain spot, such as a road, the scent will have drifted far to the right or left. I have known a good hound, in full cry, to cross a road 100 yards from where the deer had crossed.

It has always seemed to me that the glands inside a deer's back knees give off a stronger scent than those between his hoofs. A really good hound works on the bushes, as if he knew where the strong scent was to be found.

In the country before my son and me, the brush was so dense we couldn't see the hounds. But they were coming fast for us—Jeff and Thunderbird, Music and Southwind. As I've said before, you can rarely tell the exact location of a deer by listening to the hounds. They may be half a mile back and off to your right, while the buck is passing you on your left within easy range. A stander has to be silent and alert.

I was standing in a swampy area, and my son was on the elevated bank above me, and to my left.

Suddenly, in the thicket of water oaks in front of me, I heard a deer crack the brush. The foliage was so thick I couldn't tell just where he was. Almost immediately, though, I heard my son shoot twice.

The hounds swept by me on the trail, passed my son, and kept on going. I didn't like that, since they were headed for the broad reaches of the river a mile away. My driver came up running; so did my youngest son and my grandson. For a dismayed moment, all we could do was listen to the retreating hounds.

"He's turned," I told the boys, as the hounds began to make a wide circle. "I don't believe he can make it to the river."

All of us broke into a run. My driver, with unerring instinct, seemed to anticipate where the buck and the hounds were headed. He vanished into the thicket ahead of us. Then there was silence as the hounds stopped running.

We found the buck near a little pond, dead where he had fallen. He had run about half a mile from where he'd been shot.

His body was only medium-size, his coat was very dark, and he had a rugged, wildwood look. But his antlers amazed me.

Ever since early boyhood I have been a nut about deer horns. I used to collect them, and I would travel miles to examine a reputedly fine pair. I have seen thousands, but none like these.

In conformation, they are normal. They have eight points, and they spread only eighteen inches. But in color they are almost black. The circumference of the beams at the bases is eight inches (an American record, I believe). The beading is the heaviest I have ever seen, extending almost to the tips of all the tines. This great rack has an indefinable ruggedness and majesty, taking one back in imagination to pioneer days. Old deer hunters out of the swamps and backwoods have traveled far to see these remarkable horns.

When I first got a good look at this buck, I thought he must be a stranger (a few bucks were imported here from Michigan). But the fact that he ran to that secret crossing convinces me that he was born right here. His horns make the kind of trophy few men ever have the good fortune to bring home, even in a lifetime of hunting.

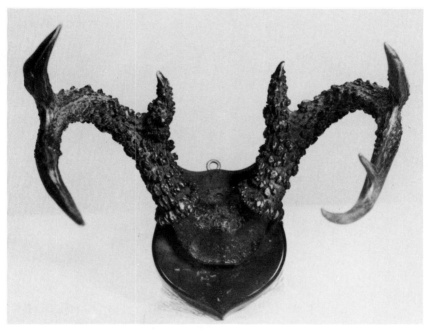

These are the remarkable antlers of "The Beaded Buck."

The Arizona Coues Deer

Jack O'Connor

Most intelligent game animal I have ever run into on this side of the world is the pint-size Coues deer, also known as the Arizona whitetail. He's a little guy, about half as large as the mule deer he often ranges with. He is, on the other hand, about five times as smart as the mule deer. The little rascal makes up his mind quickly and gambles coolly with his life. When he knows he can no longer stay concealed, he comes out like a quail, depending on his sudden and noisy appearance to befuddle the hunter.

The only North American animal I've hunted that I'd put in the same strategy class with the little Arizona whitetail is an *old* desert bighorn, one that has learned the facts of life by dodging the bullets tossed at him by prospectors, fishermen, and vaqueros. Yet the wild

This chapter originally appeared in the February 1958 issue of *Outdoor Life* under the title "Our Smartest Game Animal."

sheep gets smart the hard way. The Coues deer imbibes craft and cunning with his mother's milk.

He's a great fellow to size up a situation, work out an escape plan, and stick to it. On one hunt I used binoculars to watch two distant whitetails go into a little patch of chaparral under a rimrock about thirty feet from a spring. Soon after that a cowboy rode his horse up to the spring, where he made a fire, boiled a can of coffee, ate his lunch. Then he snoozed in the sun for about fifteen minutes before he mounted and moved on. The Coues deer stayed put. I hadn't been able to see antlers even with my 8X glasses, but the color of the deer and the way they carried their heads made me think they were both bucks.

I approached the chaparral where the bucks lay upwind and inconspicuously, but both deer sneaked out ahead of me. I just caught a glimpse of one, moving like a gray shadow with his head down and his tail clamped between his legs. Before I could shoot he was out of sight. Those deer knew the cowboy's heart was pure as driven snow but mine was full of guile. How, I'll never know, but they did. That's why so many Coues bucks live to a ripe old age.

The only animal I ever ran into anywhere that seemed smarter and harder to hunt than the Arizona whitetail is Africa's greater kudu. This elk-sized, spiral-horned antelope has many things in common with the little whitetail—super hearing, coolness, a gambler's instinct. He's considered one of the very top African trophies and the hardest of all the fairly common antelope to bag.

The little whitetail, although tough to hunt and about as smart as a kudu, is not so famous. In the United States, he's found only in a strip near the Mexican border, and his head is a very rare one in trophy collections.

One afternoon years ago another hombre and I were hunting in southern Arizona. We had separated, and in late afternoon I saw him pussyfooting down a point about 400 yards from me. Presently I saw a deer jump ahead of my friend, and from his obvious excitement I knew it was a buck.

The deer continued off the point as if to run along under the rimrock toward the main mountain. My friend hurried out to the brink of the ridge and stood there with his rifle ready. He was watching the spot where the oaks ended, where the buck was sure to break out of cover on his way to the mountain beyond.

But instead of doing the obvious, the buck put on his brakes as soon as he was out of sight in the scrubby little evergreen oaks under the rim. Then he turned back around the point, sneaking along under the rim with head down, tail plastered between his legs. He came out in the open about 200 yards to the left of where my pal was expecting him. Then, with the last concealing bush behind him, he flirted up his big white tail and ran. My friend threw a hasty shot at him and missed. It was difficult to make him believe that this deer he shot at was the same one he'd jumped a few minutes earlier.

I know of no animal that's better at finding a strategic bedding ground than this smart little whitetail. This was firmly impressed on me one fall day when I was hunting a long ridge on horseback. I saw four bucks, but every single one of them was bedded so that he needed but one jump to be out of sight.

I have never seen an animal make better use of cover than the Coues deer. I recall a time years ago when I was hunting with two friends in the Canelo Hills not far from Patagonia in southern Arizona. We were climbing up a trail toward the top of a low range. When we got to the top we'd figure out how to team up and work out the heads of some canyons. Then one of my friends saw a buck flip up its white tail and jump over the ridge toward a big canyon.

This is a trophy-size Coues buck. The antlers follow the typical whitetail pattern with one main beam.

Yelling for us to follow, he took after it. We knew the country and thought it highly probable that we'd get another look at the deer. The big canyon into which he'd gone was quite open — golden slopes of frost-cured grama grass with an occasional ocotillo and oaks in little groves in the side draws. There was so little cover that it would be almost impossible for a deer to move without one of us seeing it.

But nothing did we see. That deer hadn't possibly had time to run out of sight, yet he was. A couple of us searched the valley with binoculars. Not a thing could we find except a couple of crows slithering along with a lofty wind, cawing and snarling at each other against the flat blue of the sky. We decided the deer might have stopped directly below us, where the contours of the ground and a few scattered patches of mountain mahogany and cliff rose would afford cover. We rolled big stones that went crashing through that growth. Nothing moved.

Right beside us was a little patch of brush about large enough to conceal a cock pheasant. We hadn't given it a thought. Presently one of my pals decided to roll a cigarette, so he walked over and leaned his rifle against a bush. Instantly a fine whitetail exploded out of the little patch, head up, antlers back, snowy tail looking as large as he was. His first jump kicked leaves and twigs all over us. He passed so close to me that if I'd been less astonished I might have grabbed him by an antler. (Don't ask me what I'd have done after I got such a hold.)

Meanwhile the man who'd leaned his rifle on the bush made a lunge for it and fell flat. The other hunter and I were so busy bumping into one another that the buck buzzed over the ridge without a shot being fired at him. We agreed that this buck was too hard on our nerves and set out to find a more docile one.

The career of a mossy-horned old buck that lived near Patagonia, Arizona, illustrates the amazing ability of these little deer to survive heavy hunting without much cover. The buck's home range was a canyon-cut ridge that ran about three miles from north to south. Thin brush grew along the talus slopes below the rimrocks. Oak, mountain mahogany, and cliff rose was fairly thick in a few places in the draws. The rest of this long ridge was open — slopes of grama grass, limestone outcrops, an oak here and there. The ridge was within half a mile of a ranch house containing three hunters, within three miles of the village, and a mile from a good automobile road.

The buck lived out his long, long life almost as publicly as a goldfish in a bowl. He probably was born on the ridge and he lived about five years after his antlers had grown so large and many-pointed as to cause comment. Deer hunters came down from

Tucson to try for him. High school kids matched wits with him after school and on weekends. Cowhands sniped at him.

It wasn't difficult to see the buck. Almost anyone could see him. But armed men only saw him just as he was disappearing into the brush, crossing a ridge at 400 yards, fading around a point. Yet I'm sure two-hundred shots were fired at that buck, maybe more.

I had a hand in this buck's undoing. Arizona rancher Frank Siebold and I knew the buck had a habit on chill fall mornings of taking the sun on a flat between a big canyon and the south slope of the mountain. If hunters came up the canyon, the deer faded over the south slope and hugged a belt of oaks as he eased away. If hunters came up that south slope, he dropped over into the canyon.

Frank and I framed him. We sent his sister Doris and my wife Eleanor up the canyon while we skirted the bottom of the south slope of the hill. When the buck came sneaking along through the belt of oaks, I took a crack at him. The bullet struck a bit low in his left shoulder. He went down, but got up as we were scrambling toward him, and climbed over the rimrock. There he ran into Doris, who nailed him.

The old buck had a beautiful head with nine points to a side,

O'Connor, left, and Frank Siebold tie a Coues buck over a saddle. These bucks seldom dress-out over one-hundred pounds.

but the meat was so tough it was only edible in a stew. His teeth were about gone and he showed every sign of extreme age and decrepitude. He was probably somewhere between twelve and fourteen years old and probably would have died of old age within a year.

Arizona whitetail is a misleading name for these little deer. That's a handle they got when they were first classified from specimens taken near Fort Crittenden, Arizona, in the days when that old army post was on guard against Apaches. Coues (pronounced *cows*) is a more accurate name for these little deer, and the scientific name for them is Odocoileus virginianus couesi. Other common names are fantail, Sonora whitetail, Arizona whitetail. Mexicans call it the venado, which simply means deer. They keep things straight by calling the mule deer the buro.

Coues deer are found in southern Arizona in all the hills and mountains high enough to support live oaks from the little border town of Sasabe east to the New Mexico line. Their range is by no means continuous, but there are scattered herds as far north as central Arizona along the Mongollon rim. In New Mexico they are found in mountain ranges west of the Rio Grande as far north as the Datils and are quite plentiful in the Mongollons and San Franciscos. Some are found in the Davis Mountains in the Big Bend of Texas and in the Glass and Chisos mountains in the same area.

They are most plentiful in the Mexican states of Chihuahua and Sonora, and there are many in western Choahuila. In the United States, Coues deer are generally found at altitudes above 4,000 feet, but in Sonora they range from 10,000 feet in the Sierra Madre clear down to little hills that are in sight of the Gulf of California. Distribution maps do not show them down near the salt water, but I have seen them there by the hundreds and shot many.

Outside of the Southwest, these wonderful little deer are almost unknown. They have also undergone the ordeal of being written about by people who knew but little about them. I mentioned that distribution maps do not list them as occupying the western desert portion of their range in Mexico. Writers often promote another error by making Coues deer seem smaller than they actually are. One piece I read about them says to imagine a jackrabbit with horns. That's silly. Vernon Bailey, Fish & Wildlife Service biologist, wrote that bucks reached a maximum weight of a hundred pounds (presumably live weight) and does seventy-five.

I have weighed dozens of them. The average grown buck will weigh from eighty to ninety pounds after he's field dressed, and hundred-pound bucks are common in any area I have hunted. It's true that a buck weighing more than a hundred pounds field dressed is large, but a hundred pounds is certainly not a maximum weight. I wrote a story some years ago about a 117½-pound Coues buck. I killed it in the Tortolita Mountains near Tucson, Arizona. I thought I'd win a rifle in a heavy-buck contest, but the next day my shooting pal Carroll Lemon brought in one that weighed 128½.

Generally speaking, the little whitetails are just about half the size of Southwestern mule deer or the larger varieties of Virginia whitetail. Coues bucks weighing a hundred pounds are just about as common as buck mule deer that dress out to two-hundred.

Coues deer look like Eastern whitetails done in miniature, except that their skulls are smaller and shorter in proportion. Does and young bucks are a beautiful dove gray, but old bucks are grizzled and darker. Their antlers, ears, and tails are larger in proportion to their bodies than those of their Eastern relatives. Tails range from a grizzled brown on top to a bright orange, and when they toss them up to take off the deer appears to be all brilliant white tail.

Although the little fantail is only about half the size of his Northern and Eastern cousins, his antlers are larger in proportion to his body. As is the case with all whitetail deer, all the points on the antlers of the fantail come off one main beam and the eyeguard points are long and conspicuous as compared with the short ones of the mule deer. However, whereas the mature Eastern whitetail generally has four points to the side in addition to the eyeguard, the Arizona deer has three. On the other hand, I have shot Coues bucks with as many as five points to a side and have seen one with nine on one side and eleven on the other.

The heads do not freak as much as those of mule deer, and are generally very regular and symmetrical. A head with a 16-inch beam usually will have about a 16-inch spread, and so on, and a four-point buck with a 16-inch beam is a good one. A buck with a 17-inch beam is extraordinary, and an 18-incher is getting far up in the records if the antlers are massive. The heads may not knock your eye out, but they are one of the rarest trophies in North America. Because they are an entirely different animal from the orthodox whitetail, they are given a separate classification in Records of North American Big Game.

No matter where he's found, the little Coues deer is a hill animal. On the Sonora desert, the mule deer like to range out on the flats, but the whitetails cling to the hills like ducks to a pond. The long, rather narrow tracks of the desert mule deer are found all over the flats, but usually the hunter doesn't run into the smaller heart-shape tracks of the whitetail unless he's close to a hill.

The most heavily populated whitetail area I ever ran into was in

Peculiar to mature bucks of this species, spread measurement and length of the main beam are usually about the same, in this case 17x17 inches.

the Sonora desert—a chain of low, rolling hills southwest of the little placer-mining town of La Cienega. I was in there for a hunt during the winter of 1937–38, and the deer were so thick that they obliterated the horse tracks on a trail between dusk and dawn. Apparently they soon got too plentiful and died off. I was in there a few years later and didn't see one where I had formerly seen ten.

In spite of their wide distribution in respect to altitude, I always think of the little whitetails as creatures of what scientists call the upper Sonoran climatic zone, which means a zone with the climate and vegetation common to the higher elevations in Sonora. This is one of the most pleasant regions on earth, a zone where it seldom gets very hot or very cold, a land of eternal fall and eternal spring. In the warmest months the nights are always cool, and in the coldest months the sun is out bright and warm at noon. This is true of high and hilly Sonora, and also of the Arizona hills running along the Mexican border clear to the Big Bend of Texas.

All of this area has hills and mountains rising from grassy, rolling plains. It's a region where the ocotillo and the prickly pear of the desert meets the oaks of the mountains, a land of piñon and juniper, cliff rose and mountain mahogany. In this belt of country the animals of the Rockies meet those of the semitropics. From the far north have come the bighorn sheep, the mule deer, the elk, the black bear. Up from the south have come our little whitetails, the peculiar coati-mondi, the mountain lion, the wild turkey. Once

35

the grizzly ranged this country in good numbers, but it has been hunted out in the American Southwest and survives only in a few parts of Chihuahua. Of all these animals, to me the most typical of the region is the little fantail. I always think of him as running along a grassy hillside, waving his snowy flag, and disappearing into the head of an oak-filled draw.

Because the little whitetails occupy many different types of country, there are many different ways of hunting them. Down on the Sonora desert I have hunted them by walking around the bottom of the little hills, where they bed down, and letting my rising scent flush them out. When they're found in brushy canyons, a good way to get venison is for two hunters to work together, one hiking up one side of a canyon and his companion taking the other. The hunter seldom sees deer that he himself moves. Instead he can nail bucks on the other side of the canyon that have been put up by his pal.

As I write this I can still see in memory one of the finest whitetails I ever shot. A friend and I were hunting together, he on one side of a draw and I on the other. I saw a buck get up about fifty feet in front of my companion and sneak off, head down, tail between his legs. He was almost as inconspicuous as a cock pheasant sneaking through the stubble ahead of a dog. My pal wasn't aware that he was in pebble-tossing distance of a fine buck, but I could see both of them on that steep hillside opposite me. I sat and carefully put a bullet right behind that buck's shoulder.

But the sportiest and in many ways most pleasant whitetail hunting is done with horses, riding cattle and game trails along the sides of the draws and canyons. Then every time a deer flashes a white tail and takes off, the hunter has to see if it's a buck or a doe and take action accordingly. I always carry my rifle in a scabbard on the left side of my saddle, with the rifle butt to the rear and pointing up at about a 45° angle. It takes only seconds to get off the horse on the left side, grab the small of the stock with the right hand, and yank the rifle out of the scabbard. Then you sit down and open up.

Fantails are small deer, and their light, tender bodies don't offer much resistance to bullets. This calls for relatively light, easily expanded bullets traveling at high velocity. More often than not the bucks are shot running, and fast bullets make it easier to figure the right lead. I have used the 87-grain bullet in the .250/3000 Savage and have found it excellent on these diminutive deer. The 7 mm. Mauser with the old Western 139-grain open-point bullet was powerful whitetail medicine, and so is the .257 with good

100-grain bullets. The new .243 Winchester and .244 Remington with bullets weighing from 90 to 100 grains should be made to order—fast, flat shooting, and quick opening. The 150-grain bullets in the .30/06 and the 130-grain bullets in the .270 are poison on fantails. Generally, 180-grain bullets for the .30/06 open up too slowly. Some of the 150-grain bullets are excellent.

I did a lot of whitetail hunting in Mexico, from one to four trips a year for many years. I have no exact record of how many whitetails I shot there and in Arizona, but I took a good many. One thing I learned for sure is that they call for a fast-opening bullet. Back when the .257 was newly hatched, the bullets for the most part had thick, heavy jackets, and when I used them I spent half my time chasing wounded whitetails that were well hit but still going.

The main enemy of the fantail is the mountain lion, and until hunters get more skillful and are allowed to shoot does as well as bucks, predation by lions is necessary for healthy whitetail herds. In areas where lions are kept killed down, the deer become too plentiful, destroy their own browse, and die off from disease. The best Mexican deer ranges have a lot of lions—and a lot of deer. Coyotes take many fawns, and I have found where they have killed grown deer. Bobcats are likewise fawn killers.

But nature has seen to it that the little whitetails can survive. The twin fawns, born in the off-beat months of July and August, mean a great rate of increase. The stealth and cunning of the deer make them difficult for predators to get. Because of their size, an area can support about twice as many whitetails as mule deer.

The hunting pressure Coues deer can stand is amazing. There's excellent whitetail hunting, for example, in the Catalina mountains overlooking the city of Tucson, the second largest city in Arizona.

If a country is brushy, the little fantails like it. If it's open, they can make a little cover go a long way. Many times when hunters are working out the brush in the draws and along the rimrocks, fantails bed right out in the grass where no one would expect to find them. I once jumped a dandy buck out of tall grass under a lone oak on a big grassy slope. I shed my surprise in time to nail him, but I had no more expected a shot at a whitetail than at a tiger.

Another time I was sitting on a ridge glassing some country below when it dawned on me that some dark points sticking out of the grass about fifty yards in front of me looked more like antler tips than dead sticks. I turned my 9X binoculars on them. They were antlers. The buck had been lying there in the grass taking the sun when I came over the ridge, and he apparently decided the smart move was not to move at all. He didn't jump until I was almost on top of him.

A Coues buck in Sonora jumped out of the grass so close in front of my horse that he frightened my poor beast of burden almost out of his wits. By the time the resulting rodeo was over the buck was long gone.

I've seen grown fantail bucks sneak along in tall grass with their knees so bent they appeared to be crawling. Once I missed getting a shot at a fine buck I'd watched for five minutes as he crept through tall grass and thin brush. I couldn't believe it was a deer, it was so close to the ground I thought it must be a coyote.

I can think of no hunting more pleasant than a November or December shoot for fantails in Mexico. It's a hunt for a rare trophy worn by a shrewd and intelligent animal.

The deer don't rut until February and March, so the late-fall venison is always good, one of the choicest pieces of big-game meat in North America. The weather is perfect then—crisp nights and balmy days full of sun. Generally the dude will hunt from horseback and cut the deer down on the run, which takes some doing. Then there are always the nights around the campfire of fragrant mesquite, the coals cooking steaks from the little venados and a pot of frijoles. Ah, me!

Deer and Deer Rifles

Jack O'Connor

The scene was the Arizona desert and the time was about two generations ago. One of the actors was a skinny, long-legged kid, a clumsy lout with big feet, green eyes, light hair, and a hide so browned by the sun that on the rare occasions when he wore a hat and his straw-colored hair could not be seen he was often taken for a light-eyed Mexican.

The other was an equally skinny, three-year-old buck mule deer, slab-sided and probably beset with worms. The kid called the buck a blacktail because in those days everyone in Arizona called mule deer blacktails. The buck was not very well nourished but it had a spindly four-point head, which in the East would be considered a ten-pointer.

Anyway, when he was hunting quail, the kid had found an area all tracked up by desert mule deer. In addition, he had actually

This chapter originally appeared in the September 1962 issue of *Outdoor Life*.

seen a doe and a fawn. In those lawless days, the sight of a deer was rare on the Arizona desert since the animals were hunted in season and out.

So, saying nothing to anyone about his plans, the kid had gone out the next day with a rifle instead of a shotgun. It was a .30/40 Krag with a 30-inch barrel. The kid had paid $1.50 for it. He had bought it from a bindle stiff (tramp) who had been camped down by the river beneath a wrecked railroad bridge. The bindle stiff had found himself in great need of a bottle of corn squeezings and in no particular need of a rifle just then. His asking price for the Krag was $3, and the lowest price he would accept was $1.50. By a curious coincidence, the price of a bottle of popskull was $1.50, and the kid happened to have that much scratch with him.

So the bindle stiff got his jug and the kid got his rifle. Ammunition, as he now remembers it, cost about $1.25 a box. The cartridges were loaded with the long 220-grain bullet with a lot of lead exposed. The bindle stiff had evidently known a thing or two about a rifle, as he had put on a homemade front sight that lined up with the military rear sight so that the old musket shot at point of aim at about 150 yards.

So, that frosty winter morning the kid was sneaking cautiously through that tracked-up desert forest looking for a deer. Generally he couldn't see over 100 yards since this was a country of paloverde and ironwood trees, saguaros (giant cactus), and cholla (jumping cactus). Then the kid became conscious of a movement on the other side of an ironwood tree about 50 yards away. He suspected it was a deer, and the shock was so violent that afterward he had a headache.

Next he knew it was a deer, as the animal moved a bit and he could make out gray hide and dingy white rump; then he saw the deer's head as the animal reached up and delicately nipped off a delectable bit of browse.

After what seemed like an hour but was probably less than a minute, the buck was fairly well out in the open. The kid could see the gray-shiny antlers. It was time to shoot. Shaking, he lifted his rifle and tried to keep the homemade front bead in the middle of the deer.

He was trembling so violently that the front sight jerked off and on the buck. He tried to remember to squeeze the trigger. He tried to make himself quit shaking. He hated himself because he could not. He was desperately afraid the buck would see him and take off.

Finally he yanked the trigger. The buck was gone, and the kid stood there, his heart pounding, his head aching, his hands still trembling, his legs weak. After the roar of the shot, the desert seemed deathly still. He heard a quail call, and far off in the quiet desert air the sweet and melancholy whistle of a freight train. He had blown his chance and he'd probably never get another.

Slowly he walked over toward the spot where the deer had been. There were the tracks all right; he could see how they had plunged through the soft, sandy soil as the deer had run. Desperately he tried to think of an alibi. It was that damned, long-barreled rifle, he decided. What he'd wanted was a real deer rifle, a .30/30 Winchester or Marlin carbine. But those cost $15 down at the hardware store, and as far as he was concerned they might as well have cost $1,000.

Hopelessly he followed the tracks. He had gone about fifty yards when he got another violent shock. He saw blood. He could hardly believe it. At first there were a few drops. Then he found a big splash, then more. He followed the blood. Then he saw something gray and quiet beside a bush ahead of him. It was the buck—and the buck was dead. The old 220-grain soft point had struck just forward of the flank and had come out behind the left shoulder.

Maybe the fact that that old Krag happened to wobble on just as the kid yanked the trigger had a lot to do with making him a hunter. Anyway, the kid grew up, became a father and a grandfather, and almost every year of his life he has hunted deer—whitetails and mule deer, big deer and little deer, deer in brush and deer in open country, deer on the flats and deer in mountains almost rugged enough for sheep, deer far north in Alberta and British Columbia and deer south in tropical Sinaloa.

He has hunted deer with that old .30/40, with a .256 Newton, a .250/3000 Savage, a .30/30, a 7 mm. Mauser, several .30/06 and .270 rifles, a .35 Remington, a .257, a .348, a .35 Whelen, a .300 Weatherby. He has killed deer with a .22 Hornet, a wildcat 2-R Lovell, and a .22 rimfire.

How many deer this chap has shot he does not remember, but it has been quite a few. He has done a little deer hunting in Pennsylvania and South Carolina and quite a bit of it in Texas, but most of the deer he has shot have been mule deer (of the desert and Rocky Mountain variety) and Arizona whitetails. He has heard of mule deer that have dressed out at 400 pounds and more, but he doesn't believe such an animal exists. The heaviest buck he ever weighed field dressed was, as he remembers it, 235 pounds, but he has shot two bucks that weighed about 175 in the quarters, and he thinks they might have gone 250 field dressed. The heaviest Arizona whitetail he ever shot weighed 118½. He once shot a whitetail buck with nineteen points in all and has shot several mule deer with thirteen and fourteen points altogether. He once killed two deer with one shot and once helped a couple of companions put fourteen shots into a 110-pound buck before it went down. The antlers with the widest spread he ever shot went 37½ inches, but he has seen mule deer heads that went from 45 to 48 inches.

This hunter has missed more deer in the brush than anyplace else. The best shot he ever made on a deer was with a scope-sighted .30/06 at 330 paces. He could see only the buck's head and neck, took a rest over a log, held what looked like about nine inches over the top of the neck, and broke it. His worst shot was a clean miss—before two witnesses—at a standing buck broadside at not over 125 yards. He was afraid the deer was about to jump, and he yanked the trigger.

A good deal of deer hunting has convinced this chap that deer are easy to kill if the bullets hit in the right place and behave properly. He also knows that if the bullets don't hit in the right place deer are very hard to kill.

Almost always this deer hunter, if he has the opportunity, tries to place the bullet through the lungs back of the foreleg. If the deer is not broadside, he aims to drive the bullet up into this area. He likes the lung shot because it is a large target easy to hit, and because if a bullet placed there behaves properly, the deer seldom goes far and is generally dead within a few yards of where he is hit. Furthermore, the bullet that goes through the buck's rib cage from side to side destroys no edible meat.

This hunter thinks there are two very different kinds of deer rifles—one to be used in brush and forest and the other to be used in hilly, open country. For the kind of brush and forest hunting done for whitetail deer in the East, for blacktails west of the Coast Range in northern California, Oregon, and Washington, for mule deer early in the season in thick spruce and fir at high altitude, and for mule deer in the brushier parts of the Sonora desert he likes a light, fast-operating rifle with a short barrel. He thinks such a weapon should be chambered for a reasonably heavy bullet at moderate velocity.

The reason for this is that the heavy, round-nose bullet that isn't traveling at breakneck speed gets through brush with less deflection than faster, lighter bullets with sharp points. But he also knows that any bullet can be deflected by brush. He remembers one time when he took a shot at a moose through heavy brush at what he remembers as being about 30 yards—and missed the whole moose. His next shot at the moose was in the clear and he killed it. He remembers also three shots at a whitetail buck that foolishly ran in a semicircle around him through heavy brush. The first two shots, he afterward found out, did no damage except to nick the

This Remington Carbine Pump Model 760 "Gamemaster" handles .30-06
and .308 calibers.

Here is a .300 Weatherby Magnum Mark V Deluxe bolt action with 4X
Weatherby Imperial Scope.

Browning automatic rifles come in calibers from .243 to .338 and can be
used for all sorts of hunting.

The Winchester Model 94 in .30/30, like that shown here with low-power
scope with long eye relief, is a favorite for woods hunting.

buck with some fragments of bullet jacket, but on the third shot
the buck went through an opening and the 180-grain .30/06 bullet
piled him up.

Unlike many hunters who look down their noses at the .30/30,
he thinks it an excellent cartridge for this sort of thing. And he
likewise regards the .32 Special as a good brush cartridge with
adequate killing power—at moderate ranges and with well-placed
shots—for any North American deer that ever walked. He also
thinks that the light, fast-handling Winchester and Marlin lever
actions in such calibers are about right for deer.

Because there is always a possibility that the first shot at a deer
in brushy country may hit a limb or a twig and deflect, he thinks
that for hunting of this sort a lever action, a pump, or a semiautomatic is a good idea for the woods hunter. All of these are faster

43

than the bolt action. The Winchester Models 94 and 88, the Marlin Model 336, the Savage Model 99, the Remington Model 760 pump, and the Remington Model 742, the Ruger carbine, and the Winchester Model 100 are all light, handy, fast-operating weapons.

This old deer hunter, as we have seen, has killed deer with a .22 rimfire. They were killed at a Mexican waterhole at very short range. He has likewise killed deer with carefully placed shots with varmint calibers like the .22 Hornet, the 2-R Lovell, and the .22/250. However, he has seen the high-speed .22 bullets go to pieces on large bones (if a deer can be said to have large bones) and even on ribs, and doesn't think deer should be shot with any bullet weighing less than 90 grains. He thinks a minimum of 100 grains is better.

For short-range woods shooting, he thinks any fairly heavy bullet that opens up quickly is adequate for deer. The old .44/40 cartridge with its 200-grain bullet at a muzzle velocity of 1,310 ft. seconds has probably killed more whitetail deer than any other cartridge with the possible exception of the .30/30. The .44 Magnum revolver cartridge shot in the Ruger carbine should be deadly.

But if he were going in hock for a new brush rifle, he thinks he'd acquire a Marlin lever action or a Remington pump for the .35 Remington cartridge of a Model 88 Winchester or Model 99 Savage in .358.

He regards the neglected .358 Winchester cartridge with its 200-grain bullet at 2,530 or its 250-grain bullet at 2,250 as probably the most deadly woods cartridge in existence—not only for deer but for elk and even moose. The .358 has the power and weight to drive deep on the rear-end shots which the woods hunter all too often has to take.

Over the years this deer hunter has had more trouble with bullets that didn't open up fast enough than he has had with bullets that penetrated too deeply. He thinks that if the deer hunter has a choice he should take the fast-opening bullet.

For woods shooting he hasn't got much use for open sights. Under the stress of excitement, it is easy to shoot over with them since the tendency is not to get the bead down into the notch. Receiver sights are better, but the best iron sights were the peeps close to the eye—the old Lyman tang and cocking-piece sights. They were not the most accurate sights in the world, but they were adequately accurate for 50- to 100-yard shooting.

The best sight he has ever used in the brush is a low-power scope (2½ or 3X) because of the wide field of view and because of the ability of the glass sight to resolve detail, to "look through" the brush, to tell deer from limbs and twigs.

For open-country deer hunting at longer ranges, this chap likes a flat-shooting cartridge giving a fairly light bullet a velocity of from 2,700 to 3,200 foot seconds. Then he likes to sight-in for the longest range that will not give him midrange misses. The world is full of good, open-country deer cartridges — the .30/06 with the 150-grain bullet, the .270 with the 130-grain, the .280 with the 125-grain, the 7 mm. Remington Magnum with the 150-grain, the 7 x 57 Mauser with the 140-grain, the .300 Savage and the .308 with the 150-grain. He has never shot a deer with the .243 but considers it entirely adequate with the 100-grain bullet. He bases this opinion on a good deal of use of the now-dying .257 Roberts on deer.

However, he has done more open-country shooting of mule and whitetail deer with .30/06 and .270 rifles than with anything else. The quickest-killing .30/06 bullet he ever used was the old 150-grain Western hollow point. Bullets he liked for the .270 were the Remington 130-grain Bronze Point, the 130-grain Speer and Sierra, the Western Silvertip, the 120-grain Barnes. Some of the controlled expanding bullets don't open up quite fast enough, he thinks, and don't give kills quite so quick. He remembers a buck he shot with his rifle rested over a rock at about 325 yards. Dust could be seen to fly above the deer's back as it stood on a hillside. "Over," his companion said. But before he could shoot again, the buck was down. If the bullet had opened faster the deer would have collapsed in its tracks.

For this open-country shooting at deer, this hunter now uses 4X scopes. They have sufficient field and they give a better picture of the deer and more precise aim. However, this hunter admits that probably a 2½ or 3X scope will do just about as well for any big game, even at ranges of 300 yards and over. Before World War II, he used 2½X scopes almost exclusively and never felt himself underpowered.

Flat-shooting, high-velocity, bolt-action rifles, such as those described, are also excellent for those Eastern hunters who shoot from hillside to hillside at deer when the leaves are off the trees and bushes and for those who plan to shoot across pastures at deer coming out of the woods to feed.

But they are by no means ideal for ordinary woods hunting. The fast bullets deflect badly in the brush, this deer hunter thinks. In addition, the 4X scopes are a bit shy of field for brush hunting, and the bolt action is on the slow side for the fast second shot.

Likewise, most of the brush cartridges are not much good for open-country shooting where shots will often be taken at 300-350 yards. Used as it should be, the .30/30 is a good killer on deer. Shot wildly at deer 250-350 yards away, it isn't so hot. When this chap got out of college his pocketbook was thin and he had sold his rifles so he would have enough jack in his jeans to take pretty girls dancing. He ordered the then brand-new Model 54 Winchester rifle in .270 caliber, but until it came he tried to make do with an ancient Model 8 Remington automatic for the .35 Remington cartridge. He hunted in semiopen country of juniper, piñon, and yellow pine, and the shots he got were long. It was a pretty frustrating experience.

But cartridges like the .308, the .300 Savage, and the .30/06 when used with suitable, round-nose 180-grain bullets do pretty well for the brush as well as for open country. The .270 and .280 with the round-nose 150-grain bullets are usable in the brush and shoot flat enough for much open-country shooting. Once this chap hunted in the jungles of India, shot everything including hog deer, spotted axis deer, wild boar, and even peacocks with the 150-grain Core-Lokt and Hornady round-nose soft-point .270 bullets. He didn't have much to complain of.

The old deer hunter in this little piece is, of course, your correspondent. The piece is directed mostly to the many thousands of *Outdoor Life* readers who have done little or no deer hunting but who will be out for deer this fall. The old deer hunter wishes them well and hopes they get a good bullet in the right spot. If they do, they'll find that almost any reasonably potent rifle will get them venison.

Deer Cartridges

In this chapter, O'Connor discusses many of the cartridges shown here. Ben East discusses his favorites in the next chapter. And other cartridges receive mention throughout the book. The following cartridges are close to actual size, arranged sequentially from small to large calibers. The grain with each name corresponds to that shown; though many of these cartridges are also available in other grains.

6 mm. Remington
Magnum, 100 gr.

.243 Winchester, 100 gr.

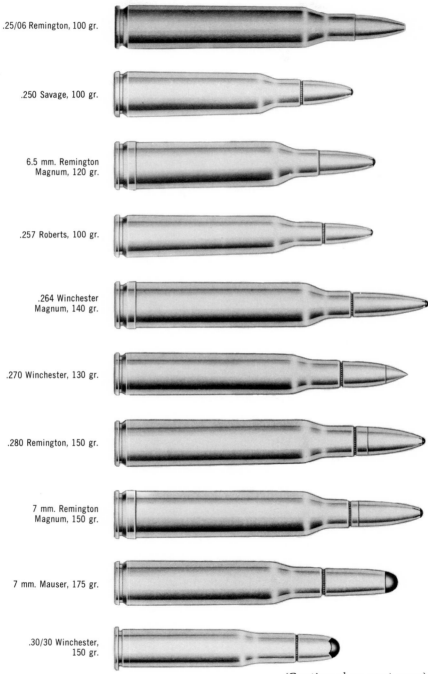

.25/06 Remington, 100 gr.

.250 Savage, 100 gr.

6.5 mm. Remington
Magnum, 120 gr.

.257 Roberts, 100 gr.

.264 Winchester
Magnum, 140 gr.

.270 Winchester, 130 gr.

.280 Remington, 150 gr.

7 mm. Remington
Magnum, 150 gr.

7 mm. Mauser, 175 gr.

.30/30 Winchester,
150 gr.

(Continued on next page)

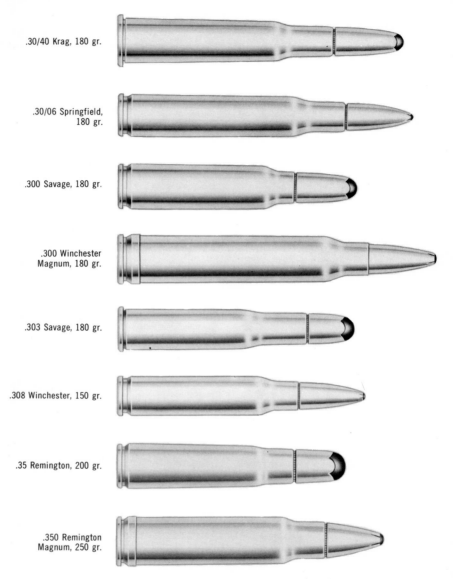

.30/40 Krag, 180 gr.

.30/06 Springfield, 180 gr.

.300 Savage, 180 gr.

.300 Winchester Magnum, 180 gr.

.303 Savage, 180 gr.

.308 Winchester, 150 gr.

.35 Remington, 200 gr.

.350 Remington Magnum, 250 gr.

Photos by Remington Arms Co., Inc.

Guns
for Whitetails

Ben East

$\mathbf{T}$he most important item in any hunter's outfit is his gun. But let me follow that quickly by saying that the man behind it is far more important than the gun itself. There is a wide range of firearms that will do a top job of killing either whitetail or mule deer, in the hands of a hunter who can shoot where he wants to. But the best firearm made is far more likely to miss or cripple than to kill if its user lacks the ability to place his shots properly.

If the gun is the Number 1 item in deer hunting, it is also the most debated. To begin with, although the whitetail and muley are the foremost game animals on this continent for the rifleman and the majority of hunters prefer a rifle to a shotgun for deer, thousands are using shotguns successfully these days for the reason that the law gives them no choice.

This chapter appears in print for the first time.

49

Many heavily populated farmland states now have thriving white-tail herds. If cover is in short supply the deer have even learned to hide out in cornfields. And the majority of those states ban rifles, both as a safety measure and also in response to overwhelming landowner demand. Farmers just don't want deer hunters traipsing around with firearms that can carry a mile. When Michigan first opened a deer season in its southern farming counties, for example, the governor found it necessary to convene a special session of the legislature to limit hunters to shotguns. At the short ranges at which most whitetails are killed a shotgun will do the job nicely, too.

The shotgun hunter has his choice of two loads, buckshot or rifled slugs. Round or pumpkin balls are no longer loaded by American ammunition makers. Of the two available, it's far better to use the rifled slug if the laws of your state permit.

Buckshot is a reasonably good killer up to sixty yards. Beyond that, although kills are made at seventy-five yards and even up to ninety and a hundred, the pattern opens up and the pellets lose their punch, so it's much more likely to cripple than kill cleanly. As an oldtime buckshot user remarked to me years ago, "Unless you're close enough to spoil meat, you ain't close enough to lay 'em down."

As for the rifled slug, there is no question about its great killing power. In 12-gauge it has been used successfully at ranges up to seventy-five yards on such game as caribou, elk, moose, Alaskan brown bear and even African lions and buffalo. And in a shotgun equipped with the right sights its accuracy will amaze any shooter who has not tested it. By the right sights I mean a good visible bead in front and a rear peep adjustable for elevation and windage.

Several sight makers now offer equipment of that kind for the benefit of deer hunters using shotguns. Such sights help in two ways. First, for practical purposes they convert the shotgun into a rifle, enabling the shooter to do a better job of aiming. Second, they make it possible to correct any defect in the accuracy of the gun itself. Not every shotgun will throw a slug true center, exactly where held. The receiver sight allows adjustment for this, just as a rifle sight does, and enables the shooter to get the best out of his gun by sighting it in ahead of time.

The Williams Gunsight Company at Davison, Michigan, not far from my home, has done a great deal of research and experimental work in this business of shotgun sights. I once watched Dale Williams test a 12-gauge, full-choke Winchester Model 12 with rifled slugs in standard factory load. At seventy-five yards he laid five in a group I could cover with my hand. That's better than many deer hunters can do with their favorite rifle. Williams told me that 4-inch groups at 50 yards and 7-inchers at 75 are not unusual. Now and then an exceptional gun will perform well up to 125 yards but 100 yards is considered the maximum effective range of the rifled slug, and even that may be stretching things a little. Advance work on the range will tell you what your gun will do and enable you to take any kinks out of your shooting.

For deer the gauge of the gun is not of great importance. Of course the 12 is more powerful than the 16 or 20, for the reason that it throws a bigger chunk of lead, but any of them packs ample wallop for muley or whitetail. And while it can hardly be recommended as a deer gun, the little .410 has put quite a bit of venison on the table.

The rifled slug in 12 gauge as loaded by Western weighs 1 ounce and leaves the gun at 1,470 feet per second, with a muzzle energy of 1,995 foot-pounds. At 50 yards it's still moseying along at 1,270 feet with a 1,485 foot-pound punch. Slugs in 16- and 20-gauge travel almost as fast and shoot about as far, but because of their lighter weight are not as powerful. At 50 yards, for example, the $7/8$-ounce 16-gauge slug delivers 1,205 foot-pounds, the 20-gauge, weighing $5/8$ ounce, 923 foot-pounds. Plenty for deer in each case, although many firearm experts are inclined to rule out the 20 as too light.

On the other hand, I have a friend, an experienced deer hunter and also a taxidermist, who contends that the 20 gauge is the ideal shotgun for whitetails. The bigger gauges do more damage than is necessary, he says, and leave a needlessly big exit hole if they go all the way through.

The hunter who wants or is required to use a shotgun for deer can make out all right with the same gun he uses for upland game or waterfowl, if he will equip it with a good set of sights, rely on rifled slugs, and limit his shooting to the effective range of his equipment. He can shoot slugs in any bore from cylinder to full choke, although a modified choke or skeet bore is likely to prove best. Choke devices handle them very well.

One hunter of my acquaintance carries a 12-gauge side-by-side double, from which he has cut about eight inches off the barrels to reduce it to brush-rifle length. Equipped with front bead and rear aperture sights, its accuracy just about matches that of a rifle and its owner counts it the perfect firearm for whitetails.

In most whitetail range—excepting farming country where the deer feed in fields and must do much of their moving in the open—the shotgun with rifled slugs has one final advantage.

The heavy, slow-moving slug punches through brush as if it

Browning Buck Special automatic fires
rifled slugs and buckshot in 12, 16, 20
gauge — has interchangeable 24-inch barrel.

Savage Model 30 (Slug) Field Grade fires
rifled 12-gauge slugs. Barrel lengths/types
can be interchanged.

Ruger M-77 bolt action rifle comes in two
barrel lengths for six calibers ranging from
.25/06 to .338.

Savage Model 99-A (saddle) lever action
rifle is made for .250 and .300 Savage, .243
or .308 Winchester calibers.

were not there, and that's a lot more than can be said for a high-speed rifle bullet. I have never heard of a deer missed because a shotgun slug was deflected, unless it whacked somewhat solidly into a tree. Every experienced rifleman knows what brush or even a single twig can do to his shot. Most have learned by hard experience.

There are firearm experts who contend that at extreme close range a 12-gauge shotgun loaded with buckshot is the greatest game stopper of all, on anything up to the African leopard. In fact many African white hunters pick that as their weapon when they have to go after a wounded leopard in thick cover. Certainly there is no reason for any deer hunter limited to a shotgun to harbor doubts about his firearm. The gun will deliver the goods if the hunter does his part.

When it comes to deer rifles, the arguments are endless. But there is one thing to remember first of all. Most whitetail hunting is done in brushy cover or timber, a lot of it in cedar swamps or the dense thickets of stream bottoms. Therefore, the first requirement of the whitetail rifle is that it be no heavier than is necessary, well balanced, and short and compact enough to handle well in brush. And within reason, light recoil is to be preferred to hard kicking.

I never owned one of the .35 caliber autoloaders that Remington made many years ago, but a hunting partner of mine did and I always considered the rifle an abomination, for one somewhat surprising reason. It was a good caliber, with plenty of power for deer, it shot fast, and the length was right for easy handling. But the clip magazine protruded just ahead of the trigger guard, and there simply was no convenient way to carry the gun. On the shoulder the clip cut in. In the hand the rifle had to be held ahead of the clip, and that threw it completely off balance.

So pick a rifle, first of all, that feels right to you and that you can take through cedar or alder tangles with a minimum of fuss.

It's the subject of calibers that provokes the most disagreement among whitetail hunters. On that score there are a few basic considerations to keep in mind.

In its day, the .30/30 was close to the universal whitetail gun, with the .32 special — which is almost identical so far as effective range and killing power are concerned — a close second. In the deer woods of Michigan, Wisconsin and Minnesota, where I have done the bulk of my hunting, those two were seen two generations ago more frequently than all other calibers put together.

They are still good deer calibers and they're still being sold. Also, there are a good many old ones around, for the reason that if a deer rifle is given care it lasts for many years. But in recent years modern calibers that speak with more authority have supplanted them to a large degree.

In the whitetail country of the Great Lakes states today you are likely to see such calibers as the .280 Remington, .284 Winchester, .308, 7 mm Remington Magnum, .30/06, or the .348. Occasionally you run across a .270, .300 H & H Magnum or .338 Winchester Magnum. Some of these are logical rifles for the job, some have drawbacks.

To begin with, the whitetail hunter has no need for a high-velocity, flat-trajectory rifle. Such guns have their place in mountain hunting and in the West generally, for sheep, mule deer, antelope and so on. But what you need for such game in open country is not what you need for deer in brush.

One of the top hazards of whitetail shooting is brush deflection, so why not pick a rifle and bullet most likely to get where you want it to go? That means something on the heavy side and slow moving. And round or flat points are better than sharp ones. There is no guarantee that even the burly, lumbering messenger will make the grade, but at least it has a better chance.

I began my deer hunting, back in the 1920's, with a .38/55 Winchester. It was too heavy and the barrel was too long by today's standards, and there were good reasons why it became obsolete years ago. The shell is no longer loaded, so far as I know. But there was one thing about that old rifle that I liked. The slow and heavy bullet was not easily turned aside from the business at hand.

Of the deer rifles I have shot, the one I like best (and the only one I have carried in years) is a Savage Model 99 Featherweight in .300 caliber. I make no claim that that is the best of all calibers for deer. But it is an excellent and entirely adequate cartridge, and I have killed elk and a polar bear with it with no difficulty. My reason for preferring that rifle over any other I have used, however, is the fact that I like its weight, balance, hang and action.

As for its killing power, any time I can't floor a deer with that .300 I certainly wouldn't do any better with an elephant gun — and I'd probably do a lot worse.

I have always preferred the 180-grain bullet to the 150 in the .300 Savage load, for the reason that, because it is slower as well as heavier, it is more likely to punch through brush. But there was one time when it failed me incredibly.

I was sitting that wet November afternoon at the edge of a thicket-bordered logging road, with my back against a stump. Fifty yards to my left, something moved in the brush and I made out a deer's head. But I couldn't see horns, and I was hunting under a buck law.

Very carefully I freed my binoculars from my jacket front and brought them up. The antlers were there, a good six-point rack.

While I was putting the glasses out of the way, the buck walked across the road, in no hurry, and stopped with his head and shoulders screened in thick brush on my side. The back half of him was out in the open, but that was not what I wanted to shoot at. I rested my left elbow on my knee, found what looked like a patch of shoulder free of brush, took very deliberate aim and squeezed off.

Nothing happened. The deer didn't jump or even flinch. In the belief that my shot had paralyzed him, I waited a second or two for him to fall. When he didn't, I levered in a fresh shell and tried again. The result was identical.

It's hard to believe, but I fired four careful and well spaced shots at that deer without cutting hair, and he did not move out of his tracks. Obviously, he had not located me and wasn't going to run until he knew where the danger lay.

When I racked the action to load the fifth shell he decided where the noise was coming from. He pivoted and crossed the road in one soaring bound, back the way he had come. I threw my last shot as his flag went out of sight in a thicket of young hemlocks. It also was a clean miss. That was the only time in my life I ever suffered a full-blown case of buck fever. When I had time to think things over I concluded that brush deflection was entirely to blame for what had happened. Not long after that I had lunch in New York City with Jack O'Connor. He got a big kick out of my story, and he also supported my explanation completely. For the benefit of any reader who may think I just missed those four shots, let me say that I'm no expert rifleman but neither am I that bad.

So pick a whitetail rifle and a load that is most likely to get through brush. A twig can deflect a 250-grain bullet from a .348, but the same twig is far more likely (almost certain, in fact) to turn aside a 130-grainer from a .270.

One of the heavy slowpokes that quite a few brush-wise deer hunters are buying today, for example, is the recently revived .45/70 Winchester. The bullet leaves the muzzle at only 1,320 feet a second, but it weighs a whopping 405 grains, more than twice that of almost any other deer caliber, and it's a real brush cutter.

Of course it has to be remembered in choosing a rifle that the man who wants an all-round gun and intends to hunt moose, elk and bear with the same weapon he uses on whitetails must keep in mind his all-round requirements. He's not likely to want a .30/30 or a .300 Savage, for example. What he needs is a compromise, a gun that handles at least one load not too fast for deer brush, but with enough knock-down power to deal with the biggest, and even dangerous, game he plans to go after.

But under no circumstances do the big magnums, such as the .338 or .375, have a place in the deer woods, and because of their wicked recoil it's a rare owner who fires enough rounds with them on the target range to get on easy terms with his rifle.

When it comes to actions, I do not pretend to have advice to offer. Some hunters lean to the bolt, some to the lever, others to the slide and a few to the autoloading.

Experts like Jack O'Connor rate the lever action faster than the bolt, the pump or slide still faster and the autoloader fastest of all. But the difference is very slight, and I know of few situations in whitetail hunting where that tiny fraction of time really matters.

The experienced rifleman can get off a second or third shot plenty fast enough with any of the actions, and in heavy cover a fleeing deer rarely gives him the chance for more than that.

For the man who uses a horse—which whitetail hunters rarely do—the lever action has the advantage of fitting easily into a saddle scabbard and being easy to draw when game is sighted and the hunter steps down. I'm no horseman and I'm clumsy getting on and off. But I have pulled my .300 Savage from its boot and had a shot on the way to a mule deer about as soon as my feet could hit the ground. When all is said and done, the individual deer hunter is likely to be happiest if he picks the type of rifle action that he likes best.

What about scopes? They have advantages and disadvantages, but the former probably outweigh the latter where whitetail hunting is concerned. In thick brush, and especially for shooting at a running deer at close range, a scope can be a real handicap. But in seeing a standing deer and, above all, in making out antlers, and also in finding a hole through a thicket, a telescope is a big help. Many a hunter kills whitetails regularly with a scoped rifle who would go home empty-handed with iron sights.

A scope of low power is best for brush shooting. Three-power is plenty. And the hunter who does not want to use any scope is likely to do better shooting with a good aperture or peep rear sight mounted on the receiver. Never on the tang if the rifle is a hard kicker. The danger of eye injury with that combination is very great.

One final word about scopes. When a man grows old enough to need reading glasses he'd better resign himself to a scope whether he thinks he'll like it or not.

Not too many years ago, I missed three easy shots at a running buck in northern Minnesota, for no better reason than the fact that to my aging eyes the rear sight was a blur in which I simply could not find and properly place the front bead.

If you are not going to use a scope, by all means carry a good pair of binoculars. They won't improve your shooting but they will be a big help in finding and identifying deer.

Sighting-in the Rifle

Jack O'Connor

I well remember my first attempt to sight-in a rifle. I was then about nine years old, and the rifle was a .22 pump with open sights. It was nicely blued, and the stock was shiny. Everything worked smoothly, and I took great pride in the fact that my little pet handled .22 short, long, or long rifle cartridges interchangeably in its tubular magazine.

In those days my eyes were young, keen, and flexible. I was a pretty sharp hand with my Daisy BB gun, but with my new .22 I couldn't hit a thing.

I took the rifle back to the hardware store where I had bought it and asked the owner what I should do. He knew about as much about sight adjustment as I did. I found myself a wide plank with a conspicuous knothole and used it for a target. I discovered that

This chapter originally appeared in the October 1971 issue of *Outdoor Life*.

my little weapon was putting them high and to the left. But since the open rear sight was already in the lowest of three notches and as far as I could determine there was no way to move either the rear or the front sight left or right, I did not know what to do.

I finally enlisted the help of my uncle, Bill Woolf, who was a crack rifle and shotgun shot, a captain in the Arizona National Guard, and a member of the Arizona rifle team that competed at Camp Perry. We went out into the country. My uncle put up a target at fifty yards, and by deepening the notch of the rear sight with a file and knocking the rear sight over to the right in its slot with a hammer and punch, he finally got the little rifle putting them where it looked.

I used the little .22 pump for years, knocking off doves, quail, cottontails, jackrabbits, and a coyote or two with it. From the time my uncle got it sighted-in it always performed pretty well, but sighting-in remained to me a pretty mysterious business.

Today shooters, even young ones, are better informed and more sophisticated than they were in the days of my youth. There are more and better magazines publishing articles on hunting and shooting and more and generally better gun and shooting departments. Nevertheless I still get letters which show that some of my correspondents are as innocent of sighting-in know-how as I was at the age of nine.

Until comparatively recently most factory rifles came into the hands of the consumer equipped with the same sort of sights as my old .22 pump wore. Elevation was obtained generally by raising or lowering the rear sight by crude steps that were of no standard value. If the rifle still shot high when the rear sight was on the lowest step, the only thing to do was either to deepen the notch itself with a file or lower the step by filing it. Elevation changes could also be achieved by installing a higher or a lower front sight, as raising the front sight lowers the point of impact.

A rule to remember is that the rear sight is moved the way the shooter wants the point of impact to move; the front sight is moved in the opposite direction. If the rear sight is lowered and moved to the left the bullet will strike lower and to the left. If the front sight is moved low and to the left the point of impact moves higher and to the right.

The telescope sight, which I shall write about presently, is both front and rear sight. The scope tube acts as the rear sight. Move the rear of the scope to the right, and the point of impact moves to the right. Raise it up, and the point of impact moves up. The reticle, on the other hand, is the front sight. Lowering it makes the rifle shoot high; moving it to the right causes the point of impact to move to the left.

Rifles still leave the factory equipped with open sights, although today many of these open sights are adjustable. It is possible to buy some rifles with factory-installed telescope sights. The open sights are inexpensive and consequently do not add unduly to the retail price of the rifle. The manufacturers know that soon after purchase the better-grade rifles will be equipped with scope sights or possibly with adjustable receiver sights.

Rifles factory-equipped with open sights, from the humble .22 to the magnums, are sighted in at the various plants by men who specialize in such work. In the main they do a good job, and generally a good shot can pick up a factory big-game rifle and hit a standing deer with it at 150 yards or a cottontail with a .22 at 40 yards.

However, such accurate shooting should not be taken for granted. Workmen have their quotas, and sometimes they rush a rifle through the sighting process with the sights poorly adjusted. In addition, there is no guarantee that the factory will use the same bullet weight as the purchaser. Other factors are that no two shooters see sights alike (particularly open sights) and no two people hold rifles exactly the same. Anyone buying a rifle should verify the sighting with the ammunition he is going to use and should *never* assume that his rifle is correctly sighted-in.

Until comparatively recently dealers and gunsmiths who installed scope sights lined up bore and scope by "bore-sighting." To do this the rifle with the scope attached but with the bolt removed is put into a vise and the bore is lined up with a conspicuous object 25 to 100 yards away. One gunsmith I knew used to line the rifles up so that he could see in the center of the bore a light-colored brick about 50 yards away. Then the scope is adjusted so that the aiming point (intersection of crosswires, top of post, center of dot, or whatever) rests on the spot centered in the bore.

The average shooter who does not have a vise can do the same thing by cutting notches into a cardboard box and resting the rifle in the notches. Then he can line the bore up on a conspicuous object and adjust the scope so that the reticle rests on whatever is centered in the bore.

This is simply the first step in sighting-in. All it does is to make certain that sights and bore are pointing in the same direction. Bore sighting is equally useful with either peep or open sights.

Today the dealer or the gunsmith generally lines up bore and sights with an optical collimator. This is a gimmick with a "spud" that is inserted into the muzzle of the rifle. The "spuds" are of various diameters to fit the different bores. An optical gadget is aligned with the bore of the rifle by the spud. Looking through the scope of the rifle, one can see the crosswires or other aiming point in the scope and also crosswires in the form of an "X" in the collimator.

To collimate the scope, adjustments are made with windage and elevation dials to bring the "X" in the collimator and the aiming point of the scope reticle together. When this is done the scope is lined up with the axis of the bore.

A great advantage of the collimator over bore-sighting is that it can be used on lever-action rifles, on automatics, and on pumps since it is not necessary to remove a bolt in order to look down the bore.

Sometimes a bore-sighted or collimated outfit is so well lined up that is is perfectly sighted-in and does not need to be touched. Some years ago Earl Milliron, the Portland, Oregon, stock maker, bore-sighted a .280 Remington that he had stocked for me. My first group on the range at 100 yards was right on the button for all-around hunting — about 2½ inches high and right in line. I have had this happen a few other times.

However, no one should depend on such luck. Usually collimating or bore-sighting simply means that the first shot will be on the paper, often in the bull, and sometimes almost at point of aim. The reason these methods of preliminary sighting can't get those first shots just right is that barrels vibrate and rifles jump when they are fired. A barrel vibrates a little differently with bullets of different weight, and a rifle will shoot a little differently when shot from a rest, from offhand, from prone, or from sitting. The only sure way to know just where a rifle will shoot is to shoot it.

But let us suppose that our rifleman doesn't have a collimator (as most of us do not!), and suppose he doesn't even have enough credit at the grocery store to get away with an empty cardboard box to cut notches in. I'll let you in on a secret — an easy and just about fool-proof way to line up rifle sights which as far as I know I originated about thirty-five years ago — a method that requires no expensive equipment and little time, but which is surefire.

The method involves doing the preliminary shooting at 25 yards and adjusting the scope to put the bullet at the point of aim at that distance. Properly sighted-in for a practical distance, the scope-sighted big game rifle puts the bullet across the line of sight the first time at 25 yards. The second time the bullet crosses the line of sight (and the distance at which it is said to be sighted-in) varies from 200 to 275 yards depending on the velocity of the bullet and the height of the scope above the line of bore. But more of this later.

To do the preliminary shooting at short range, the essentials are a target, a supply of ammunition, and some sort of safe backstop. A barren hillside stops bullets nicely; so does the face of a quarry or

In bore-sighting, the intersection of crosshairs in scope (top) is adjusted to rest on the target seen through the center of the rifle bore.

When the X of the collimator and the + of the scope line up, the scope and bore are aligned.

The elevation dial of Leupold 4X scope has arrows to indicate Up and Down. Each graduation is one minute of angle.

As the elevation dial in Weaver K2.5 is turned, it clicks in ½ minutes. It is marked in 1-minute and 5-minute graduations.

the cut bank of a sand pit. If the shooting can be done at a regular rifle range, so much the better; but rifle ranges, alas, are in short supply in this country today.

A simple way to shoot is to put a target on a frame or on a cardboard or wooden box so placed that the bullets will not ricochet, then measure off 25 yards from the muzzle and shoot. The good shot who can hold steady and squeeze his shots can well shoot from the sitting position. The not-so-good shot should use a padded rest of some sort.

Mrs. Eleanor O'Connor uses a notched cardboard carton to bore-sight this bolt action rifle.

O'Connor points to a five-shot group, with center of impact a bit left (index finger covers one bullet hole). A group such as this, one inch left at 100 yards, would be only two inches left at 200 and three inches left at 300.

He should shoot about three shots, and then he should measure the distance from the center of impact of the three shots to the aiming point. Let us suppose that the center of impact is 1½ inches left and 1 inch low. A minute of angle has a value of 1 inch for each 100 yards of range. At 25 yards the point of impact is four times 1½ or 6 minutes left, and four times 1 or 4 minutes low.

Scope sights and receiver sights are graduated in minutes of angle and often click at changes of ½ or ¼ minute. The well-known Weaver K4 and K6 scopes click in ¼ minutes, for example, but the Weaver K2.5 and K3 scopes click in ½ minutes.

Now let us suppose that the rifle is equipped with a scope with adjustments that click in quarter minutes. We know our point of impact is 6 minutes left and 4 minutes low. We therefore come left 24 clicks by turning the windage adjustment dial in the "Left" direction and up 16 clicks by turning the elevation dial 16 clicks in the "Up" direction.

The next step is to check and refine the adjustments at 100 yards. This is necessary because any error at 25 yards is multiplied by four at 100 yards, by eight at 200 yards, and by twelve at 300 yards. When we shoot at 100 yards it is a good idea to use some sort of a soft or padded rest if a regular bench rest is not available. I have shot prone with the rifle rested over a rolled-up bedroll, from the back seat of a station wagon with the rifle rested on a pillow.

Generally this 100-yard shooting will reveal that a little refinement is necessary. The group should be centered and for all-around use to 250 or 300 yards about 3 inches high.

Then a bullet like that of the 180-grain .30/06 that leaves the muzzle at about 2,700 f.p.s. will be at point of aim at 200 yards, about 9 inches low at 300. Bullets that start out at 3,000 to 3,100 like the 125-grain .280 Remington bullet, the 130-grain .270, and the 150-grain 7 mm. Remington Magnum bullet will be 3 to 4 inches high at 200 yards and will cross the line of sight the second time at 250 to 275 yards, depending on the ballistic coefficient of the bullet, the height of the scope above the bore, and so on.

Usually such sighting and such trajectories make possible dead-on holds behind the shoulder at most practical game ranges. However, if the rifleman has the range facilities at his disposal he should shoot at targets at 200, 300, and 400 yards to determine the exact trajectory with his particular rifle and load.

The rifleman should never take it for granted that if he is sighted-in for one bullet weight he is also sighted-in for other weights. Sometimes he is, but often he is not. Generally a heavy bullet will land near enough to the point of aim at 100 yards so that it is practical to shift for short-range shooting. Some like to change from a 180-grain to a 220-grain bullet in the .30/06 for brush use, for example.

Anyone who plans to use two weights of bullets should fire at 100 and 200 yards. I use a 180-grain bullet in a pet .30/06 with a scope sight. Sighted to put the 180-grain bullet at 2,700 f.p.s. 3 inches high at 100 yards, it puts the 220-grain at 2,300 exactly to the point of aim at that distance. However, whereas the 180-grain is at point of aim at 200, the 220-grain is about 6 inches low.

This initial shooting at short range will save the man trying to sight-in a lot of headaches. Many times I have seen people who have just installed scopes or receiver sights try to do their first shooting at 100 yards. They miss the target completely and have no idea where their bullets are hitting. Consequently they do not know what adjustment to make.

I remember an incident during World War II when I was living in Tucson, Arizona. Three friends of mine had put Weaver 330 scopes on their rifles with the now-obsolete Stitch Install-It-Yourself mount made in San Antonio, Texas. Two of the rifles were Model 99 Savages in .300 caliber, and one was a Model 70 Winchester in .30/06.

The lads went out into the desert, found a hill for a backstop, paced off 100 yards, and set up three cardboard boxes with 100-yards small-bore targets pasted on. Then they sat down in a row and opened up on the boxes. When they walked up to inspect them they found that not a bullet had hit. They moved the adjustments this way and that and still did not connect. Presently each had used a box of twenty rounds of hard-to-get and carefully hoarded ammunition.

Finally one of them suggested that they tell me their troubles, since I had recently been installed as the shooting editor of *Outdoor Life* and presumably knew something about such arcane matters as sighting-in rifles. I went back to the improvised range with them. I took each rifle in turn, fired one shot at 25 yards, made the necessary adjustment, fired another shot for verification, then turned the rifles over to the owners. They checked at 100 yards and were delighted to find they were on target.

There is yet another method of preliminary shooting. This is to fire one carefully squeezed-off shot at 25 yards from a good solid rest and then, keeping the rifle rigid with the reticle still against the aiming point, to adjust the scope so that the aiming point of the reticle rests on the bullet hole.

This sounds slightly cockeyed, but it works. Here is the reason. The rifle itself always points in the same direction. When we sight-in we simply move the sight so that our point of aim and the spot where the bullet hits coincide. That lone bullet hole is where the rifle is shooting. We adjust the scope to point at the same spot.

An outdoor bench rest is ideal for sighting-in.

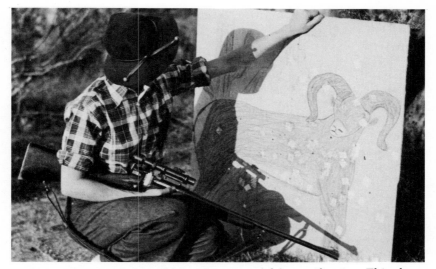

A target colored and shaped like game is useful for verification. This sheep target was used for checking bullet deflection through brush and for fast shooting at undetermined ranges.

If the shooter does not have perfect confidence in his shooting, he should fire three shots, determine his center of impact, and adjust to put the scope reticle there. But if the good shot uses a rest, one shot should do. As is the case with any short-range sighting, further checking and refining should be done at 100 yards.

For all-around use on big game, the point of impact that is 3 inches high at 100 yards is about right. On a big-game animal a 3-inch departure from point of aim does not amount to much. No one will miss the chest of a deer at 100 yards with a center hold on the chest, because the deer's chest is 14 to 18 inches thick. On the other hand, if the .30/06 with the 180-grain bullet is sighted-in for 100 yards and a 200-yard shot presents itself, the bullet will land about 7 inches low and a miss may well result. If an animal is 250 yards away the bullet will land about 14 inches low.

However, sighting-in for varmints is another thing. A mid-range rise of the bullet of 3 or 4 inches is too much and will cause misses in case of a jackrabbit or a rockchuck lying down. I generally sight-in my varmint rifles so that the bullets strike 1½ inches above the point of aim at 100 yards. This means that with something like the .22/.250, with its 55-grain bullet approaching 4,000 f.p.s., the bullet will be on at 250 and about 3 inches low at 300. With the slower .222 sighted to put the bullet 1½ inches high at 100, the bullet crosses the line of sight the second time at about 200.

The .22 rifle used for small game and plinking is probably most useful when it is sighted-in to hit the point of aim at 75 yards. With high-velocity ammunition the scope-sighted .22 is on at 25 yards, 1 inch high at 50, and on again at 75. At 100 yards the bullets strike 3 inches low, and at 125 yards they're 8 inches low. As can be seen, the useful .22 is by no means a long-range varmint rifle!

This habit that scope-sighted rifles of various calibers have of putting the bullet across the line of sight the first time at approximately 25 yards is a useful thing to remember. Shooting from the sitting position, I have clipped the heads off many juicy blue grouse with a .30/06's and .270's. To give the bullet a little leeway I hold where the neck joins the body. This knowledge of where the bullet crosses the line of sight at short range enables the hunter to shoot the head off a snake.

Rifles that are to be used on dangerous game at close quarters should be sighted-in for 100 yards. Special rifles like the British double rifles for such cartridges as the .450/400, the .465, and the .470 are usually sighted for 100 yards with open iron sights. This means that at 50 yards the bullets will strike 1 inch high—certainly not an excessive deviation from line of sight.

Today many African hunters are turning to scope-sighted bolt-action .458's. These are also sighted for 100 yards, and at 50 yards the bullet is only about ½ inch high. This close adherence of the bullet to line of aim is important in shooting dangerous game—to make a brain shot on an elephant or to shoot through a hole in branches to drive a bullet into the vital area of a grizzly or a buffalo.

The .375 is generally looked upon as an all-round rifle and is sighted to put the bullets a bit higher—2 inches above point of aim at 100 yards and, if scope-sighted, on at about 175. My .416 Rigby, the most powerful rifle I have, is scope-sighted to put the 400-grain bullet hand-loaded to 2,450 f.p.s. at point of aim at 100 yards. So sighted, it is practically at point of aim at 50 yards and the bullet strikes only 2 or 3 inches low at 150.

Whether the hunter uses his factory-installed open sights or has a scope or receiver sight put on and lined up by a gunsmith or a dealer, he should carefully check the rifle's shooting on paper. Banging away offhand at a rock on a hillside, as I have seen many people do, is no way to check the sights, as a shot that misses by a foot or two may be mistaken for a hit.

The finest rifle in the world is no good unless it shoots where it is aimed. And many a hunting trip has come to naught because the hunter neglected the simple precaution of sighting-in his rifle.

Preseason Scouting

Erwin A. Bauer

My friend Frank Sayers has been hunting whitetail deer with firearms or bow and arrow for longer than he likes to admit, and he has bagged about as many bucks as the law allowed. That's not easy to do, because the whitetail ranks with the wariest game animals on earth. I believe that a good whitetail buck is the most difficult trophy to take among all the game animals that I've encountered all over the world.

A good part of Frank's success must be the result of a hunting tactic he has long used. It has nothing to do with still-hunting, driving, tracking, or accurate shooting, although Frank is skilled at all of them. Most deer hunters ignore it. Let me cite a memorable example that happened years ago.

This chapter originally appeared in the October 1971 issue of *Outdoor Life* under the title "The Big Secret."

The Michigan deer season opened in mid-November as usual. Normally the weather is cold at that time of year, and there is a carpet of snow on the ground with more in prospect when the army of hunters heads north into the best whitetail country. A steady stream of traffic forms on all highways leading out of southern Michigan and northern Ohio the night before opening day.

Frank was never one to buck that traffic. He had driven to School-craft County in the center of the Upper Peninsula a week before. While most sportsmen were driving their cars, Frank was already ensconced in a comfortable camp on the shore of Blazed Trail Lake. When I arrived, a fragrant pot of stew was brewing on the two-burner camp stove, a week's supply of birch firewood had been cut and stacked just outside the tent, Frank was sipping a hot toddy while he honed his favorite hunting knife to razor sharpness. The scene would have been a splendid subject for Currier & Ives or Norman Rockwell.

Frank's secret should be obvious to you by now. He had come early and had made a comfortable camp on the very best site available in the Hiawatha National Forest. Bad weather wouldn't bother us, because of that secure camp. There was no rush to set up a tent in the darkness in a spot that might later prove to be very inconvenient. Frank had done all the chores, and that meant that the coming week could be devoted to hunting and nothing else.

Frank had a far more important reason for setting up camp early. It gave him several days to scout the area thoroughly in order to see just where most of the buck deer were located.

Morning and evenings, Frank had driven slowly along the back roads and fire trails, looking for places where deer had crossed. Tracks were easy to see in the soft sand of the roads where the wind had blown the snow away. And where the snow was undisturbed, tracks showed up clearly too. During the middle of the day he hiked along the birch and maple ridges looking for sign. One day he made a float trip on the Big Indian River to see if any deer were yet using the balsam swamps that the river drains. By the time I joined Frank in camp, he had collected evidence on where most of the whitetails for miles around were likely to be found. That's a huge advantage.

I won't go into the details of Frank's opening morning, because it was over almost as soon as it began. He bagged a four-point buck even more easily than is usual with him.

At daybreak he'd stood beside a runway that was deeply etched in the snow. His scouting had indicated that it was the hottest spot in the woods. When the buck came along, prancing nervously, Frank shot the deer handily. I helped my friend to drag the animal

Antler rubs on trees betray deer. Closer examination should yield pawings, runways and tracks that spell venison.

Even under dry conditions, tracks show up in soft earth and mud along the streams and roadsides.

Newly-fallen snow reveals heavy traffic on this deer runway.

In early fall a bedded buck might remain motionless while hunters tramp by unaware. In snow with thin cover a wise buck shows only an empty bed.

out of the woods, and by midmorning the buck was completely dressed out and hanging from a limb in camp.

"Scouting early really pays off," Frank mused that evening as he fried fresh deer liver.

Numerous similar incidents have convinced me that the very best way for the average Eastern or Northern whitetail hunter to collect his venison is to do some preseason scouting. Opening day may be much too late to begin looking for your deer.

Whitetails go largely unmolested during most of the year, but their quiet daily routines are disrupted early on opening day when a host of hunters hits the woods. The bulk of the kill is made on opening day, and the number of deer taken declines rapidly thereafter as each day of the season passes.

Deer behavior changes abruptly from normal to abnormal, and finding the animals becomes increasingly difficult. Old bucks become especially unpredictable and elusive. They actually seem to vanish from the earth. So I contend that the hunter with the best chance of success is the one waiting in the best possible position at daybreak on opening day. And only preseason scouting can locate that place. Hunting groups that make big drives often benefit from the preseason scouting too.

Assume that you are an enthusiastic deer hunter and have set aside a week or so of your annual vacation time for deer hunting. A recent survey in several Midwestern states revealed that the average

Buck and does emerge to feed at dusk—good scouting time.

deer hunter spent 3½ days in the woods, although he may have intended to spend seven or more. More significantly, most of those surveyed hunted on the first 3½ days of the season.

Instead of scheduling vacation time to begin with opening day as most men do, why not go early and spend several days scouting before the other hunters hit the heavy cover? That way, you get the jump on them as well as on the deer.

Preseason scouting has a fascination all its own. You're not under any great pressure, and buck fever isn't a factor. So you'll probably be a better observer, and you'll learn more about whitetails than you would if you were carrying a firearm. When you're reconnoitering on foot, you can also brush up on your woodsmanship—trying to walk more quietly, for instance.

In some states it is perfectly legal to combine some form of hunting with preseason scouting before the firearms deer season. For example, the archery deer season may immediately precede the firearms season. In such circumstances you could be bowhunting while you look for a deer to take with your rifle later on. Elsewhere the season on such species as ruffed grouse and snowshoe hares may be open, and that also provides an opportunity to double up. But because of the shooting involved in upland gunning and the con- centration it requires, it isn't as helpful as bowhunting. You won't spot deer so often if you're blasting away at birds.

In some regions that are crisscrossed by many roads, the bulk of

One delight of preseason scouting is seeing deer undisturbed. Here a buck may be skulking nearby.

the scouting can be done by car. In rough country, a four-wheel-drive vehicle is a great help. It is wise to get a county map, available in almost every county courthouse, or if you're hunting in a national forest, a forest map available at regional headquarters and most ranger stations. Large-scale topographic sheets may also be very helpful.

Sighting the animals themselves is obviously the best possible evidence. But in some areas, especially when the weather is very mild, deer may not move about much until after dark. So you may have to rely on tracks and other testimony.

Fresh tracks are a good indication that deer are in the area, and keep an eye out for fresh pellets, pawings in the earth, and rubs on saplings and trees. Rubs are easy to spot. They are made just before and during the rut by bucks that are scraping the velvet off their antlers. That rubbing often peels off the bark, leaving a bare spot that is noticeable from a distance. You'll often find the ground pawed up nearby.

Another preseason scouting method is to drive about at night and use a spotlight to locate deer. Their eyes show up clearly when the artificial light hits them, and you can often see antlers too. Never carry both a spotlight and any kind of firearm in your car at the same time at night. Having both during darkness is usually considered to be good evidence of deer jacking—illegal everywhere. Whenever I have gone out at night with a spotlight, I've always informed the local game warden or forest ranger beforehand about what I was going to do, so that there could be no mistake.

Small areas are best scouted by simply hiking across them, perhaps once from north to south and then from east to west. Two or more hunters hiking on parallel paths can inspect an area even more thoroughly. Although the hikers should certainly take note of actual sightings, a man afoot usually must depend heavily on the fresh sign he finds along his route.

There are many places, particularly in the Northern States and southern Canada, where a canoe float tip or cruising slowly around the edge of a lake can reveal a great deal. Tracks on sandy or muddy beaches are easy to spot.

Several years ago Lew Baker and I made an expedition to Ontario's Manitoulin Island in Lake Huron. We arrived well before opening day so that we could scout for deer and enjoy the autumn walleye fishing. What we found while fishing one day was enough to give any serious deer hunter a case of buck fever.

There are many lakes on Manitoulin Island, and there are small islands in many of those lakes. We found numerous fresh whitetail tracks on the shore of one such island where we stopped to cook lunch. And among them were exceedingly large hoofprints.

"Yearlings didn't make those," Lew commented with considerable excitement in his voice.

For the first time since my first boyhood deer hunt, I did not spend opening morning waiting on a stand or stillhunting. Although it was so cold that a crust of ice had formed around the lake's fringe, Lew and I launched a canoe and cruised around the island at daybreak toward the spot where we had spotted the multitude of tracks. Both of us had visions of getting our venison the easy way. In Ontario, it is legal to shoot deer from a canoe or rowboat, though swimming deer aren't legal.

It would make a great success story if I could say that we scored quickly by bagging a fine old buck at water's edge. Things didn't work out that way. We paddled completely around the island but saw nothing. We finally beached the canoe on the island and considered what to do next.

"Let's drive the island," Lew said. "You take a stand at one end. I'll still-hunt in your direction from the other. One of us should connect."

"All right," I said, "but give me enough time to get set."

I needed about fifteen minutes to paddle to the island's opposite end, where I disembarked and pulled the canoe up onto the sand. Right at that very spot were more very fresh deer tracks. Perhaps the animals had even seen me approaching. And at the same time I

Clicks of author's camera unsettle two bucks at their regular drinking place.

noted that there was crosswind from the west, so Lew's scent would not precede him.

The interior of the island was very rocky. The cover near shore was very dense. By pushing inland a short distance I found that the cover opened up slightly. I chose a pair of crisscrossed deadfalls for my stand and sat on one of the trunks. The other one concealed me. The natural blind was quite comfortable.

Waiting on stand or in a blind isn't my longest suit. I'm impatient, and I'd rather be up and moving around even though that seldom pays off so well. But I didn't have long to wait at the crisscrossed deadfalls.

Ten minutes or so after I'd gotten into position, I heard a single shot from Lew's direction. Shortly thereafter I heard deer hastening through the cover toward me. When they're really frightened, deer can make plenty of noise.

The first animal to appear on the other side of a small clearing was a doe. She paused and looked directly at me before turning abruptly and running off. I was motionless, and I doubt that the doe spotted me. Right behind her came two more does and two fawns, but they didn't pause. One of the does might have been a spike buck, but the glimpse I got of the animal was fleeting, so I couldn't be certain. Besides, I heard still another animal running toward me and slowly raised my .270. Then I was staring at a scene that could have been an *Outdoor Life* front cover.

A six-point buck stepped out into the open and hesitated. I don't remember raising the rifle, but I did hear it go off a split second before the buck bounced away. Although I have been hunting deer for thirty years, I found out that I had to fight off a sharp onset of buck fever. Next thing I knew, Lew appeared from the cover.

"I've got one deer down," he said, beaming. "How about you?"

"I'm not really sure," I answered.

We found plenty of blood immediately and followed it easily into a tangle of willows. On the opposite side, we found the buck, stone dead with a bullet through the lungs. Not many hunts end so soon or so successfully as that one did.

"It sure paid off," Lew said, "to go walleye fishing before the deer season opened."

Preseason scouting for whitetails is productive, and the general idea is also worthwhile if you plan to hunt any big-game animal. Because of the heavy turnout practically everywhere on opening day in antelope country, for example, it is virtually impossible to get a really large male without locating the animal before the season opens.

Going afield early can make you a better, more confident hunter. No matter whether you're fishing for brown trout or hunting cottontails, you're more likely to succeed when you have confidence and are familiar with your surroundings. It's a simple matter of psychology.

If you know where the deer are on opening morning, you are sure of yourself, so you're much more likely to hunt skillfully and shoot well.

And if all the camp chores are done and you have enjoyed a good night's sleep, you're even more likely to do your best. Going out on a hard day's hunt relaxed and refreshed means more than most hunters realize.

Any hunter needs every small advantage he can muster when the whitetail buck is the game.

Strategy
for Whitetails

Erwin A. Bauer

On a bitter morning late last fall I had a ringside seat at an uneven contest between man and beast. From high atop a white-oak ridge in southeastern Ohio, I watched three whitetail deer enter a dense woods of about twenty acres in the valley. Apparently they bedded down; thirty minutes passed and they did not emerge.

One of the animals was a very good buck with heavy, whitened antlers that had been clearly visible at a great distance. A second also had antlers, but they were small. I wasn't certain about the third deer. Perhaps the animal was a doe. The time was the tag end of the rut.

While I was thinking about the best approach for a shot at one of the bucks, a car came along the dusty township road not far from the woods. That ended my planning because three red-jacketed hunters

This chapter originally appeared in the September 1971 issue of *Outdoor Life*.

stepped out of the car, uncased their shotguns (only smoothbores loaded with rifled slugs are legal for deer hunting in Ohio) and headed directly toward the timber in which the deer were concealed. Any experienced whitetail hunter knows what happened next.

The hunters barely had time to penetrate 100 feet into the woods before the whitetails exited at the other end. The three deer were in no hurry. They walked along slowly in single file, but they were careful to stay hidden in a brushy draw. If I had not been up on a ridge, I would not have seen them. At intervals, all three animals stopped to look back, listen, and test the cold wind. Only when they were well away from the woods did they break into a trot and then bound gracefully across a brook. They disappeared among the trees on the opposite bank.

It was an adept escape. I don't think any of the hunters ever realized that so much as a single deer had been in the woods. Later I met those three hunters at a checking station, and all of them complained about the scarcity of deer. That is a common lament.

And yet the men probably would not have been embarrassed if I had told them about the deer. They were hunting Odocoileus virginianus, the whitetail, and nowadays a good whitetail buck is one of the most elusive game animals on earth. Even in the Northern

A whitetail with a rack like this has survived many seasons. He's as difficult to hunt as any animal on earth.

and Eastern States where the species is most abundant, a good set of whitetail antlers is a difficult trophy to come by. A substantial head on the wall is the result of considerable diligent effort or great good luck, or both.

There are three basic ways to hunt whitetails — stillhunting, standing, and driving. Which is best depends on the time of year, the weather, the ground, and the skill and experience of the hunter.

No challenge to a hunter's skill quite matches stillhunting for whitetails. This method is called stillhunting because the hunter makes as little noise as possible as he moves through the woods. He does not stay in one place. Formerly, European noblemen hunted antlered game on horseback with a pack of hounds, and that made a great deal of noise. Stillhunting is often the most exciting technique, and if you score, it is always the most rewarding. But stillhunting is also the most difficult method.

In today's heavily hunted whitetail range, the odds are stacked against even the best woodsmen, and an inexperienced hunter has little or no chance of bagging a trophy whitetail by stillhunting. The hunter must move noiselessly through noisy woods and remain always alert. He must be capable of fast, accurate shooting at surprise targets, almost always in motion, through a screen of underbrush.

The proper way to stillhunt is to do so very slowly. You stop and go. In a fairly open woods you might move 100 feet or so and then pause for several minutes to look and listen. If you're hunting dense woodland, walk less and wait longer.

It is very important to blend into the woods as you move along. If the day is bright, keep to the shadows as much as possible. Always take each step deliberately to give yourself a chance to find solid, quiet footing. A whitetail can hear the crunching of leaves or a twig snapping at an amazing distance. Never make any sudden motions and do not smoke or cough. When stillhunting, travel into the wind, or across it, at the very least. Never move with the wind at your back.

A soft blanket of snow is helpful because it muffles sound and makes spotting a deer possible at longer range. Crusted snow, however, is noisy under foot and a great disadvantage to the stillhunter.

Any really good stillhunter is attuned to the forest and its sounds, and the only way to become attuned is to spend a lot of time in the woods all year long. A man soon learns to relax when he's out alone, but at the same time, he becomes aware of the slight movements and noises that could betray a nervous whitetail. He also learns to identify the sounds made by juncos, jays, woodpeckers, and squirrels, and other sounds that might be mistaken for the sounds made by deer.

Two or three men can stillhunt better than a lone hunter. One worthwhile tactic is to travel very slowly and deliberately on parallel courses. A deer spooked by one hunter may blunder into another's sights. It also pays off to station standers ahead of any stillhunter.

Suppose, for example, that two of those three hunters in the opening incident of this story had circled around and taken stands on the opposite side of the woods. One of them should have covered the draw through which the whitetails eventually escaped. The third man could have stillhunted through the center of the woods. Almost certainly, someone would have gotten a shot.

Playing the waiting game on a stand is almost anyone's best bet to bag a buck even if there are no drivers at all. That is doubly true for the sportsman who has limited experience with deer. But taking a stand and waiting is not as simple as it sounds, and a good stander must be exceptionally patient.

By standing, a hunter eliminates the noise and movement that betray the still hunter to deer. If he remains still, and I mean perfectly still, he can be betrayed only by his odor.

The first consideration of the stander is to choose the right place to wait. You'll find good spots along busy, well-worn deer trails, near known feeding, bedding, or rutting areas; or beside deer "crossings" from one patch of cover to another. A ravine or brushy

Heavily-used deer runways are often mistaken for man-made trails. Deer tracks resolve the question.

A weakness in a deer's defense is that he seldom looks up. Where legal, deer blinds, or scaffolds, work well.

draw often connects one whitetail woods with another, and it will be used by deer in preference to traveling across an open area.

No matter where you take your stand, be sure the wind blows in your face. You should be well concealed, but you should have an open field of fire at an approaching deer.

It may be possible to use a natural blind behind a deadfall or a tangle of vegetation, or it may be necessary to build a blind out of natural vegetation that will at least break up your silhouette. Wearing neutral-colored outer garments would help, but many states require deer hunters to wear brightly colored clothing during the firearms season. Most veteran deer hunters, however, believe that movement rather than bright color alarms the whitetail.

One glaring weakness in the wary whitetail's armor is his failure to look up or sense or even suspect danger from above. Keep in mind that in some states it is illegal to hunt from an overhead stand and that in several others the height of the stand is strictly regulated. In most states, however, a tree blind is legal, and it is worth every bit of time and effort spent in its construction. Choice of location depends on the same factors already mentioned for locating any deer stand. Care should be taken to build a firm, comfortable platform that does not creak underfoot or make noise when the wind blows. Some kind of old carpeting on the floor helps to muffle the foot sounds that you inevitably make.

Success depends heavily on the stander's ability to wait motionless for long periods.

The first and best advice is to dress properly. That means wearing the warmest possible clothing in much of the whitetail's range. If a hike is necessary, however, carry your heavy garments during the hike to avoid working up a sweat. Put them on after you have reached your stand. Handwarmers stuffed into your pockets can be very useful, and a thermos full of hot beverage breaks up a long vigil.

Some hunters have a tendency to lose interest on stand. The mind wanders after a long, tedious wait. But that is invariably when the buck of a lifetime comes silently along the forest trail.

A stander's chances of success also depend a great deal on how much the deer are moving. If the deer are up and traveling, the hunter gets more opportunities to shoot. The hour or so after daybreak and the short time just before sunset are the periods when natural deer movement is greatest, and those are the best times to be on your stand.

Other hunters on the move also cause deer to shift about, and that is true at any time of day. Certain farming activities stir the deer up too. Of course whitetails can also be moved by making organized drives.

In typical whitetail cover in the Eastern United States and Canada, the best strategy is often to spend the mornings and evenings on the best available stands and stillhunt during the middle of the day if you're alone or make organized drives if several hunters are along.

In order for you to make a successful drive, the terrain must be suitable. It should be broken up by lakes, roads, meadows, cultivated strips, streams, or other geographic features so that the deer tend to move along predictable routes. Large unbroken stands of timber are unsuitable. At least one member of the party should know the area very well so that the drive can be planned in advance. All hands must follow the plan to the letter.

Driving whitetail deer can produce extremely good results, but even a well-planned drive can be an utter waste of time if the hunters ignore the plan.

At least two hunters are needed to make a drive — one to move the deer and the other to wait in ambush for them — although any number may participate. If the number exceeds eight or ten, however, the drive usually becomes too cumbersome to succeed.

To make a drive, a party of hunters is usually divided into two groups — standers and drivers. After the area to be driven has been decided upon and everyone is briefed, the standers are placed in positions to best intercept the deer. Then the drivers systematically hunt toward the stands, trying to flush deer toward the standers or sandwich them between the two groups. At the very least, a deer or two should pass within shooting range of someone. Of course whitetails do not relish these tactics and do not always cooperate.

This buck pauses to test the wind before entering new cover.

The hunter who knows the country best should lead the drive, and he should select the places to be driven. These areas should never be too large. If possible, it's best to drive isolated tracts of whitetail cover bordered or surrounded by natural barriers.

An island, for example, is the perfect place to drive because there is a water barrier all around, and deer are usually reluctant to swim, perhaps because it puts them out in the open. Almost as good are peninsulas and bottomland almost surrounded by the meanders of a winding stream. Remember, however, that it is illegal to shoot deer in the water. Strips of unlogged timber bordered by cut areas are good and so are brushy draws and large farm woodlots bordered by open cropland.

Summing up — it's best to drive good deer cover that is surrounded as much as possible by water or open areas that whitetails are reluctant to cross. Whitetails do not like to be out in the open.

Once the area to be driven has been selected, the standers are posted where they can cover one or two sides of the cover. The stands should be along known deer trails and at crossings where there is some concealment for the stander. All standers should know where all the other standers are located and the exact direction that

82

the drivers will take. Standers should never leave their posts until the drive ends.

When the standers are in place, the drivers move toward them from the opposite side of the cover, traveling on parallel courses so as to thoroughly scour the area. In a few regions of the Southeast and Canada where the terrain is particularly difficult and the cover dense, hounds are often used to supplement the drivers or to replace them entirely. But in most other places, using dogs for deer hunting is illegal.

One or two very experienced woodsmen can often do a better job of driving than a whole gang by zigzagging toward the standers or changing direction now and then to root deer out of thick patches of cover. But of course a wise old buck can easily double back and escape around one or two men.

When flushed by hunters, whitetails seldom run downwind if any other choice is open. They usually bound away upwind, and therefore often scent standers waiting ahead of them. A calm, cold day provides the best conditions for driving, and a crosswind can be very helpful too.

There's a lot of disagreement about whether the drivers should move quietly—stillhunting as they go—or as noisily as possible. There are advantages and drawbacks to both approaches.

The stillhunter who drives deer toward standers is less likely to alarm the deer and drive them right out of the area. In fact a buck may choose to stay just far enough ahead of a quiet driver to be unseen and yet keep "in touch" with the intruder. If so, the deer may not watch for danger lurking up ahead where a stander is posted. Of course the stillhunting driver may also get a shot himself when he flushes the animal or if the deer turns back through the drivers.

Many experienced drivers prefer to whoop and yell when making a drive. Hearing a lot of noise, the deer are less likely to lie low and let the drivers pass them by, and the deer are more likely to be so frightened that they blunder into the standers. The shouting also indicates the drive's progress and the location of the drivers to the standers. A noisy drive often works best if the drivers move silently at first and only begin to shout after they are certain that deer have been flushed.

Trail-watching

Norm Nelson Jr.

My best buck in thirty years of deer hunting was all but handed to me by a stranger. But getting that trophy wasn't luck so much as it was a testimony to the effectiveness of trail-watching as a deer-hunting technique.

It was a dead-calm fall day when stalking was impossible in the forests of northeastern Minnesota's big St. Louis County. A twig's crack could be heard at fifty yards, even by human ears. So before daybreak I settled down at a good trail-watching spot I knew about, hoping a deer would come to me.

About an hour after sunup, a sound in the thick alder swamp to my left indicated that I might be in business. But it was only another hunter, picking his way through the shintangles. I mentally cussed

This chapter originally appeared in the September 1972 issue of *Outdoor Life* under the title "Trail-Watching for Deer."

him for the noise he was making. He would spook any deer within a quarter-mile.

The hunter kept going, however, and never saw me. After his red jacket had disappeared in the gray blur of the swamp, I heard another crack and a thump. I thought the heavy-footed stranger was now bulling right through the windfalls rather than climbing over them. But I was wrong. Two deer came bounding through the swamp in my direction. The first was a doe. My heartbeat doubled, however, when I saw the sun gleam on the rack of the huge buck following her.

The two deer slowed to a walk to skirt the knoll I was on. That's a typical whitetail maneuver—to stick to a swamp or other heavy cover rather than head straight through a clear area. At fifty paces the buck loomed as big as a pony in my Bushnell scope. When my 6.5 x 55 mm. Swedish Mauser cracked, he froze. Then he crashed down into the alders.

The buck was so heavy that I couldn't drag him up onto the knoll for easier field-dressing. The job had to be done right there in the swamp. But first I had to sit down and have a long smoke to get over the shakes. He was the kind of trophy I'd dreamed of.

Fortunately I didn't have to get the buck out of the woods single-handed. Within a couple of hours I was joined by my thirteen-year-old son Peter and two hunting partners, Sonny McFall and my uncle Ralph Nelson. Those two have taken many deer in their time, but they were impressed with my buck. I don't know what he weighed, because we had to quarter him and pack the meat half a mile to our hunting camp.

A good trail-watcher makes his own luck. True, the other hunter had probably jumped those two deer, which then circled him and walked almost into my lap. But it wasn't by accident that I was at the right place at the right time.

There's nothing new about trail-watching. Most deer hunters know of it. But I doubt whether more than a small percentage of them really know how effective it is—when it's done right. I've found it deadly on whitetails in Minnesota's North Woods country, where I was born and spent half my life. I've found it effective on mule deer in the West, in both timber and open country. In the incredibly thick forests of the coastal Pacific Northwest, where I now live, trail-watching is about the only worthwhile way for a man to hunt deer.

Trail-watching overcomes your biggest problem as a deer hunter: the inability to move silently through woods under quiet or dry conditions. It offers you good chances to bag deer in early morning or late afternoon, when they're most likely to be on the move. It is

The author scouts for deer trails and feeding sign in a logged-off area before taking position for the watch.

also worthwhile during midday, because other hunters, roaming about, often serve unintentionally as beaters or drivers for you.

Trail-watching is also one of the best ways to pick up a big buck prowling at odd hours during the rutting season. It's about the only way to catch a black bear unaware in forest cover without using bait. Finally, it's usually the best method for the lone hunter.

Many sportsmen seem to think trail-watching is both simple and dull. It's neither. Doing it right demands some complex planning. Some deer trails are much better bets than others. Some trails are merely little-used auxiliary escape routes for deer. Other trails are main day-to-day thoroughfares. You'd better know in advance which kind you'll be watching.

The physical condition of a trail can tell you something about how well it's used. But you should also know the feeding and bedding areas of deer in the area you want to hunt, as well as the hideouts and escape runways they're likely to use under hunting pressure.

I learned these rules the hard way, long after my first deer season, when as a boy of twelve I hunted with Uncle Ralph and my dad. They were highly skilled, experienced hands at hunting whitetails. Their classic system was the drive. Ralph, who is a federal forester, is a great woods walker. Dad has been a crack rifle shot since his boyhood days on a YMCA rifle team. For the deer of Gnesen Township north of Duluth, those two comprised a bad-news combo for over two decades.

But conditions changed. After World War II the number of deer hunters quickly doubled and then continued to increase. The added hunting pressure soon taught surviving deer to skulk and circle when a drive came through the woods. Even the forest changed. The timber, recovering from the great fire of 1918 that burned over 300,000 acres in northeastern Minnesota, had become thick enough again to hamper drivers and obstruct vision of standers on the ridges. Hunting success at our little camp dropped to the point where sometimes no one got a shot.

That's when I started convincing the others that we had to change our tactics. Trail-watching was the logical move.

Trail-watching calls first of all for good reconnaissance. If you don't know something about the area, you'll waste a lot of time in the wrong places. In the case of my trophy buck, I had done my homework. I chose the knoll because it covered the intersection of three pieces of brushy swamp—a favorite terrain of whitetails. A fairly open ridge from the lake to the knoll offered me reasonably quiet access to my stand.

Preseason scouting had revealed four major deer trails in those swamps, all within fair rifle range of the knoll. I increased my elevation, thus improving my visible coverage of those trails, by building a crude platform six feet up in a clumped birch tree. (Check your state's game laws before you build a tree stand. Most states allow elevated stands, but Minnesota, for example, limits an artificial stand to a maximum height of six feet.) Even a low stand helps you keep an area under better surveillance.

So my setup was ideal—but only because the triangle of three swamps was likely to have a variety of deer activity including rutting traffic, normal feeding activity, and animals moved by other hunters.

Here's an important point: don't pick your trail-watching site just because it offers a good view or is convenient to reach, or because it provides a comfortable natural seat such as a rock or a stump. Instead, pick your site on the hard-nosed basis of the chances it should give you to see deer. It's better to be rather poorly situated on good trails than to be well set up on seldom-used trails.

Start your scouting by looking for a feeding area. A forested ridge with acorns or dogwood for browse is good, Clear-cut logging areas are always magnets for deer, until the new crop of timber shades out and reduces the browse plants that quickly spring up after logging. You may find deer feeding in clear-cuts at dawn and before dark, and you'll certainly find deer runways going to and from such areas.

Next, you can take a cue from the story of the village moron who found the lost horse after everyone else had failed. He simply figured out where he'd go if he were a horse. You should size up the surrounding terrain and cover, and decide where you'd bed down during the day if you were a wise buck. It could be a thick swale or swamp — what they call a pocosin down South. The deep grass or brush in such a place camouflages a buck and shelters him from cold wind or hot sun. It also causes an enemy to make a noisy approach.

When you're looking for deer-bedding areas, remember that forest deer usually don't range far between bed and board. Mule deer in open country will travel a lot farther as a matter of routine, a habit that gives you a better choice of trail-watching sites.

Once you've picked a likely bedding area, look for proof. Deer beds — circular areas of crushed-down grasses or ferns — aren't large but are easily recognized. How often they're used will be revealed by the number of dropping piles, since deer frequently evacuate their bowels after a snooze on a full stomach. Though deer don't always return to the same beds, an area that contains a number of beds and numerous droppings in various stages of weathering is certainly being used.

Saplings that show severe scuffing and peeling from antler rubbing indicate that bucks are using the area.

After you've found feeding and bedding areas, look for trails connecting them. There will be more than one. Deer typically move into the wind, scenting what's ahead. Some trails will seem to meander, but they actually allow the deer to approach a feeding area into the prevailing wind. If the wind shifts, the deer use a different approach trail.

You'll usually find another set of trails circling in a different direction. These the deer use in returning to the general bedding area, again making a final approach upwind to scent out any ambush.

Mule deer often travel along the path of least resistance, but blacktails and whitetails are natural skulkers. They frequently make trails in the best available cover, even though the route takes them out of their way.

The best site is a spot from which you can cover more than one major trail. The classic is an intersection of two or more trails. Remember that you must be posted downwind of the trails or junction.

Nevertheless, situating where you can thoroughly cover one trail is better than trying to watch two trails that are too far apart for good visibility or decent shooting. Failure to follow that rule one morning cost me chances at two bucks, one of them a whopper.

When hunting deer in heavy forest, limited visibility may require that you set up close to a main trail. At such sites you must operate with catlike silence. This is where many hunters make their mistake.

You may not see a soft-footed deer until he's only a few yards away. Random throat-clearing, fiddling around, or any other noise you make can alarm a deer well before he ankles into view.

Keeping silent is easier said than done. For one thing, it means little or no smoking. The odor of tobacco smoke isn't the problem. If the deer can whiff that, he can smell you too. But fishing around for smokes and matches and then striking a light makes noise.

Even a low cough can carry in the woods for many yards. Occasionally sucking astringent hard candy, such as sour lemon drops, cuts phlegm buildup in your throat, reducing your need to cough or clear your throat. Eating chocolate or smoking tends to make you cough.

Other common noises that can blow your chances include the metallic rasp of a zipper and the clink of a gun breech being closed. If you're out for the day and have a lunch, it should be wrapped in a bandanna rather than in noisy waxed paper or crinkly foil.

When you feel the call of nature, your only recourse is to answer it a considerable distance from your trail-watching site — at least 200 yards away. Human body wastes can be sniffed at considerable distance by a keen-nosed deer and easily identified as human.

Your setup must be reasonably comfortable, because most men find it impossible to remain quiet for long periods if uncomfortable. Some hardy hunters need only a convenient log to sit on. But good trail-watchers aren't above moving old chairs back into their favorite spots.

Another of my uncles, George Nelson, once tobogganed a cast-off easy chair and a horsehide robe to his favorite trail for a day-long watch. His brothers meanwhile were running ridges all day long. When they returned to the cabin at dark, tired and without a deer, George was enjoying a glass of stump-lifter while frying liver from the buck he'd nailed after three hours of trail-watching in comfort.

An elaborate blind isn't needed. Forest deer have a hard time recognizing a motionless human, even when fairly close to him. Mule deer have better eyesight, so don't perch up on the skyline to watch a good muley route through a draw or canyon.

If you're trail-watching close to the trail, however, some concealment behind brush or a tree will give you more freedom to move your head, shift your rifle to ready, or sneak a candy bar without being spotted by an unseen deer. Be sure that the concealing brush doesn't block your vision or field of fire. Action in a trail-watching situation is likely to be quite close and very fast, and sometimes unexpected.

An elevated stand, in addition to offering better visibility, gives you another advantage. Whitetails and blacktails don't seem to worry about danger coming from above their normal line of sight.

This buck pulls a sneak over a ridge, making use of cover.

That's not true of muleys, probably because at times they're preyed on by eagles. But any time you can trail-watch safely and legally from a tree platform or other elevated perch, you've got a big edge over forest deer.

Play it safe. When Lee Kuluvar was Minnesota's firearms safety director, he told me, "Over the years, we've educated hunters to unload guns before crossing fences. So we don't have many accidents of that type anymore. Instead, hunters climb trees, drop their guns on the way up, and shoot themselves from the bottom up, usually with pretty grim results."

Even with the gun slung on your back, it's foolish to climb a tree or a deer-stand ladder without first unloading the gun. The carrying strap or swivel might break, dropping the gun butt-first, and the impact can jar the sear loose and cause the gun to fire — straight up in your direction.

You'll find that an unadorned tree crotch is murder to sit in after the first five minutes. A stiff boat cushion in a safe red or yellow color is handy to have along in a haversack. Even better is a seat or platform rigged in the tree before the season.

If your state has no legal restrictions on deer-stand height, you may be inclined to build a stand too high, which can put you above the canopy of nearby trees, sharply reducing your view. In a typical deciduous forest, a stand should be just above the brush but below the overstory of tree branches.

The need for stealth and alertness, both at your stand and when approaching it, can't be overemphasized. If you slam a car door and then noisily march a few hundred yards to your stand, you've sent a telegram to every deer in the area. They'll either quietly mooch away or, just as bad, hide out and stay immobile.

Alertness means conditioning yourself to constantly expect action. After hours of seeing nothing but a passing raven or a squirrel, it's hard to keep that frame of mind.

The most thrilling thing about trail-watching is the way deer suddenly show up without warning. One moment, the vista of trees or brush is as empty as it has been for several hours. The next instant, a twig cracks or a black nose protrudes past a low hemlock bough.

Even at this stage you can still very easily blow your chance. First, you must be certain that what's approaching is a deer—or perhaps a black bear. If it's a doe and you're not interested in taking her, it's vital that you don't spook her. There's a good chance that a buck is following her.

In dense forest you may get only one shot; it had better be a good one. Once, a hunter in our camp shot too soon when a buck's head stuck out of the cedars. The shot broke the deer's jaw, and the shooter didn't get another chance. Fortunately my kid brother Alan, who was on another stand, got a poke at the wounded buck a few minutes later, and he dropped it for keeps.

At close range in the forest, I always try to wait until a deer isn't looking my way. Then I mount the gun, throwing the safety off as the sight comes on target—not before. If the deer hears the safety or hammer click then, it's too late to do him any good.

But circumstances vary. Your buck may have been spooked by other hunters and come past you really carrying the mail. Or he may suddenly get your scent on a back eddy of wind and be instantly alarmed. In either case, you've got a fast-draw contest on your hands—your gun-mounting and straight-shooting speed versus the buck's ability to bound into the nearest cover. It's all-important to have the "off" position of your gun's safety memorized well before this moment.

Blood no doubt has been spilled on hunting-camp floors in arguments about whether the neck shot is better than the chest shot. My vote is to try for a shot through one or both front shoulders. A deer's neck isn't a big target, and much of it is nonvital tissue. Also, the neck is more likely to be moved without warning than the torso is. The heart shot placed low and behind the shoulder is notorious for galvanizing the animal into a jet-propelled takeoff.

He then drops dead some distance away, where you may not find him or where some larcenous clown may already have tagged him when you come down the blood trail.

For trail-watching in forest ranges, you can depend on any reasonable deer weapon to shatter one or both front shoulders. If, miraculously, the deer does move after you've made a solid hit in the front shoulder, his mobility will be drastically reduced. You'll have plenty of time for a follow-up shot with anything other than a muzzle-loader.

Your choice of sighting equipment is more important than resolving the usual hot-stove hairsplitting about the virtues of the .308 versus the .300 Savage and so on. Iron sights are fine for close or medium-range trail-watching. But a good low-power scope is even better—if it has the right reticle. With a scope you can pick out a deer's shoulder outline in thick brush or bad light—conditions in which iron sights would fail. In woods country I like a 2½X scope. If you're trail-watching at longer ranges, such as in covering a good mule-deer canyon route, a 4X scope is hard to beat. High-power scopes don't have the field of view to follow a running deer.

Conventional crosshairs and even the heavier dot reticles give problems at close range against a dark backdrop. Even a big six-minute dot is a tiny aiming point at twenty yards or more in a spruce swamp. A post reticle is better.

All told, trail-watching has a lot going for it. At our Minnesota deer camp it broke the venison drought in a hurry when we switched over to it in the 1950's. My father bagged a fine six-pointer during the first hour on opening day.

In the years I've hunted with Sonny McFall, he has always been hard to keep still for five minutes. Despite having lost a chunk of one leg to a German mine during the Battle of the Bulge in 1944, Sonny is the greatest ridge-runner I've ever seen. But even he will admit that trail-watching is effective.

One of the best things about trail-watching is the planning that goes into it. The preseason scouting is fun, especially in areas where you can combine it with a little fishing or upland gunning.

Best of all, the stump-sitting system provides a day-long thrill of watchful anticipation. Your patience—and, in chilly or damp weather, your stamina too—will be severely tested. But you'll be repaid by a real involvement in your surroundings as you make friends with an inquisitive Canada jay or watch a weasel—a fellow hunter—checking out a hollow log.

And when a big black-nose buck suddenly glides past that far hemlock, every minute of your days of trail-watching will be worthwhile.

Small Drives for Big Bucks

Norm Nelson Jr.

Mention deer drive, and many sportsmen picture a whole line of beaters playing dogs for a large number of standers. But a small hunting party—two to five hunters—can stand and drive deer effectively if they know a few basic facts about deer behavior. The trouble is that the deer have been changing their ways.

That fact has been made very clear to me during thirty-four years of hunting whitetails, mule deer, and Columbia blacktails. I have hunted deer in the northern forests of the Great Lakes States and Ontario, the high plains and foothills of the Rockies, the semi-deserts east of the Cascades, and the thick coastal forests of the Northwest.

Years ago life was simpler, and so were the deer. Increased human pressure has made deer much smarter. When I was cutting my

This chapter originally appeared in the September 1973 issue of *Outdoor Life*.

This hatrack buck was driven past the camera by a single driver.

teeth as a hunter in the late 1930's in northern Minnesota, there weren't many hunters. My father and my uncle Ralph Nelson, a forester, and I hunted deer on weekends without seeing another hunter, and we hunted within twenty miles of Duluth. When I began hunting mule deer in Wyoming in the early 1950's I was the only hunter on a 15,000-acre ranch. These days I'm one of a dozen or more who hunt on that ranch.

Nowadays many forest areas are full of humans all year — timber cruisers, forest-research crews, tree-planting crews, hikers, fishermen, birdwatchers, and many others. Hunters know too well that nonhunting recreational use of forests has zoomed. We spend about fifteen percent of our gross national product on leisure, and outdoor recreation easily tops the list. Just think of the booms in backpacking, camping, rockhounding, crosscountry skiing, and snowmobiling. I work for a forest industry in my home state, Washington, and I'm constantly aware of the invasion of the woods.

The result is that deer are no longer the seldom-disturbed wilderness animals they once were. With people in the forest all year instead of only during the hunting season, deer have developed routine methods of avoiding close contact with people. Today you can't move deer to standers with old-fashioned straight-line, panic-them-out-of-the-cover drives.

Effective driving today requires a knowledge of the deer's new defensive tactics so that you can employ effective countermeasures. They work best when you're familiar with the lay of the land. The hunter who hop-scotches around to different areas never really learns much about the terrain. Good topographic maps and preseason scouting are important.

Small-party drives work well for me and my two sons during the firearms hunting season and when we go camera hunting. To take worthwhile pictures you must get closer to the deer than you do when you're hunting. Basically our tactics work with all woodland deer, and that includes mule deer in forested areas. Some of these tactics can also be used to take mule deer in fairly open country.

The simplest small-party tactic is the circle drive. It's particularly useful in dense cover. (This drive and all the others discussed in this story are shown in the accompanying drawings.) Ordinarily, two hunters in a large forest have a tough time with the old-fashioned straight drive. With one hunter on stand, the solo driver can't stop deer from evading him unseen, which is exactly what they do nine times out of ten if the driver moves in a straight line toward the stander.

In the circle drive the driver makes a meandering circle around

CIRCLE DRIVE
The stander stays put and quiet while the driver circles around him. A
jumped buck often circles the driver to get his scent, and this may set up a
shot for the stander.

his partner's stand. He may even circle two or three times along slightly different routes if the cover is dense.

After hearing us oldsters discuss this drive's frequent success, my son Peter, then sixteen, tried it with his younger brother Paul, age fourteen, one noon when I was hunting deer by radar from my bunk in camp. Within ten minutes Pete ran two whitetails past Paul, who bagged one, his first deer.

Deer jumped by the driver but not shot at are likely to circle back or move to his flank, depending upon the wind direction. There's a very good chance that the deer will cut in front of a stander posted in the center of the area that is disturbed by his partner.

The radius of the circle drive depends on the cover. In thick stuff the driver may be no more than 100 yards from the stander as he swings around his circuit. That makes for a short drive, but remember that it's worth doing it more than once in thick cover in order to flush deer that are holding tightly. In open forest the radius of the driver's circle may be 200 to 400 yards.

The circle drive works best when it prompts the deer to stalk the driver. Few hunters realize how often they are shadowed by their quarry. Whitetails and blacktails do it more often than mule deer. I spend much time in the woods, and deer frequently follow me at a distance or discreetly tail me off on a flank.

I was camera hunting in southern Oregon's Klamath country when I jumped a mule-deer buck in a ponderosa forest. Not at all uptight about human activity, the buck had been watching truck traffic on a nearby forest road from a comfortable shady spot.

I simply concealed myself by leaning against a pine trunk and waited. Within ten minutes the buck came sneaking back on my flank. He was trying to work downwind in order to pinpoint me. An easy target at 60 yards, he was lucky I was hunting with a camera instead of a rifle.

I learned the circle drive by accident. On a family-owned tree farm in northern Minnesota my younger brother Alan and I built a tree stand prior to the season. I climbed up onto the stand and directed Al to move to various spots on three nearby deer trails so that I could check for clear shots through the intervening brush.

Al was 70 yards away when movement caught my eye. Silent as a cougar, a huge whitetail buck was stalking Alan. The deer was about 50 yards behind him. After hearing my brother, the deer had apparently decided to trail him in order to keep track of the potential danger.

When not really frightened, deer and some other wild animals have a lot of curiosity. In Wyoming I once saw a whole herd of mule deer sneaking along for a quarter of a mile to investigate the noisy trail bike of my hunting chum, airline crew officer Don Hendrickson. I believe that curiosity often prompts deer to follow human beings.

The buck that was stalking Al did his work beautifully. The animal slunk along as low to the ground as a hunting cat and sank down out of sight whenever Al stopped.

Al was completely unaware of the deer, and the buck was unaware of me, even after his silent trailing brought him downwind of my position in the tree stand. Al's scent by that time completely saturated the whole area and probably masked my odor. Besides, I was high up in a tree stand.

I could have put that buck's liver in the frying pan fifty times over, if the season had been open. And I didn't even have a camera.

Before a circle drive is begun, the stander should move into position very quietly, to avoid alerting nearby deer. Sometimes it can't be done, because the cover is dry and noisy. If so, both hunters should go to the stand together. Then the stander stops and takes pains to remain quiet while the driver keeps on going and starts his circle. A listening deer is almost certain to be unaware of the silent stander unless the animal actually sees him.

This brings us to the dropout or shadow drive. It works best in dense cover. In this drive there's no stationary stander. Both hunters move, but again, the deer is fooled into believing there is only one hunter.

Both hunters go upwind together, making no effort to walk quietly. After a short distance one hunter temporarily stops while the other goes ahead 50 to 75 yards in heavy cover, 125 to 200 yards in thinner timber.

Hunters move noisily into the wind, but then one stops temporarily. A buck may sneak around the lead man to get his scent. This gives a shot to No. 2, the "dropout" man.

Once the distance has opened up, the dropout hunter or shadow starts following his noisy partner, but he moves very slowly and quietly. The first man makes plenty of noise with his feet, but he must go slowly or he will get too far ahead of his pussyfooting partner.

If all goes right, deer moved (but not panicked) unseen by the noisy front man will usually circle to get downwind of him. The deer wants to catch the scent of whatever is making all that noise. When a deer starts this maneuver, he often winds up in the sights of Silent Sam bringing up the rear.

The shadowing hunter must be careful not to fire at a deer that comes between him and the front man. He watches off to the side for his shot.

I began learning about the dropout drive in northern Minnesota years ago when my uncle Ralph and I cut a big deer's tracks, obviously fresh in falling light snow. The deer was heading across a muskeg swamp toward a small island of black spruce. We moved in on the island from opposite directions, hoping for a squeeze play.

For the next hour the buck led us a merry chase in those few acres of thick spruce. Never a shot was fired. Would you believe we never saw him? Since we had approached from opposite directions, the deer knew he was contending with two hunters and avoided us both. Our tracks and the deer's soon made a hopeless jumble, and the game was called because of darkness.

A few seasons later I was hunting in northeastern Washington's forested hills above Spokane with my son Peter. I spotted a buck at the edge of a forest atop a steep hill. Remembering the spruce-island fiasco, we moved toward him together. Fortunately it was possible to do so with the wind coming from the deer to us.

Of course, the buck moved into the trees long before we got within effective rifle range, but the animal wasn't really alarmed. Once Peter and I were inside the trees, I stopped to let my son get ahead. Then I followed.

Within five minutes I spotted the three-point whitetail circling off to my left. The deer was moving around Peter to get downwind of him. I shot the deer well off to the side to be perfectly safe. The backstrap slices tasted all the better that night because we knew that we had learned something important about deer hunting.

Another drive that works well for a small party calls for two or three hunters to move through the woods with the wind quartering from the rear. We call it the staggered drive.

The hunters are spaced out in echelon, and the rear man, who is upwind of the others, moves along slightly behind as well as to the side of his partners. This trailing driver moves quietly, but the lead man makes a certain amount of noise.

Deer alarmed by the front man often swing to head into the wind as they move from his line of approach. That brings them across in front of the slightly trailing hunter, 50 to 100 yards away (farther in thinner forests).

Depending on the circumstances, the rear hunter can often take a stand off somewhere on the upwind side. That may sound foolish, but a stationary hunter doesn't broadcast as much scent as a moving hunter. If the stander has a vantage point on a ridge, high stump, or windfall, he has a good chance of spotting the deer sneaking around the two other hunters before the deer gets into the stander's odor cone.

As a variation—which we call the parallel drive—the two drivers move somewhat abreast with the wind coming at a 90° angle. Deer jumped by them will usually cross in front when they head into

STAGGERED DRIVE
Two drivers move in echelon with the wind quartering from the rear. A spooked deer moves into the wind across the front of the stander (No. 3). No. 2 man may get a shot too.

PARALLEL DRIVE
With only two men moving, No. 1 is noisy, but No. 2 is silent. Deer almost always flee into the wind to scent danger, and that sets up No. 2's shot.

DRIVER NO.1

WIND

DRIVER NO.2

VALLEY DRIVE
Drivers walk toward each other. The stander waits upwind since deer seldom run with the wind. A high stand puts stander's scent above deer.

the wind. Again, the hunter on the upwind flank should move quietly. He ambushes the deer when the animal crosses in front, preoccupied with giving the other hunter the slip.

Many hunters still try to drive deer downwind into the laps of standers. The theory is that the deer can't scent the standers. That's great in theory, but forget it. Most deer today simply will not move straight downwind. They seem to know that the standers are down there, thumbs on their safeties.

Always remember that a deer depends more on his nose than on his other senses. When disturbed, the deer moves into the wind in order to get advance notice of any trouble ahead, and when possible the animal will then circle to get downwind of anyone or anything that disturbs him. Not knowing that your nose is almost useless in comparison to his own, the deer doesn't want you to be downwind of him. Knowing this, you can often predict where the deer will go and arrange a surprise party for him.

Good drives can be made in a canyon or valley when the wind is coming from the side. Three men can do it. One hunter takes a stand on high ground on the upwind side of the valley. His partners flush out the canyon or draw by heading toward each other from opposite directions. If a fourth and fifth man are available, post them as additional standers if the valley is a long one, or use them as extra drivers if the valley is wide.

The deer hear the drivers approaching from opposite directions, and they are likely to bail out to avoid the pincer movement. They exit into the wind, and you would think they'd catch any stander's scent. During most daylight hours, however, the scent of the stander on high ground rises on thermal air currents, and the deer doesn't catch it. Only in late afternoon, when the air is growing cooler and the thermals are flowing downhill, is the deer likely to get wind of the uphill stander.

The valley drive is deadly on mule deer and works well with blacktails, but smart whitetails are hard to flush out of a brushy draw or ravine unless the area of the cover is quite small. Mule deer and blacktails are likely to make an uphill break for it at a good clip via the easiest, fastest route. They often head for a saddle in the high ground above the valley. Whitetails often ghost out through the heaviest sidehill cover they can find, and the stander should be posted accordingly.

All these drives can be modified to suit exact local conditions, but a few rules always apply:

- Safety is always important. Never risk a shot toward your partner.

- Short drives are best. Nowadays deer are much too smart to be pushed long distances, and even if you could do it, you'd probably be moving the game into the sights of another hunting party.

- If you want to drive deer in a fairly straight line, try it on a windy day. With their sensitive hearing jammed by the noise, deer become jittery. When spooked, they almost always take off straight upwind in a hurry.

- When it is calm and quiet, deer hear an approaching driver early enough to try the sneaking, circling game. Under those conditions it's almost impossible for a small party of hunters to kick whitetails out of dense cover unless the area is very small. But as cited earlier, there are ways to put the deer's circling tactics to work for you.

- The best way to drive deer out of dense cover is by moving slowly and very quietly with long, silent pauses. Unless the deer already has you pinpointed by scent, the ominous silence of those pauses really worries him, particularly if you're hunting in cougar country.

- By the same token, a noisy driver's approach doesn't worry a deer too much, given good cover. A smart buck, knowing where the noisy hunter is, is well aware that he can stay out of the clod's way all day if necessary. The only virtue of a noisy drive nowadays is that it sets up the deer for the driver's silent partner.

- When you're a driver, check your flanks and rear frequently. You will often spot deer circling around you or tailing you. Big mule deer have a habit of lying doggo until a hunter passes and then getting up to amble off over a ridge behind him.

- Any deer drive is only as good as the planning and coordination that go into it. That's why a small party actually has an advantage over the big, hard-to-coordinate gang. Make sure that each man knows what he's going to do, where, when, and for how long, and where to meet afterward.

Some hunters think deer drives are unsporting. My guess is that the critics have never tried small-party drives. They require a great deal of hunting ability. It's a challenging and enjoyable way to hunt, and it is productive as well.

Games
Whitetails Play

Erwin A. Bauer

For the last quarter of a century I have spent many days each fall hunting, filming, and just watching whitetail deer. During that period I've learned some of the games whitetails play. Many of those games were played on me, but last fall I had a ringside seat for a game played on somebody else.

It was a bright day in November, slightly warmer than normal for that time of year in the Midwest. I had built a platform blind in an oak tree near a point where two heavily used deer trails crossed and bordered an abandoned apple orchard. It seemed to be a good spot both for filming and for getting a good shot with bow and arrow before the firearms season opened. I climbed into the blind and sat down to see what might happen along.

I hadn't been in the tree long when a good buck came mincing

This chapter originally appeared in the May 1970 issue of *Outdoor Life*.

down the trail. He moved slowly and suspiciously, his antlered head held low, looking in every direction except up at me. About seventy-five yards away he stopped in some tall grass beneath an apple tree and began pawing the ground. Then, like a weary hound dog, he circled the trampled area several times, settled down in it, and remained still. I could only see his antlers.

Perhaps an hour passed. Then a station wagon stopped on a farm road several hundred yards away, and two men stepped out of it. Through binoculars I recognized them as surveyors. One man set up a transit on its tripod; the other grabbed a range pole. The rodman then walked out into the apple orchard, following the buck's exact trail. He walked within fifteen feet of the animal without ever seeing it.

The buck did not spook; he held fast!

For at least ten minutes the two surveyors worked in the surrounding area — the rodman very near the buck, both men shouting instructions. But not until they were back in the station wagon and driving away did the deer stand up and leave the scene. His nerves apparently couldn't stand the pressure any longer.

But that wasn't all. A moment later another, bigger buck, which had been bedded near the first and which I had not seen, stood up and hurried away. I can only guess that this second deer was already bedded down when I climbed the tree and that he had decided to wait me out.

Nothing else happened that morning, but I had seen enough to serve for many mornings. I wondered how many other times I had been close to trophy bucks without knowing it.

"Whitetails play amazing games," I mumbled to myself.

In the early years of my whitetail hunting the only glimpses I had of bucks were of white fantails evaporating into the underbrush, usually too far away for even a snap shot. And even those glimpses were rare. So my personal experience seemed to prove what I'd read in every book I could find on deer hunting: that whitetail bucks invariably try to escape by running — that they run the instant they detect any false sound or smell in the forest. But now, after much more exposure to whitetails, I'm convinced that they don't always follow that behavior pattern.

The truth is that a good many of the biggest bucks escape by doing nothing at all. Last fall furnished me with another excellent example.

I'd been photographing deer on a government reservation in Kentucky that contains a substantial whitetail herd. But each fall these animals are hunted hard during a series of weekend hunts, so they are as wild and wily as any whitetails anywhere. On the

In heavily hunted areas, big bucks may venture into the open only at dawn and dusk—if at all—and stay within a bound or two of cover.

morning before the hunting, I'd had fair luck filming with the aid of a telephoto lens at very long range. But by noon most of the animals had bedded and were hard to find. When I spotted an Osage orange sapling that had practically been shredded by a buck's antlers, I parked my vehicle and walked the hundred feet or so to take close-up pictures of the damage.

The tree practically exploded. A splendid buck had been bedded unseen in grass just on the far side of the tree. He had waited until I'd approached to within ten feet of him before he flushed out and raced for safety. Again I wondered how many other times I had passed very close to a stationary buck without seeing him.

On that same afternoon, I drove out onto a high ridge from which I could look down into a brushy, meandering creek bottom. There I stopped again, and through field glasses I soon spotted the ears of a doe bedded under a large sycamore. Then just off to the right in a tangle of honeysuckle, I saw a bedded medium-size buck, which was staring directly toward me. Recalling my earlier experience, I figured I just might be able to approach near enough for close-range pictures. I picked up a Hasselblad 500C with 500 mm. lens (about 6X) and headed down the ridge, being careful not to walk directly toward the buck.

The doe spooked and bounded away almost as soon as I left the vehicle. I couldn't see the buck as I descended the ridge, but I could keep an eye on the telltale green of the honeysuckle. I would certainly see the buck if he jumped up—or so I thought.

What followed would have been comical to watch. I stalked up to the honeysuckle as carefully as I could, inches at a time, tense, holding my camera at ready. I *knew* I'd get a good shot, at least of a buck bounding away. But when I got there the buck's bed, though still warm, was empty.

The escape was fairly easy to reconstruct. The buck, by staying on its belly and actually crawling, had retreated into a small draw that led away into the main stream channel. Its footprints were etched at water's edge. If whitetails could laugh, that one was probably guffawing.

I now have a couple theories to offer, for whatever they are worth. Bucks *do* prefer to escape by running — by evacuating the vicinity of danger. But the longer and more comfortably they are bedded, the more reluctant they are to make the break. Thus, a hunter who can locate a bedding area (or better still a bedded deer) is in a good position to score.

My other theory is that whitetails that live anywhere near human habitation or activity year-round become accustomed to human noise. Voices, for instance, alert them but do not unduly frighten them. So a noisy hunter has as good a chance as a stealthy stalker to approach close to such a whitetail in its bed — maybe even a better chance.

Perhaps I should insert another reason for that noise theory. In my years of filming many kinds of wild and semiwild big-game animals, I've found that my chances of getting close to them are better when I approach casually and openly, but not directly, than when I try to make a silent, hidden stalk. Animals with very good vision seem to be less apprehensive about what they can see than about what they cannot see. And whitetails have extraordinary vision.

The behavior of whitetails varies throughout the year. In spring and summer they are most scattered. Bucks and does with fawns are likely to be anywhere. In the winter whitetails are most concentrated, with bucks and does grouping up where the foraging is best. In between comes the rut. Because the rut normally coincides with most state hunting seasons — and because it's the most active period in a whitetail's lifetime — it is the time that most concerns hunters.

First let me explain the rut, or annual breeding season. It does not occur at exactly the same time every year, though very nearly so. In Ohio, for example, what might be termed the peak of the rut occurs in mid-November. North of Ohio it occurs somewhat earlier; south of Ohio, later.

Nor is the duration of the rut the same every fall. Occasionally most of the breeding activity may be concentrated in one week or so. More often it is spread out over a month or more. During the rut, short periods of great activity are interspersed with longer periods of relative inactivity. Cold weather seems to stimulate activity, while high temperatures slow it down.

Technically the rut probably begins in late summer when bucks begin to shed the velvet from their fully grown antlers. Though the velvet falls away naturally, bucks hasten the process by rubbing their antlers against trees, shrubs, and one another. I have even seen them rubbing against telephone poles, as well as against an old outhouse at a long-deserted Michigan logging camp. This rubbing gradually becomes an aggressive display—a duel against a sapling or another deer—and continues for months after all the velvet is gone. Thus, the presence of many slashed trees from which the bark has been peeled should be a sure sign that many bucks are in the area.

But is it?

Not at all. It is only another game whitetails play.

Two years ago in October, while I was on a weekend scouting and filming trip, I found an area of about ten acres where trees had been slashed and barked wholesale. I have never seen so much slash damage concentrated in any other place.

"We'll build a couple of blinds," I said to Lew Baker, "and when the foliage is down we'll do some serious filming."

The blinds were erected in ideal places. Two weeks later most of the leaves had fallen from the trees, and I went hopefully into the woods.

I have always wanted to film whitetail bucks fighting. Actually, fighting occurs far less frequently than most sportsmen believe, and when it does it usually happens at night. In all my time in deer woods I have seen conflict only twice, and both incidents were merely brief pushing matches. Another time I saw two bucks with antlers locked; one was practically dead from the long struggle.

But now, as I entered my blind, I was hopeful from so much sign that I would see action.

I shouldn't have wasted my time. Not only did I fail to see bucks jousting; I didn't see any bucks at all. Only does. What happened?

On my desk is a beautiful scene on an outdoor calendar, very well done by the artist except for one thing. It shows a splendid whitetail buck with massive rack in a woodland opening. His swollen neck and his stance indicate that it is the rut. He is surrounded by three does. But the scene should be the other way around: during the peak of a whitetail rut a single doe is far more likely to be surrounded by several bucks. Elk acquire harems; whitetails do not.

So where you find one good buck you are likely to find others

This doe and her fawn have spotted the author, but low flags indicate that they aren't alarmed yet.

nearby. And all will be where the ready does (but not *most* of the does) are, rather than where they rubbed the tree trunks a few weeks —or even a few days—before.

This concentration of breeding bucks into groups accounts for the generally accepted belief among whitetail hunters that year after year certain places are "big-buck places." From my own experience, I'd say that theory is no more true than the elephant-graveyard theory.

On a snowy, gusty evening last November I spotted eight bucks in the vicinity of one doe at the edge of a hardwood forest. There may have been other bucks and does nearby, but my count in the failing light was nine deer. Four of the bucks were huge old busters; the others had pretty good heads. Each was trying to outmaneuver the others, but no actual head-on clashes occurred. It was too dark for photography anyway, but I resolved to be on the spot first thing next morning. It was a very exciting prospect, and believe me: buck fever is possible even before the hunting season opens.

But as I've been saying, whitetails play games. In a whole year of Novembers there wouldn't be more than a few days as perfect for photography as the next morning. It was crisp and clear. Shortly after daybreak I drove out to the trysting spot, cameras ready. And found? NOTHING! Brush had been trampled, and leaves on the ground had been raked with sharp hoofs, but frost covered the evidence, and the deer were gone. Soon, so were my high and hopeful spirits.

109

Finding one buck often means others are nearby.

Luckily I located those deer again late in the afternoon. I'm almost certain it was the same group because there were eight bucks and one doe. They were about 2½ miles as the crow flies from where I first saw them. My conclusion is that if there are big-buck areas, they are not necessarily in the same places day after day, let alone year after year. At least not during the turbulent time of the rut.

Perhaps I should make a further explanation here. After the rut subsides, the bucks in an area might very well retreat into deep winter cover and gather there. And these might be traditional wintering areas, most often very remote, where a serious deer hunter stands a good chance of getting a fine trophy if the season remains open long enough.

My whitetail filming during the past few falls has been in areas of both light and heavy hunting pressure. From these experiences, one fact has become very clear: the heavier the pressure, the more nocturnal are the bigger bucks in all their activity, and of course the harder they are to see. About the only chance you have of seeing them in the open in heavily hunted areas is very early and very late in the day right at the edge of the forest.

At the tag end of my whitetail-watching last fall, on the eve of open hunting season, I sat in a tree blind that a bowhunter had built several years before. It was flimsy, and I didn't really enjoy the precarious perch. But enough fascinating things happened on the ground to keep me up there awhile.

110

Around midafternoon a handsome buck appeared from the heart of the forest and strolled toward the edge of the woods. He didn't go out into the sunlight, but stayed in the shadows, moving quietly and scanning the forest all around. Eventually he vanished as silently as he had arrived.

Before dusk four more deer, including two bucks, passed below me within point-blank gun range. Again, none of them stepped beyond the forest shadows. Then and there I decided to spend opening day in that same tree, certain that I could collect my venison.

But I ended the first day without firing a shot. This time, however, I was tricked by other hunters rather than by whitetails. When I arrived on the scene opening day, five hunters were in the process of organizing a drive. Three of them were going on stand, one directly beneath my tree. The other two would make the drive from the opposite side of the woods. The strategy seemed to guarantee some shooting.

Later in the day I again saw the leader of the hunt. I asked him if they had scored.

"Naw," he replied. "No deer in that woods. Scarce everywhere this year."

I wish I knew how the deer eluded those drivers. The next day I again saw deer from the tree stand, and I bagged one. It was so easy that I almost felt guilty. Because deer seldom look up, getting above them is one very effective game that hunters can play.

An Eye for Parts

Byron W. Dalrymple

Don't move a muscle—I saw an antler point!" I whispered.

Terry, my younger son, was hunkered down behind a tree trunk. He had his rifle slung over his shoulder and a pair of rattling antlers in his hands. I was almost completely hidden by another tree a few feet behind him. Although I had my rifle, I intended to shoot only with my camera, to give Terry the first chance.

More of the antler showed just above the top of a bank a few yards away from Terry. Then it moved. The deer was turning his head, listening intently.

As many deer hunters know, bucks in rut can be "rattled up." A pair of antlers are whacked and rattled against each other. Hearing what he assumes to be two bucks fighting over a doe, a buck

This chapter originally appeared in the December 1971 issue of *Outdoor Life* under the title "An Eye for Deer."

Motionless antlers may look like branches until other parts materialize.

often comes running to fight or comes in quietly to abduct the doe. The buck behind the bank was the quiet kind.

The time was opening morning of the 1970 deer season in our part of south-central Texas. Terry and I had started out before dawn on that warm and hazy morning. The heady excitement of opening day made us eager, and it was shortly after dawn when I saw the antler tip.

Terry had a problem. He should have propped his rifle against the tree, within easy reach, but it was still slung over his shoulder. Intending to make a practice run with the antlers, he had only tickled the tines together and whacked them gently one or twice, but I spotted the antler tip almost immediately.

Before Terry could change postion, the buck hit the top of the bank with a sudden bound. The deer stood there tensely, broadside to Terry. It would have been an easy shot, but Terry remained frozen.

Both of my boys—Mike, who couldn't get home for opening day, and Terry—are very sharp deer hunters. Terry knew that he couldn't unlimber his rifle without spooking the buck. He was waiting for the deer to move off to the left—the direction in which the animal was looking—so that he could quickly drop the antlers he'd been rattling, spin the rifle off his shoulder, and shoot.

113

Then it hit me like a whack on the noggin that the deer was staring at something to our left along the bank. I cautiously took the buck's picture and then slowly turned my head. Where the bank curved around to our left, I could see over it. A buck twice as good as the one in front of Terry was standing behind the bank with only his head and the top of his back showing.

Zooming my lens out, I photographed the big one, but that didn't help Terry. I was sure he realized that there was a larger buck beyond the first one. The boys have learned a lot about whitetails on our ranch. They've been able to hunt there every weekend during the open seasons. They both know a lot about whitetails and how to spot them. It's an art.

A buck coming to rattled antlers usually looks over his shoulder and in every direction other than at the rattler. He's worried that another buck may try to horn in on the fight. Terry knew that. If another buck shows up and is a big one, the smaller buck becomes nervous and often withdraws. That's just what happened.

Wanting no part of a fight with the big buck, the smaller one whirled and fled. In one big scramble, Terry dropped the antlers, got his rifle off his shoulder, and dodged around the tree trunk. He hadn't seen the big one yet, but Terry knew he was there.

It was a good try, but it wasn't good enough. The old buster dodged behind the bank, and we heard him crashing into the timber. Terry got a glimpse of the deer, but his rifle didn't come up in time.

"Oh, no!" he groaned, but with a grin finally spread over his face. "Well, it was exciting. He sure was big. Darn!"

I felt sorry for him, but I didn't want to show it. On the bright side, we had both learned one more lesson about hunting whitetails. Terry should have been placed to give him a wider view, and his rifle should have been ready. As it was, any attempt to drop the antlers and unsling his rifle would have spooked either buck. He was pinned down.

I have been hunting whitetail deer for a good many years in many different states, and I have taken dozens of them. I have also spent weeks on end observing them and photographing them. Some of what I've learned, I've tried to pass along to the boys. I've also urged them to observe the deer as much as possible. I'm convinced that the whitetail deer is the most difficult to hunt of all the North American big-game animals. I also believe that you improve your chances for success if you know their habits, particularly their preferences for different kinds of cover and learn what to look for—usually one small part of the deer, not the whole animal.

The light on any day or at any time of day has much bearing on what to look for. I'm thinking particularly of dull days in the open brush and cactus of south Texas. When poorly lighted, this terrain is one vast, monotonous sweep of dull gray-green, and a deer blends in very well. If you look for deer at a distance, you'll never see one unless you are extremely conscious of opposing lines—the horizontal line of the back, for example, which seems out of place in the upright vegetation.

A deer with only a small part of the body or head showing usually remains unseen unless you look for a small part of the animal—an antler tine, perhaps, the pale-white ring around the deer's nose, or the light blotch on the neck under the chin. Too many hunters expect to see the whole deer. They miss the pieces.

When we hunt our ranch, we always start at dawn at the east end if the wind is right. That orientation puts the rising sun behind us, and the light shines on the deer, not in our eyes, and allows us to see much better. There are cedar and oak woods, however, and if we intend to hunt where the trees are large, we try to hunt with the light the other way. The deer are in these brakes sometimes as early as 9 a.m. By that time the sun is high enough for the upper foliage to keep direct rays out of our eyes, but underneath the trees, enough light streams through to silhouette a deer or part of a deer. The light comes from behind the animals, and spotting them is much easier.

I recall prowling one stand of cedars a year ago with Terry. We moved with extreme caution, so slowly that we covered no more than 100 yards in half an hour. Suddenly Terry tugged my arm and slightly inclined his head to our right.

"Those four small trees," he whispered.

I studied the spot through my binoculars. Terry had seen what looked like four shin oaks maybe an inch or two in diameter, but they were just too neat and orderly, and that had caught his attention. He had actually seen the four legs of a deer. The animal's body and head were screened by low cedar limbs. But we stood still and studied the spot, and we finally made out the neck of the animal. Then we saw part of one antler.

Terry raised his .243 Winchester and took a rest across a limb. Then he cranked the 3-to-9X Redfield scope up to 6X. There is a popular belief that high-power riflescope magnifications are no good in brush. That's nonsense. It depends on how you use them. At 6X, Terry could easily see a hole to shoot through. The buck, imagining himself undetected, remained immobile. I'm sure that if we had taken a single step after stopping, the buck would have fled. Suddenly the rifle cracked, and Terry had a cleanly shot buck on the ground. He had looked for his whitetail with commendable skill.

After our rattling debacle, we moved on and fell to reminiscing about that cedar-brake kill of his.

"Whitetails are difficult because their habitat varies so much," I said. "Right here, we find them in dense brush and heavy woods and on the hills and in the draws. You can learn all sorts of rules about where to locate them, but a lot of hunters never really learn what they're looking for—silly as it sounds."

It is a fact that many whitetail hunters do indeed hunt where there are many deer, but think of how many come home without even seeing one. And many men only see deer when it is too late for a shot at the fleeing animal. Some hunters never see anything except a rear end. I have repeatedly told my boys never to shoot at that kind of target. Oh, I suppose there could be an exception if the buck had a tremendous trophy rack, but rear-end shots at whitetails too often mean a wasted deer. We found two wasted bucks on our own place during the 1970 season. Both had been shot from the rear. Apparently they were wounded on the next ranch and jumped the fence afterward. Both lay dead in heavy cover a few yards inside our fence line.

Sometimes a hunter is too quick to shoot and thereby misses a chance to take the real trophy. Before the 1969 season, we were scouting a big ranch where we had an invitation to hunt. As usual I had my camera and long lens. We found a great deal of sign near a pond that was surrounded by large mesquites. The bucks had been rubbing their antlers on saplings. We moved along quietly

A third, and bigger, buck may try to horn in on this fight if the rattling stirs him up enough.

and had the good fortune to see an astonishing sight—a whole herd of whitetails, mostly bucks. "Would I ever like to take that buck on the right during the season," Terry whispered.

Through my telephoto lens, I could see that the buck was a good one. His antlers extended well beyond the tips of his ears—one of the first things to look for when you want a big rack, as Terry well knew. There was a spike and a confusion of so-so bucks in the herd too, but I didn't stop looking after I'd glassed them. A trophy white-tail almost never precedes the small bucks and the does. He's a tag-along, wise enough to let the others go on ahead so that they'll run into danger first.

"If you shot that one on the right, Terry," I finally said, "you'd be passing up a real trophy. Look behind all the others. He's screened by mesquite."

Just then the deer stepped out. He was stunning ten-pointer. I regret to say that we did not get him when the season opened, but seeing him at the tail end of the herd was a good lesson for Terry.

During the morning of the 1970 opener, the haze finally lifted and the sun came out bright and warm. We prowled around for an hour and then sat on a ridge to look down into the canyons and glass the slopes. Not a deer stirred.

"What do you think they're doing right now?" Terry asked.

"Probably standing in the shade or lying down," I replied. "But it's so warm I'm sure they'll be on the ridges."

We talked about how weather affects the animals. They dislike being out in the open when the sun is bright and hot, so they hole up under cover, usually on ridges where the cooling breezes blow. Sometimes, though, they dodge the heat on the high, shady side of a canyon or up at the very head of a draw. By mid-morning they'll usually be lying down, so you keep looking for deer very close to the ground, thinking in terms of seeing only an antler or perhaps the rounded curve of the rump. At other times, deer stand in shade, so you must look high too.

Almost everyone thinks deer are much taller than they really are. Our small whitetails in hill-country Texas seldom stand taller than thirty inches at the shoulder. Big strains of deer elsewhere may be as much as forty inches tall, but that's not very tall either, so don't look for antlers up in the branches.

We didn't know it right then, but Terry and I were about to have an excellent illustration of that point. We decided to take a turn back to the vehicle and break out our lunch since we had eaten breakfast mighty early.

"Give me the camera," Terry said. "Maybe you can get a shot at a buck on the way."

"Sure," I told him jokingly, "you mess up the good chance and then let me hunt when the deer aren't moving."

We walked along the rough vehicle trail, and talk tapered off as we grew warm, weary, and hungrier. But I can never really stop hunting. As we passed a rather narrow strip of cover, mostly cedar, I was struck by the way the sunlight on the other side of it brightened the dead grass there. The grass was pale-yellow, and the trees and stumps were etched against it in stark black. Then something clicked. Branches seemed to be growing out of one stump's top, and they curved symmetrically upward.

I stopped and reached my left hand out behind me to warn Terry. He had my camera and binoculars, so it was easy for me to bring my .308 Winchester up and look through the 4X Redfield scope. I was looking at a nice buck. He wasn't as large as the big one Terry had rattled up, but I decided to try for him.

Then I could see another deer moving, perhaps more than one. I couldn't be certain. The first buck switched around to move toward my left. I picked out a small opening through the cedars where I could get the crosshairs on the deer, but I hesitated a moment. Something told me not to be hasty. A doe showed. The buck and the doe bolted, and then I saw a larger buck in the shadows beyond them.

The spirit of the hunt really hit me then. The big buck leaped out into the dried grass. Just as the scope view enclosed the animal, I was conscious for a split second that the crosshairs had touched base and instinctively squeezed off a shot. I heard the solid whunk of the bullet hitting home, but the buck kept going.

I ran, trying desperately to keep the buck in sight and hoping I had not made a bad hit. Terry was running into the oaks.

"He's down!" Terry yelled. "About fifty yards out in the grass."

Sure enough, instinct had prompted me at the correct instant. We hurried over to have a look. The buck was a pretty fair eight-pointer.

"Not the biggest one here," I said, "but I looked in the right place at the right time."

We dressed out the buck, got the four-wheel-drive vehicle, and loaded up.

"You know, Dad," Terry said, "we both get more kick out of the hunting—knowing how to look and what to look for—than we do out of the shooting." Then he paused and said, "I'm not saying I didn't hate losing the chance at that big one this morning."

During the afternoon, we jumped several does and fawns but saw no antlers. Toward dusk we sat down where we could watch the shore of our lake and an open flat nearby.

In areas where the deer are bedded or standing in the cover

The setting sun behind a lake silhouettes moving game.

during the day, you have to look very closely to see them. It's easier to spot deer at dawn and dusk because the deer move a lot then. And yet, there are inexplicable times at dawn or dusk when you'd think the woods would be alive with moving deer, and not a single one stirs. Nevertheless, the hunter's eye should always be tuned to pick up even the slightest movement during the early and late hours.

I've often watched deer coming down to drink in the evening, and when I hunt late in the day near water, I'm always careful to take a stand looking toward the water, if possible. The deer are silhouetted against the sundown glow on the water, and if the glare isn't overpowering they make clear targets. Seen from any other direction, deer blend into the darkness of the shore.

Terry and I watched two does creeping out onto the edge of the flat. The last rays of sunlight touched them, and their legs, rumps, and necks were outlined in lines of pale-gold light. A deer in the shadows at dusk is all but impossible to spot, but it is amazing how a sleek hide and long guard hairs reflect fading light and tell a sharp-eyed hunter that a deer is there. Well-rubbed antlers also pick up that kind of light. I've bagged many a buck in the evening because I spotted the wigwag of a single shining antler tine.

Next day we were out at dawn again. My wife Ellen went along to help us take pictures. She doesn't hunt. Terry and I decided to separate until midmorning while Ellen relaxed in the jeep. I did not intend to shoot unless I got a chance at a really big buck. Terry insisted it was my turn to sit where we'd seen the big fellow the previous morning, so, I sat there for an hour.

A deer suddenly peeked out from behind a large tree fifty yards away, but he was only a spike. That reminded me of a time when a partner and I failed to get a deer in northern Michigan because the deer was behind a tree. We didn't know he was there until the deer bolted, and then it was too late for a shot.

I've had that problem several times, but I learned long ago to get the rifle up and ready if I see so much as a wisp of white or a trace of movement. Deer often look around tree trunks and other objects if they suspect danger. Maybe it will be a doe, but maybe it will be a big buck. If you wait until you see the head before raising your rifle, you give the deer time to run off straightaway behind the tree trunk.

By the time the sun was bright, I was bored and tried rattling, but nothing happened. I went back to the jeep, and we drove away to meet Terry. I knew he was really hoping to get at least a fair buck that day. He had to go back to school in the morning.

We had a cold drink and then started hunting again. Terry went along one side of a ridge while Ellen and I prowled the other side. Just as we came within sight of him again, I saw a pretty fair buck walking along below me in the valley. I frantically motioned Terry to hurry. It was a long shot but far from impossible.

By the time Terry got there, the buck had vanished into a stand of small live oaks. I lined him up on the spot where I thought the deer would be.

"At this time of day, that deer is probably going to bed down," I said. "He may be right in that patch of live oaks."

Terry took off on the run, and we followed slowly, anticipation and excitement building. Terry disappeared into the oak motte, and we sat down to wait. Not a sound. After ten minutes I began to fidget. Terry should have seen the deer, spooked it, or given up by that time.

"Let's go," I said to Ellen, and we got up.

At that instant, the .243 laced out a shot that rattled across the valley.

As we neared the oaks, a deer burst out of the trees, turned in a circle, and fell. We started toward the buck. Terry was racing around frantically in the oak cover, sure he'd lost his venison.

"Right over here!" I shouted to him.

Terry came on the run.

"It's a wonder I got him," he said breathlessly. "I kept standing still, looking. The deer *was* bedded down. I finally spotted just his nose. When I moved to shot, he jumped and ran. I had a broadside chance for just one shot."

We dressed the buck, dragged him out, and went up on the ridge in the jeep to eat lunch. We hung the deer from a limb to drain and cool. It seemed an especially pleasant way to end a successful opener.

Terry kept looking at his deer and grinning to himself. I reflected that there is nothing quite like a hanging buck to give a hunter that inner glow that words never can describe. If more hunters knew how to look for deer, they'd feel that glow more often!

Hunting the
California Blacktail

William Curtis

I climbed out to a rocky point overlooking the mouth of a deep canyon that was blanketed by head-high chamise brush so thick that a hunter would have to crawl to get through some of it. Minor canyons and draws cut into the walls of the main canyon.

The terrain was ideal as a holing-up spot for a hard-pressed old blacktail buck. A lone gunner would stand practically no chance of killing a smart buck in such rough country. (Once, in similar cover in my native Napa County, California, I was on my hands and knees examining a large hoofprint when I spotted a big four-pointer bedded only twenty-seven steps from me. The season wasn't open, and the buck didn't crash away until I practically hit him with a rock. That I happened to see him at all was pure luck.)

This chapter originally appeared in the August 1972 issue of *Outdoor Life* under the title "A Hot Time with Blacktails."

Four hunting partners and I had planned a drive—one of the best methods of bagging blacktail deer. We knew the weather was going to be hot; it always is during California's early deer season. But it soon became obvious that this day would easily top the area's late-August average of 95°.

I had barely got settled on a slab of shale rock in the scanty shade of a runty blue oak when I heard a jay squawk well up the canyon wall ahead of me. Jays squawk a lot—sometimes for no reason—but sometimes they tip you off to approaching game.

I looked across the canyon to where Judy Kalfsbeek was standing guard. She had heard the bird too and was sweeping the area with her binoculars. Our drivers were still far up toward the head of the great canyon, but once in a while a wise deer will sneak out well ahead of the beaters.

Suddenly I caught a flash of movement in the heavy brush. A good buck slipped through a small opening, heading toward the bottom of a deep cut. I signaled a warning to Judy, but the buck apparently holed up in a brush patch somewhere below, for we saw no more movement.

Somewhere high above us, Dave Kalfsbeek was coming down one canyon wall. Judy's dad, Archie Shieber, was descending the other. Archie's son Bob was perched on a point behind them, backing the drive. Many a wary blacktail has escaped by circling around the drivers and exiting through the "back door."

All five of us live on ranches in Colusa County on the west side of California's great Sacramento Valley. We've hunted together for many years.

After maybe a half-hour Judy and I heard Dave's jump dog, Blaze, open with a series of excited yelps. No shots were fired, so we concluded that Blaze must have bounced out a doe. Dogs are popular with California gunners.

In the semi-open mule-deer terrain of most Western States the use of dogs for deer hunting is illegal, as it should be. But in California's dense blacktail thickets dogs are legal, and good ones—which are hard to come by—are a great help.

Blaze is the best I've seen. Part beagle and part pointer, he never chases a deer more than 200 yards. But if you draw blood he will stay on the track until he bays up the buck.

Regardless of a hunter's attitude about deer hunting with dogs, few gunning thrills can match the experience of hearing a dog baying toward your stand. Red-hot, he pushes his quarry—a quarry that you know could be the trophy of a lifetime.

Soon Judy and I heard the dog yipping again. A small band of does and fawns bounded across the main canyon between us. A spike buck followed. Arch and Dave were working closer now.

In early season, the California midday heat will drive these blacktails to shade and make them easier to approach.

Suddenly the canyon reverberated with wild bawls from Blaze and then three shots.

The buck that Judy and I had spotted earlier was now moving again, sneaking across an arroyo directly below where she sat. I yelled a warning, but she was already swinging on the buck. Her first shot geysered up red dirt just behind the target. The three-pointer (Western count) shifted into high gear, but at the second crack of Judy's .243 Sako the deer humped up, took a few faltering steps, and piled against a scrub oak.

Judy and I stayed at our stations. Many standers make a mistake by leaving too soon. Sometimes the biggest trophies try to sneak away at the last possible moment, when the drivers are almost on top of you.

A few minutes later Dave yelled that he and Arch had downed a buck and would drag it down the bottom of the canyon.

I crossed the formidable cut to where Judy was admiring her buck. We pulled her kill to the canyon bottom, and I headed back over the ridge to get Arch's jeep and herd it down as deep into the mouth of the canyon as I dared. By the time I reached the four-wheeler, the day was downright hot. Sweat had soaked through my shirt, and itchy, dried chamise blossoms clung to my face and arms.

I nosed the jeep down a narrow hogback, finally reaching a point no more than 100 yards from the bottom. But those 100 yards were almost vertical and covered by loose shale, and either carrying or dragging our two bucks uphill would be a rough go.

My companions seemed to be making good time dragging out the double-header. I could hear them talking as soon as I left the jeep.

I soon rounded a sharp bend and found Arch, Dave, and Judy sprawled out resting in the shade of some scrub oaks. Beside Dave lay a heavy-beamed five-pointer.

"Take a gander at this old buster," he said, "and see if he doesn't make your adrenaline boil over."

"I don't need a big buck to make my blood boil," I said. "The sun is taking care of that."

You may be wondering what we were doing hunting deer in mid-August. California's early blacktail season opens on the weekend closest to the first of August. This early season gives hunters a chance to bag prime eating venison.

In all but the highest ranges, by late July the velvet generally has been rubbed from the bucks' antlers. The rutting season begins by the first of September, and toward the end of the month the rut is on in full swing. In the northern half of the state the rut may occur as much as a month later. The best venison is what's bagged before rutting begins and just after the velvet has been shed.

We eventually managed to huff and puff our way up to the jeep. Venison taken in hot weather must get immediate attention, to prevent the meat from spoiling. We were hunting on Goat Mountain in north-central California's gigantic 1,082,642-acre Mendocino National Forest. This area, on the south border of the forest, is only about one and a half hours from our homes by pickup or jeep.

We slipped wool sacks (we like them better than meat bags) over the gutted carcasses to keep away blowflies. Then we headed for Arch's barn, where we skinned out the bucks and hung them in a walk-in box to age.

With a little extra care, you can keep venison in good shape for four or five days in surprisingly hot weather. The deer should be gutted immediately and the hide peeled off as soon as possible. All bloodshot meat must be trimmed away, and the carcass should be quickly sacked. Blowflies may get in their licks in a matter of minutes. At dusk remove the sack and hang the deer in the open, with the rib cage spread apart or the carcass split open.

The next morning, resack the deer before sunup and lay it in a shady spot, covering it with all the bedding you have. Repeat this procedure each night and morning.

If you plan to get the deer to a locker plant right away, it doesn't do any harm to wash out the body cavity. But if you won't be able to get there for a while, wipe out—don't wash—the inside of the carcass. Moisture speeds up spoilage in meat.

Dave's trophy was a real old ridge-runner with worn teeth and rough, heavy antler beams, each sporting five points. It dressed out at 120 pounds. An average blacktail buck will field-dress at maybe

80 pounds, but a few have been taken that weighed over 200.

Blacktail deer seldom grow anything but typical heads. I've seen only two or three nontypical racks. One, taken a few years ago in Napa County, California, had eleven points on one side and seven on the other, with an outside spread of 35 inches. However, any blacktail buck with four points on each side and a 20-inch spread is a real trophy.

In some areas mature bucks never grow more than two points, plus eyeguards, on each side. Old-timers considered these big forkhorns a different species, frequently calling them Pacific bucks.

Blacktail deer range from Southern California north along the coast ranges to the Alaska Panhandle. At the northern extremes of their range they are considered a subspecies, the Sitka blacktail. From California's San Francisco Bay Area southward, the deer are called southern blacktails.

Some of the largest blacktails, in both rack and weight, come from the western slopes of the Sierra. But these trophies are ruled out of contention for big-game records because there is the possibility that they may have crossbred with their cousins, the mule deer. I've frequently seen both species together in the Hat Creek country east of the Sacramento Valley. They interbreed freely.

Mule deer have a thin, white, ropelike tail with a black tip, and their "caboose" is a telltale white. Blacktails don't have a large white rump patch, and their tail is bushy like a whitetail's but is brown and black-edged on top. When a blacktail bounds away his tail may be straight up, at half mast, or clamped down tightly.

Climbing up and down rugged, brushy canyons in 100°-plus temperatures is one way to bag a blacktail, but there are less-strenuous ways. You can use the heat to your advantage.

California's late season opens during late September and runs until mid-November. Near the end of this season you might even run into early snow squalls in the high country. But I'm going to talk about hot-weather hunting because on sizzling days you can use deadly tactics that won't work at any other time.

Last year my landlord's girl, Jeannie Ramos, wanted to try her hand at clobbering a deer. So I used the most reliable of these tactics to get her within range of a nice forkhorn.

From late August through the fall months, acorns are practically the staff of life for deer in this neck of the woods. As soon as the acorns start to drop, the does and fawns drift into the oak foothills to feed.

Neither the antlerless deer nor the hunters like the brushy ovens that hide the animals so well. So, during the middle of the week, when pressure from gunners slackens considerably, the deer like to mosey away from their hideouts and feed up to the tops of ridges and knolls at midday, to take advantage of any cooling breeze that may be blowing. If there are creeks around, the deer will drift down to where the water has grown bigger and lusher oaks, which generally yield an excellent acorn crop.

If hunting pressure isn't too heavy, the blacktail's favorite watering time isn't at night, as is commonly supposed, but from around nine a.m. until noon, depending on how early the mercury soars. I've killed some of my biggest bucks by ambushing them at stock dams and water holes in drying creekbeds.

For the first three weeks of last year's early season I'd been watching a creek lined with acorn-laden valley oaks. Around the first of September, three days of hot, dry north winds produced a ground carpet of these fat oak nuts, and the does, fawns, and spikes moved in to feed.

It was getting to be that time of year when the bigger bucks would begin thinking about does. They wouldn't go completely out of their skulls, as they sometimes do at the height of the rut, but some old busters would likely desert the haunts that carried them through the first few weeks of heavy gunning pressure and move out closer to the herds of antlerless deer. With luck a hunter might catch a buck out on an open point or rim in areas the bucks shun earlier in the season.

"Ready to go look for that buck?" I asked Jeannie one sizzling day during the first week of September.

She was. We left the ranch at 10:00 a.m. The does and fawns would be working toward the shade by then, and I hoped to catch a buck off guard. Early or late in the day, the bucks would either sneak away far ahead of us or freeze and let us walk past. But any animal is more reluctant to run during the heat of midday.

I drove my pickup along an old field road that roughly paralleled the creekbed where I'd been seeing a fair number of deer for several weeks. Every time we came to a ridge that screened us from a stretch of creek, Jeannie and I would climb to the top and carefully glass for animals around the willows and oaks.

After our first climb, Jeannie got excited.

"Look!" she exclaimed. "Deer all over the place."

Heat waves danced in front of my heavy 7 x 50 binoculars, but I made out twelve deer. One had pencil-size spikes about as high as its ears.

"Think you could hit him if he were legal?" I asked.

"I don't know," she answered, "but I sure hope I get a chance to try."

She carried a slide-action .270 Remington and could bowl over

Oregon Wildlife Comm. photo

These Oregon blacktails are distinguished from mule deer by the dark outer surface of the entire tail as compared to mule deer's dark tip. Also the blacktail's metatarsal gland is about three inches long as compared to five inches with the mule deer. But interbreeding in transitional zones often makes it impossible to distinguish between the two types.

jackrabbits and squirrels regularly. But when you're shooting at deer—your first or your fiftieth—buck fever can play hob with accuracy. I see herds of deer almost every day, and I once counted over three hundred in a single morning. Yet a buck can still give me a good case of the shakes.

Jeannie and I drove around one point and almost ran into seven or eight does. Some were lying in the tall weeds and around broken snags, with only their big ears showing.

I didn't tell Jeannie, but I was losing hope of our seeing a legal buck. Then we walked across a swale pinched into a U-shaped bend of the creekbed.

"There's one," whispered Jeannie, pointing toward a blowdown of rotting willow limbs.

"Let him have it!" I said. "He's plenty legal."

I don't know where her 130-grain slug hit. At the shot the buck whirled back toward the undercut bank and out of our sight. We could see the entire creekbed on both sides of the thicket, but no deer thudded past.

"He got away somehow," moaned Jeannie.

"Don't give up yet," I cautioned.

I knew from past experience just how smart blacktails can be. One time, as I drove over the top of an open hill, I spotted two good bucks lying under a blue oak in a saddle directly below me. In two bounds both deer disappeared into the head of a narrow, open canyon. I thought I had them bottled up.

I raced to a high point where I had a commanding view of the entire canyon. The only cover was a few scattered oaks and digger pines and one garden-size patch of brush directly across from me. I looked until my eyes hurt, seeing nothing but a long-eared jack. I couldn't figure out how those bucks had managed to give me the slip.

All deer are creatures of habit. Two weeks later I drove past there with a friend. The same two bucks were bedded down under the same tree, and when they saw us they ducked into the same canyon. We looked in vain for them. In desperation I trained my binoculars on the brush patch and finally spotted both blacktails. They were stretched out flat on the ground. Those bucks had been escaping hunters by running as hard as they could for only 100 yards, then flopping down flat in chamise that was just high enough to screen them from gunners.

But back to my hunt with Jeannie.

I was sure that the forkhorn she'd shot at was still along the cut-bank somewhere. I motioned for Jeannie to move forward, and by the time she took two strides the deer stepped into sight — head low, sneaking.

Jeannie fired, and the buck humped up and started to trot up the creekbed. I raised my .270 Parker Hale for insurance but didn't need it. The buck suddenly pitched to the ground.

Jeannie's dark eyes flashed, and I helped the happiest girl I ever saw drag her buck to the pickup.

Day of Stealth and Grappling

Ken Crandall

I was sitting in a fresh deer bed that was big enough to couch a yearling steer. It had rained all night, but the ground was gouged with big splayed tracks, some of them made by animals so heavy that the dewclaws had been driven right into the sand. The willow clumps had been hooked and horned beyond belief. Little piles of shredded bark lay beside deeply scored trunks. Heavy antlers had torn and broken large branches.

I was certain my two days of hard scouting was going to pay off, but I sat there for over an hour without hearing a sound. Then I heard an explosive, heaving cough. From its deep tone, I knew it was a big deer. That deer was probably lying in its bed, and it was only about forty yards away. From the evidence around me, the odds

This chapter originally appeared in the November 1969 issue of *Outdoor Life* under the title "A Stalk to Remember."

were that it was a buck. My problem was to stalk the deer in brush so thick I couldn't see more than fifty feet.

Such problems are hereditary in my family. I was born in Okanogan County, Washington, which is noted for its fine mule-deer hunting, and I grew up in a deer-hunting family. At the age of four, I was posed for the camera with my dad's rifle in front of a row of heavy-horned bucks hanging from a meatpole. I nearly blew it at the age of nine when a fat forkhorn walked out in front of my dad and me. Dad wouldn't let me carry a rifle at that age, but watching him bag that deer is one of my treasured memories.

When I was ten, an uncle gave me an old Model 1886 Winchester lever action in .45/70 caliber, and I was the happiest kid in town. I had just turned eleven when I stood beside my dad on another quiet mountainside. He was looking at a bunch of deer through his riflescope. They were only about 80 yards away, but they were in the brush. Finally they moved out.

"The deer on the left," Dad whispered, "is a buck. Shoot!"

I've never had buck fever, but I'll never be able to explain that shot. I had the bead right in the middle of that forkhorn when I pulled the trigger, but the big slug hit him right behind the ear.

From that day on, nothing could keep me out of the mountains during deer season. With a lot of hard work and a lot more luck, I hung up twenty-three sets of antlers in twenty-three seasons. I learned that there is a lot more to hunting mule deer than wandering around hoping to blunder into one. A big mule-deer buck is sophisticatedly programmed by weather, feed, water, cover, hunting pressure, and instinct.

I once bet a friend that I could show him a buck by eight o'clock in the morning. He had hunted most of the season without seeing so much as a spike. I was pushing my luck, but there had been a heavy snowstorm, and I knew just where to take him. I was back in my office by 8:30 a.m., and my friend had a dandy four-pointer to brag about. Knowing when and where to hunt are major factors. I'm reasonably certain that before that snowstorm there hadn't been a buck within five miles of the spot I selected.

As time went by, I kept trying for bigger and bigger bucks. When the Game Department opened a special High Cascade deer season in September of 1958, I didn't pay much attention, but a friend went and came back with glowing tales of bucks all over the place. That friend was John R. (Bob) Duncan, who is now a neighbor of mine at Malott, Washington. Bob works in the supervisor's office of the Okanogan National Forest. We passed the word to Art Lucas, who is a shop foreman for the state Department of Highways and lives in Okanogan. I work for the Okanogan County Agricultural Stabilization and Conservation Committee as county executive director for their facility in Okanogan.

The three of us eventually packed into the High Cascades for the special hunt. We hunted in an area near the Spanish Camp fireguard station, which we reached via the Andrews Creek trail north of Winthrop, Washington. We saw big mule-deer bucks everywhere—sometimes in bunches—and took three fine trophy heads.

I wrote about our adventure in *Outdoor Life*. As a result of that story and other publicity, a horde of hunters hit the high deer area that fall. Some got deer, but very few really good bucks were taken, and many hunters came back empty-handed. The word was that all the big bucks had been killed in the previous hunts or had been driven into Canada. We didn't believe it.

The high area we had hunted consisted of beautiful open-meadowed ridges surrounded by miles of thick second-growth lodgepole pines. We had set up our camp with little disturbance. We even ruled out woodchopping and campfires. Yet those deer were extremely timid, and after only a few days of light hunting pressure they seemed to vanish.

We were convinced that the heavy influx of hunters had sent those bucks scooting into the dense brush just before the season opened. To test our theory, we decided to go into the High Cascade area a week before the next deer season. We had heard about some fine fishing in Sheep and Ramon lakes, which are about seven miles due west of the Spanish Camp cabin. We planned a two-week trip—a week to fish and look for deer, and a week for deer hunting. Bob and I had horses of our own, and we begged and borrowed a few more. We even included my contrary burro, Cactus Jack, in our packstring.

The author's partners and his contrary burro, Cactus Jack, are en route to high country where the author will survive a harrowing encounter.

We had such a heavy load of supplies for the two-week stay that we made only the fifteen miles to the Spanish Camp cabin the first day. We stayed overnight nearby and left the next morning. It may have been only seven miles in a straight line, but it took us all day to battle the gruelling switchback trail that led to Sheep Mountain. But it was worth the effort. Sheep Lake, cradled in the bosom of that mighty 8,300-foot-high mountain, is breathtakingly beautiful. The two little Ramon lakes nearby were dazzling.

The lakes were full of cutthroat trout, the weather was perfect, and deer were so thick that we gave up trying to count them. We did count up to forty-five of them in a big meadow and on an adjoining hillside one evening.

We saw innumerable bucks, but they didn't behave as mule deer are supposed to behave. They rarely came out into the open. They lurked along the edges of the timber and came out when it was difficult to see them even with the aid of big binoculars. One night we saw two old monarchs against the skyline; they had racks we couldn't believe. Our suspicions were confirmed. Those high-country bucks hadn't been eliminated, but they were educated.

Our other suspicions were also confirmed. We set up our deer camp the day before the season was to open, and hunters were everywhere. By opening morning nearly every deer on the ridge had plunged into the heavy brush. I did see two small four-pointers just at dawn, and I watched to see what they would do. They headed down off the ridge and zipped into the brush as fast as a nightcrawler going down its hole.

I didn't really try to hunt the first day, because I knew things would soon quiet down. I was reasonably certain I could find some of those wise old bucks, so I spent two days scouting the country. I beat my way through miles of lodgepole tangles and climbed to every vantage point I could find.

On the third day I found what I was looking for. It was a high and steep mountainside, almost completely covered with dense second-growth lodgepole pine, interlaced with fallen trees and standing snags. A brook started near the top and coursed almost straight down the mountain. There were other places almost identical to the one I picked, with one very important exception. Right in the middle of that almost impenetrable mass of brush was a patch of willows next to the stream. It wasn't more than an acre in size, but the heavy willow cover made it an ideal place for big mule-deer bucks. They are plain lazy and like nothing better than a place where they can get up out of their beds and walk a few yards to eat and drink. If you subject the big bucks to hunting pressure, hiding becomes their first consideration. They will go several miles between good feed and a secure hiding place, but they don't like it. If a big lazy buck can have his cover and eat it too, he will usually stay put.

I liked something else about that little patch of willows. A buck mule deer wants to hide in dense cover, but he also wants to be able to see out. The patch of willows was on a little flat on the mountainside, but a small fingertip ridge ran right up to the creek where it bordered the willows. I inspected it with binoculars from a vantage point about a mile away and saw quite a few openings in the willows around the end of that point. It was a perfect place for a buck to lie in the sun and gaze out.

For over an hour I surveyed the mountainside with my binoculars. I had to plot a course through dense lodgepole timber. I wanted to hit the stream about 300 yards above the patch of willows. In that lodgepole jungle, the only way to see any distance was up. So I carefully memorized the tops of the standing snags along my route.

Bob and Art were a little discouraged when I reached camp that night, but I didn't tell them of my plan. I'm not selfish, but I did know of the odds against nailing a buck in such dense cover, and I also knew that one man can hunt more quietly than two or three.

I was well equipped for that kind of hunting. In the previous week I had developed a slight growth of beard. I'm firmly convinced that one look at a pale face often sends hayrack bucks rocketing for cover.

That was clearly demonstrated once when I was mincing along a deer trail in the middle of a dense thicket. I was moving only one step every two or three minutes because I wanted to see the deer before they saw me. I crouched down to get a better look under the tree limbs and found myself looking a big buck in the eye at fifty feet. He too had his head down to peek under the limbs. It took him about three seconds to hit the panic button, and I heard him shredding brush for half a mile. I am sure he had already seen my legs, but he didn't sense danger until he saw my face. I often rub my face with mud or dirt when I'm hunting in close cover.

My broad-brimmed hat helps because it shades the upper part of my head and makes it harder for deer to see my face. I go one step further. I carry a loop of narrow elastic that I wrap about four times around the crown of my cowboy hat. In hunting where there are a lot of hunters, I use the elastic to hold a piece of bright fluorescent plastic around my hat. When I get away from the crowd on a hunt, I remove the plastic and jam four or five small evergreen branches into the loops to break up the outline of my head. The Game Department doesn't like deer hunters in camouflage, but it's legal. Nevertheless, I never dispense with my fluorescent plastic unless I'm alone in a very isolated area.

I wear crepe-soled hunting boots, an old pair of wool army pants, and a lightweight wool jack shirt. Soft, fuzzy clothing doesn't make scraping noises as you move through heavy brush.

I was carrying an old Model 95 Mauser in 7 mm. It's short and light, and it's equipped with a peep sight. I had removed the small aperture insert so that I had the large, fast rear ring for shooting at close range in poor light. Trying to use a scope in heavy brush is one of man's most confounding experiences.

The wet underbrush made movement quieter, but I also wanted to use thermal currents. From about noon on, the mountainsides get well heated under the September sun. The rising air would help me during my approach toward that willow patch from above. If the air stayed wet and heavy, however, my scent would spread all over the willow grove as soon as I got near it. I was really tickled when the air started to clear at about nine o'clock.

I had to walk a long distance to my preplanned starting place, and the brush was still wet when I started down the mountain. In ten minutes I was soaked to the skin as I crawled, rolled, and wriggled through that lodgepole jungle. I hit the little stream on the nose and disguised my hat with lodgepole twigs, swabbed my face with mud, and started Stage 2.

If a wise old buck was bedded down in or near the willows, I knew that I would need every trick in my book and a lot of luck besides to get a shot. That splashing, gurgling brook would help. It would drown out the slight noises I knew I would make. Those big ears mule deer have aren't for decoration.

Their hearing is fantastic. Sit quietly in the forest for half an hour; it comes alive. Squirrels chase each other, woodpeckers hammer, small birds tap, scratch, and flutter. Yet a wise old buck seems to have the uncanny ability to lie right in the middle of this subdued clamor and single out sounds made by a cautious hunter 100 yards away.

It took me an hour and fifteen minutes to cover the 300 yards to the willow clump. The sun came out bright and warm, and I was reasonably confident that my scent wouldn't give me away. I was completely drenched when I finally sat down in that deer bed I described at the start of this narrative. I felt as though I had swum to the spot. I slipped off my boots, wrung the water out of my socks, and hung them up to dry. Then I broke out a somewhat sodden lunch and ate it slowly. If deer were bedded nearby, they might have heard me moving. I had to give them plenty of time to forget the suspicious sounds. I was hoping that the deer would move or make some sound so that I would know where to look. That's just what happened when I heard that explosive cough.

I put on my boots and started edging down through the willows in what I could call a kneeling hitchalong. I got into the rifleman's kneeling position and inched forward on one knee. You must move slowly on a stalk, but if you try to crawl, you are at a disadvantage. Your hind end bounces up and down like a crippled camel's back, and you must drag your rifle. If a deer spots you, you can't get off a quick shot. You would also have to be superhuman to crawl along for any great length of time. I can hitchalong in a kneeling position and have many advantages. I hold my rifle in a natural shooting position and I can therefore shoot almost instantly. My eyes are high enough to see over low shrubs, but they are low enough to see under most trees. When a deer spots me, I can sit back, duck my head, and stay still as long as I need to, but I can stand up to shoot quick as a flash.

I moved a few inches at a time, and then sat on my heel to inspect every opening in the underbrush. I had to spot that deer before it spotted me! I finally reached the middle of the flat and found I could see a little farther because of wider spacing between the willow clumps. I was about ten yards from the creek and directly opposite the end of the little ridge I described earlier. The creek had washed away the end of the ridge, making a cutbank about thirty feet high. Willows growing along the creek screened most of the lower half of the bank. I was peering intently into the brush directly below me when a slight movement across the creek caught my eye. I turned my head very slowly, and sucked in a gasp of air that should have gone clear to my toes. An oversize buck with blood-red horns and flapping, bloody tatters hanging from them around his eyes and ears was rising like a devilish apparition right out of the willows.

It was at least thirty seconds before I could collect my wits. The buck had started to work the velvet from his antlers but had only succeeded in tearing it loose from the long, high tines on each side. His antlers were large but strange. They stood almost straight up from his head. The red tips and flapping velvet made a sight seldom viewed by sober eyes. He was only fifteen yards away, and now he was climbing the cutbank, nibbling at a few dwarfed willows growing on the slope. He didn't have the slightest idea that I was there.

He was such an amazing sight that I simply sat there and watched him until he turned abruptly and walked back down the bank. When I finally tried for a shot, he was completely screened by the willows and I couldn't see well enough to sight. He was feeding farther and farther upstream, and I knew those helpful thermals would soon carry my scent to him.

He finally moved his head and neck behind a few small openings. I pulled down on the thickest part of his neck and squeezed the trigger.

The buck hit the ground with a shuddering crash and slid rear-end-first down the bank and through a small hole between two willow clumps. He landed right in the creek.

I walked to a spot right above him and watched him carefully for about two minutes. It was steep and brushy down to where he lay, so I leaned my rifle against a log and climbed down through a bunch of downed poles. He had landed with his rear hanging down over a two-foot waterfall. His front feet and head were lying out in the creek on top of the little ledge.

A few small downed lodgepoles were directly in front of him, the top one about two feet above the rocks and water. I got out my sheath knife, knelt down behind that pole, and grabbed an antler. The buck gave a low moan and jerked his head away from me. I was so sure his neck was broken that I put my knife down, reached out, and grabbed his antlers with both hands. I wanted to pull his head back so I could get at him.

That buck let go with an explosive snort, rolled his eyes, and started to get up. Then he let loose with a bawl that could have been heard for miles. I was amazed, but I slammed his head against that pole and hung on. If he got to his feet, I would be in plenty of trouble.

I was right in the middle of the only place he could go if he got up, but he couldn't get good footing in the creek. Mud and water were flying as though someone had started a giant eggbeater. He never quit bawling. Every time he tried to lunge to his feet, I gave a mighty yank to throw him off balance. If it hadn't been for his long, high antlers I would have been cut to ribbons. I gained a tremendous leverage by jamming the base of one horn against that lodgepole and hauling for all I was worth against the tips.

I could feel the blood pounding in my head, and I knew I had to do something fast or lose the battle. He was getting stronger, and I was getting weaker. In sheer desperation, I released the antler in my right hand and hooked my elbow around his nose. Then I hooked my knees under the pole and gave a heave that would have ruptured a grizzly bear. I threw him clear over on his back and jammed his antlers down behind the pole while I hauled his nose straight up. For some reason this seemed to nearly paralyze him.

Then I couldn't find my knife! I sat there like an idiot, covered with mud and soaked with water and sweat, my blood pounding in my head so wildly that everything I looked at was red and fuzzy. I stupidly hung onto a very large and very strong mule-deer buck. One phrase kept running through my mind: "Fools rush in where angels fear to tread!"

I finally twisted his head clear back over the pole until I could hold his chin still with my chest. Then I reached into my pocket and dug out a very dull pocket knife. I will spare the grisly details, but I dispatched that poor buck as quickly as the situation allowed.

When I finally regained my breath, I examined the deer closely. My bullet had gone through his neck just above the spine and had only stunned him. I've often thought just how serious it might have been. No one knew where I was, and if I had been badly hurt, I could never have gotten out of that jungle by myself.

I dragged the buck out of the creek and dressed him out after I found my sheath knife in the creek. Then I backtracked to see where the deer had come from. His tracks led me down to the creek and then right out around to the sunny side of that little finger ridge. His bed was there, and it appeared that he had lain there for some time. A few yards away was an equally large and freshly used bed with great splayed tracks leading away from it. My buck's companion apparently had lain there until the ruckus started. Then he had leaped into the brush. I'm reasonably sure that the second buck was the one I had heard coughing. From the beds, droppings, and horned brush I found, it seemed two more old bucks were using that grove regularly.

The author poses with the velvet buck—antlers scraped—that he finally dispatched with a pocket knife.

My buck wasn't an old deer, but he was just plain big. We became a little more convinced of that fact the next day. It took all three of us most of the day to get him out to the closest point we could reach with the horses. We skinned him out and found him amazingly fat, with over an inch of tallow down his back and on his rump. The four quarters weighed out at 218 pounds later on a creamery scales. Allowing for the head and neck, the hide and lower legs, and all that tallow, which we cut away, I'm reasonably certain that the buck field-dressed in the neighborhood of 280 pounds. That's much heavier than the average in the area.

Two days later, we hunted another steep hillside where a stream ran down through willows and other leafy brush. The willow patch was too big and too open for stillhunting, so we set up a drive with me as the dog. The drive was well planned, but it turned out to be a complete flop because I got mixed up in the adjoining heavy timber and went through in the wrong place.

Art finally tired of waiting for my dog act and walked out onto the edge of a small cliff to look at the scenery. An old buster buck was bedded at the base of that cliff and went out of there fast. Bob was coming out of the timber about eighty yards away, and the buck was headed right at him. Bob had no idea Art was up on the cliff, and he held his fire, figuring to drop the buck at point-blank range.

Bob didn't take into account the fact that Art grew up in Nebraska and cut his shooting teeth on running jackrabbits. Art was using a Model 720 Remington .30/06 equipped with a Weaver 3X scope. He nailed that old buck through the neck while it was running flat out.

Bob was completely flabbergasted when the buck dropped out of his riflescope's field, skidded, and rolled to within thirty feet of him, stone dead. The buck's antlers were large, three points on one side and four on the other.

After helping Art dress out his deer, Bob climbed clear to the top and started hunting down through the timber at the edge of the brushy area. He jumped a big buck and got a fleeting shot as it tore through a small opening in the timber. He heard his bullet hit, but the buck kept going.

It was extremely difficult tracking because there were so many other fresh deer tracks, but Bob stuck it out and jumped the buck far down the mountain. His second shot knocked the buck down for good. His rifle was a Model 720 Remington .30/06 equipped with a 2½X Lyman Alaskan scope. The buck also had a fine rack with three points on one side and four on the other.

We were a jubilant bunch of deer hunters, but we had quite a time getting all that meat to camp. I figured it was worth every minute. We had found those vanishing high-country bucks, and I had pulled off a stalk I'll never forget.

Mississippi Backwoods Buck

Charles Elliott

I decided, after a total of twenty-four hours perched in a tree, that making like a bird was for the birds and not for me. The wooden platform that John Jared, my old hunting partner, had nailed to the trunk of a massive beech had both advantages and disadvantages. It definitely had not been designed to fit my anatomy, yet it was high enough above the swamp so that I could occasionally shift from one aching muscle to another without disturbing the creatures at ground level. Not many forest inhabitants expect to find a man sitting serenely in a tree, especially when the woods is saturated with rain.

I had proved that point on the first morning of our hunt when an old turkey gobbler flew off his roost after daylight and landed

This chapter originally appeared in the December 1963 issue of *Outdoor Life* under the title "Backwoods Buck."

The author's hunting partner John Jared scans the area from a tree stand. It's wise to check game laws before using such aids, however.

100 yards behind me in the swamp. Since turkey season was not in and I'd left my yelper at home, I cautiously fingered the yellowing beech leaves around the platform until I found one soft enough to simulate the gentle notes of a hen. The gobbler answered immediately. Then, craning his long neck from side to side, he made a wide circle around my tree.

When he started to move away, I again clucked softly, and he came back to the beech, apparently never thinking to look up until my third attempt with the leaf hit a sour note. Then he simply stepped behind a bush and vanished.

On that first day of perching in the branches, I had seen one deer, and later a second, trail through the swamp just at the limit of my vision. In the downpour, and through a screen of colorful foliage, I could not identify either animal as a buck, even through my 4X scope, so passed them up.

For two and a half days I'd scoured the platform and dripping branches around it with the seat of my pants and associated intimately with gray squirrels, woodpeckers, and a host of tiny birds.

We were hunting a corner of the 45,000-acre Noxubee National Wildlife Refuge below Starkville, Mississippi. This is primarily a waterfowl wintering area. On its lakes, rivers, and flooded, green-timber swamps, the Noxubee claims a winter population of 70,000

141

ducks and geese, with a peak year of almost 120,000 birds. No shooting of these migrants is permitted, but seasons have been established to allow the harvesting of surplus deer, turkeys, and squirrels. A split deer season is usually set up for Thanksgiving and Christmas weeks, and were were there for the early hunt.

"It's one of the fine deer areas in Mississippi," I'd been told by long-time hunting partner John Jared, who was then with a construction outfit of Meridian, Mississippi. "Whitetails were first stocked on the refuge in the early 1940's and the first hunt held in 1958, with only seven bucks taken. The high kill was in 1961, with two hundred animals brought out of the area, and a great many more were taken on adjoining private lands. This fall should be a dilly."

So far it hadn't panned out that way.

Before the middle of November, John had scouted the region and built tree stands where he found a concentration of trails and tracks. On the afternoon before the season opened, we had gone into the swamp with W. M. (Doody) Callahan, who operates a tonsorial and beauty salon with his wife in Starkville, Mississippi, and Henry Beattie, who runs a feed mill in Starkville. We established quarters in Henry's comfortable cabin in a hairpin bend of the Noxubee River.

By way of a high, swinging bridge which spanned the river between cabin and hunting area, we crossed before daylight on opening morning and worked our way through the rain-soaked forest to the burly beech in which John had nailed his first tree stand. He disappeared into the gray light, and I eagerly arranged my carcass on the wooden platform.

To a casual observer, the swamp might have been virgin woods, columned with the massive trunks of beeches, oaks, and hickories. Burton Webster, refuge manager, told me later that a small amount of logging had been done on the Noxubee, mostly for the outsize ash, which has a high market value but does not furnish food for any of the game species. Into these logging gaps have sprouted seedlings to provide low-growing browse for the deer.

I'll admit that as a stander I belong close to the foot of the class, but except for a few noonday hours when the deer are supposed to be curled up in thickets for the midday siesta, I stayed with the beech-tree platform for two and a half days. I had little choice. In that country, with the flat, open woods, there's slight chance of walking up on a whitetail.

Before noon on Thanksgiving day, however, I decided that if the refuge supported the alleged deer population, then the animals were in some other neck of the swamp. If we were to hang a buck on the front porch of the cabin, we'd have to search out a lot more territory than I could see from my platform.

We drove to the Callahan home in Starkville for a delightful Thanksgiving dinner which more than helped to supplement the cabin fare. With our paunches rather uncomfortably stuffed, Doody, John, and I were nervously watching one of the Thanksgiving Day football games on television, when Travis, Doody's wife, came in from the kitchen. She glanced from one to the other of us and laughed.

"By the looks of you, I doubt if you even know who's playing. You've been here long enough after dinner to prove you are gentlemen. I know how badly you want to get back to the swamp, so I'll forgive you if you make a mad rush for the door."

Back at the cabin, we discovered that our hunting crew had been augmented by Doody's three grown sons: Ramon, working on his master's degree in wildlife management at Mississippi State; Billy, a forester for Sears, Roebuck, and Joel, a resident of Jackson who was at work on his medical degree. Also included was nine-year-old Henry Beattie Jr., who had driven in with his father. It was midafternoon when we held a caucus in front of the cabin fireplace.

"We've got enough hunters to spread out now and do some good," I said. "I'd already planned to make a big circle at the head of the lake to look for more sign than John and I have found in the last two days. If you fellows will take stands at all the crossings and trails between the upper corner of the lake and the river, I might run a buck over one of you."

"That's a good deal," John Jared speculated. "And since you won't see any deer while you're moving around like that, why don't you take your .22 rifle, angle through some of the private property next to the refuge, and collect a few squirrels for the pot."

While I'd been sitting quietly in the beech tree with my deer rifle, the grays had trooped around me. So I quess it was only natural that when I replaced the .308 Kennon custom-built rifle with my .22 Marlin repeater, the squirrels should prove as elusive as had the bucks.

That section of forest was open and studded with magnificent oaks and hickories. Among them were huge holly trees, thick as a man's body and mingling their emerald crowns with the colorful fall foliage of the other hardwoods. Both Ramon and Billy had told me that many of the squirrels they'd killed earlier in the season had been feeding on the bright masses of holly berries.

With my standers spread in a wide semicircle to cover that corner of the swamp, I cut a circle along a shallow slough, tiptoeing very slowly and as quietly as possible, listening for a squirrel to bark or for the patter of shell fragments where the animals were cutting in one of the hickory trees. The late-afternoon woods were bright, but so still they seemed uninhabited. I squatted on my heels beside a hickory for five minutes before I heard the churr of a gray 100 yards away. I stalked him — one cautious step after another — until I got close enough to see the flicker of his tail through the lofty foliage.

I didn't know it then, but there was another hunter in the woods. I had not disturbed the squirrel and was working into position for a shot with the Long-Rifle cartridge, when a small Cooper's hawk flashed through the tree crowns. Just as I got a glimpse of the winged predator, the squirrel vanished into a knothole.

To my left sprawled a dense honeysuckle thicket in an open glade. I was moving stealthily toward it when the vines suddenly crashed and a whitetail buck, his rack a little larger than average, bounded out of the copse and stopped a few yards away to look back over his shoulder. With the inadequate .22 rifle, all I could do was mutter under my breath. Two more bounds and he disappeared in the direction of the river where I was certain one of the standers would get him. So I squatted on my heels for ten minutes, waiting for the sound of the shot. All we could figure later was that the buck had seen or winded the hunters and turned back into the swamp.

After that, I forgot all about squirrels. An examination of the honeysuckle patch showed it had been heavily browsed, and there were signs where a few deer had bedded in the thicket.

From the honeysuckle, I made a wide circle along the extreme northwest corner of the lake. Here I found the swamp crisscrossed with deer trails and fresh track impressions in the soft earth. Two of the trails showed imprints I was sure had been left by large bucks.

Not knowing whether I had spooked other deer in addition to the one I'd jumped, I sat down to wait out the fading light, with no intention of further disturbing this portion of the swamp where the whitetails seemed to be concentrated. In the last minutes of the afternoon, I discovered why at least some of the squirrels had deserted the holly trees. They were cutting on the thin-shelled, scaly-bark hickory nuts. Two trees near me were full of grays, and they were running out to the ends of the limbs, clipping nuts, and scampering back to more substantial perches to rain cuttings on the forest floor. In the two trees, I counted at least a dozen busy bushy-tails.

It was after dark when our group slipped out of the woods and followed a dim logging road to the swinging bridge over the river. Even before we put on the charcoal for steaks, we held a council of war and decided that next morning each gunner would occupy the same stand where he had sat out the twilight hours. I was to watch over the corner of the lake near the honeysuckle patch where I had jumped the buck.

We were in the swamp woods before daylight. Though the temperature was a few degrees above freezing, the leaves were covered with frost. Henry, Doody, and John took their same stands along the remains of an ancient road which Henry said was one of the first thoroughfares through that country. A small stream drained this end of the lake and followed the road from the lake to the river. Well-used deer trails crossed the rivulet in half a dozen places. Instead of stopping at the river, however, Billy and Ramon walked the extra half a mile with me to the corner of the lake and then went on deeper into the woods to a high finger of brushy land that crossed the upper end of the swamp and paralleled a man-made dike which had been thrown up along the northern border of the lake.

A hundred yards from where I had seen the buck, I cut an armload of low, bushy, water-oak sprouts and arranged the crowns of green leaves in a semi-circular blind around the base of a big white oak. I zipped up my camouflage jacket, made myself as comfortable as possible, and settled down to wait for dawn.

Shortly after first light, leaves crackled off to my left. I froze, my rifle ready, and two does came into sight. They were on the upwind side and so close I could have touched them with a cane pole. They spotted rather than winded me, paused momentarily to look me over, then moved unhurriedly along, browsing as they went.

Following at a good 100 feet was a small buck with spikes so short I knew I'd have to measure to determine whether they were legal. I let him pass, which he did without seeing me. I fully expected the three deer to be trailed by the buck I'd passed up when I'd had the .22. But if he was a part of that group, he remained out of sight in the brush.

Twenty minutes later three more does and and a fawn passed just at the limit of my vision. They were within range of the .308, and again I was cocked on hair-trigger ready, when the dawn woods were blasted by a single rifle shot, which rang like the report of a .30/30. The reverberations rolled around me in such a way that I couldn't tell whether it had come from 200 yards or half a mile away.

For another half an hour I sat perfectly still, hoping the sound of the shot might have started a buck tiptoeing toward my stand. Then curiosity got the best of me, and I angled through the woods to where Billy had perched on a tree limb and downed a small forkhorn walking almost under him.

When Ramon appeared from the other direction a few minutes later, we dressed out the buck, tied it on a pole, and marched back to the cabin.

We had only that afternoon and one more day left in the first week of the split season. Henry suggested that, since we might have disturbed that corner of the swamp, we save it until the next morning and scatter out on both sides of the Noxubee River for our afternoon hunt.

The area assigned to me lay between the northeast dike of Buff Lake and the river. I spent an enjoyable but unproductive afternoon in the radiant fall woods and got a glimpse of one doe. I met her in the trail on my way to the cabin when the light was almost too dim to see the crosshairs in my scope.

Saturday was the last day of our hunt. Billy's buck, hanging on the wide porch of the cabin, had put new enthusiasm into the party. Long before dawn, fortified with ham and eggs, biscuits, and mugs of hot coffee, we crossed the swinging bridge, and felt our way through the black swamp forest.

I intended to find the blind I'd built around the white oak but in the darkness missed it by a couple of hundred yards. With mallards cackling out on the lake, squirrels purring around me in the swamp, and light filtering into the tree crowns, I gave up my search for the oak and built another blind where I could make out the crossing of a couple of fresh deer trails.

The dawn was still and crisp enough to work its icy fingers under my hunting coat and rub a patch of goose bumps here and there, but somehow I didn't mind. It was the sort of morning that keeps a whitetail on the move.

Two rifle shots somewhere in the distance quickened my anticipation, and minutes later a report rang out from the rise about half a mile in front of me. I knew it had to be Ramon, who had gone back to the same tree he'd occupied Friday.

At the report, a flock of mallards, feeding in the shallow rim of the lake, took wing, and the busy squirrels froze into gray knots. A doe appeared out of the brush ahead, stopped, and looked back. Then she walked on toward the upper end of the lake. I put up my rifle, half expecting a buck to follow her, but the next deer was also a doe. For fully a dozen minutes after the whitetails had moved beyond my vision, I sat tense and expectant and then felt a growing sense of disappointment. I could only guess that the single shot accounted for a buck which had been following the two does.

A patch of gold appeared in the forest top, and I knew that the sun had cleared the horizon. For minutes after that, I struggled with the indecision of whether to find Ramon and help him with his buck

With mallards cackling out on the lake, squirrels purring in the swamp and light filtering into the tree crowns, the author made a decision.

or remain on my stand and hope the shot hadn't spooked the deer out of this corner of the refuge.

I felt the first sunlight on my face and had about decided to look for Ramon when the brush crashed off to my left, and a small buck dodged into sight. He had a rather odd gait, which gave the impression he'd been wounded. I watched him across 20 or 30 yards of swamp and then was not certain that my first appraisal had been correct. He passed not more than 40 yards away, but instead of going around a corner of the long slough, he waded directly into it, another indication that he might have been hurt.

I don't know what I'd have done if a granddaddy buck had broken out of the brush behind the forkhorn. Normally I will take a wounded animal over a healthy one, regardless of size. Nor do I know whether I would have passed up the small buck if he had appeared completely healthy. Those things race through a fellow's mind in much less time than it takes to tell them. This particular chain of thought ended with the decision to kill the loping whitetail.

147

How I missed that first shot, I don't know; the .308 had been sighted in so accurately that it would drive a nail at forty paces. My next shot broke his back.

I waded in over my boot tops to skid the buck to semidry swamp where I could dress him out. He appeared not to have a bullet mark on him, other than the one I had made. My decision then was whether I should try to locate Ramon and help him with the buck I was sure he had killed or wait for help in getting my own deer out of the woods. Apparently the best solution was to carry the buck half a mile through the swamp to the ancient road where John, Joel, and the two Henrys kept watch, and make further plans from that point.

After the small buck had drained properly, I worked him onto my shoulders for the trip to the old road. That, of course, is something I never would have done in ordinary deer woods, but I knew that only our hunting crew occupied this corner of the swamp, and I knew my companions well enough to be sure they wouldn't pot a deer on the shoulders of a hunter.

I waited an hour at the foot log over the creek which parallels the forgotten road before Ramon arrived with his account of the morning. A small buck had gone under his tree, and just as he decided to kill it, a deer with a massive rack passed through the brush just at the limit of his vision. At 150 yards, he had only one quick look over the open sights of his .30/30. He made the shot but could not find signs to indicate that he'd scored. He climbed into a tree much farther up on the ridge but had not seen another legal deer. The others in our party had drawn blanks.

"We've got Christmas week to finish out our job," Doody pointed out.

"By then," Henry put in, "those big bucks will be running all over one another on this end of the refuge."

From the sign I saw, I was certain they would be, but since I'd already made my legal kill, I could only look forward to another season in this picturesque backwoods swamp.

Spotting Them with Long Lenses

Byron W. Dalrymple

It doesn't make sense to me just to sit here with binoculars,"
John Ebeling said. "We can see everything for half a mile, and there's
not a deer in sight."

"You're used to hunting whitetails in the dense country in the
North," I told him. "This west-Texas mule-deer habitat looks mighty
bald to you, but you may be overlooking a dozen good deer. Mule
deer are different."

John lives in Iowa. He's in the publicity business. He had come
down to hunt mule deer with me, bringing his big all-comforts
motorhome, which served as our camp. It was parked far back in a
rough scenic canyon on the huge Catto-Gage Ranch in the Big Bend
country. We had driven out from the motorhome along a ranch trail,

This chapter originally appeared in the November 1970 issue of *Outdoor Life* under
the title "For Mule Deer Look Longer."

pausing here and there to make short hikes over the near ridges so that we could thoroughly glass the back-in slopes and rims.

As I spoke I remembered an *Outdoor Life* story in which the author claimed that some muleys—at least the older bucks—were getting as shy as whitetails. To some extent I had begun to agree. It is certainly true that the mule deer is a more-gentle animal by nature than the whitetail. But it is also true that hunting pressures and the push of civilization have been forcing mule deer to wise up.

Now as I carefully studied the open slope ahead of us I noticed something that didn't quite match the surrounding rocks and vegetation. Slowly it metamorphosed into a fair buck. Then I glassed another. They had bedded down in a spot where they could see for a long distance, where an unseen approach would be difficult, and where the terrain, though treeless, served as good camouflage.

Finally I got John oriented. One buck was now standing. John got excited. Before he could shoot, the two bucks bolted. John picked the best one, which ran along the ridge crown. He fired and missed. By the time he got into position again, the target was gone.

That was the end of the episode. But now John was enthusiastic, eager for more, and willing to "look long" to find it.

I've hunted mule deer in many types of cover—high up in the dense forests of the Rockies, in Wyoming sagebrush, in Arizona desert studded with saguaro cactus. But I think my favorite area is the Big Bend country of west Texas, wide-open terrain where I can see what's going on. And what has been going on there for some years is that good bucks, which were easy pickings when I first moved to Texas, are getting harder to come by.

Yet several friends and I have learned a rather simple way to beat that problem. Our method is far less tiring than the way we used to hunt. We sit a great deal—not waiting for deer to come to us but rather with eyes glued to binoculars or spotting scopes.

Thousands of mule-deer hunters use binoculars. Many, however, don't use them as successfully as they might, because they are not very selective in their looking. You have to learn where to look, and the open terrain I like teaches you a great deal about that angle. You also must spend much more time glassing than the average mule-deer hunter does. And you have to keep from being distracted by the smaller bucks. They're the ones, we've learned, that show themselves, while a wise old buster may be hidden only a few hundred yards away.

As the story I referred to before pointed out, the total deer kill in most mule-deer states has remained fairly constant while the number of hunters has steadily increased. Further, however, my observations over a dozen years on the west-Texas mule-deer range seem to indicate that though hunter success is extremely high—one hundred percent on some of the better ranges such as the one I was hunting and the neighboring Gage Holland Ranch—the size of the antlers the average hunter brings in keeps getting smaller and smaller.

I've watched scores of these hunters. They hunt along the main ranch trails where the going is easy. They glass the slopes only superficially and, usually, rather indiscriminately. You don't locate the bigger bucks that way. Finally these hunters get itchy and shoot just any buck.

The fact is, along the well-traveled trails the number of larger bucks has decreased in proportion as the number of hunters and the amount of disturbance have increased. And even over the ridges and in the vast unprobed spaces that can be reached only by climbing, the good bucks have learned a lot about how to stay hidden. Yet they cannot elude the patient hunter who searches diligently, carefully examining small but select patches of real estate and spending more time at this glassing than at "hunting."

At our next pause, Ebeling and I took a short hike onto ridges with more cover and scanned the area for bigger bucks. While moving along an old unused ranch trail, we saw the two other hunters in our group waving from a ridge. They came down to us.

"Did we ever find an old mossy one over in Chalk Valley!" said Jim Hayne, part owner of the huge ranch we were on. "Jumped him by a waterhole."

John Casey was just as enthused.

"He wasn't waiting around to get shot, though," John said. "Fact is, we didn't get a shot. But some of us ought to try again before this hunt's over."

Casey operates a restaurant in San Antonio. Hayne lives there too and is involved in an insurance business. He flies out to the ranch often, however, and he had urged all of us this season to get back away from ranch roads into places where he was pretty certain the larger bucks hung out.

We had discussed transportation the previous season. Many ranches nowadays use few or no horses. Cowboys ride pickups or four-wheel drives.

"I've been on many horseback hunts," I'd told them, "and though a horse can get you into good mule-deer country, horses also definitely spook deer."

We had decided to use a four-wheel-drive wagon to move us over long distances on main trails, from which we'd hike back in on numerous short swings.

The author here glasses the rimrock, spotting nearby deer that escaped his unaided eyes and those of his hunting partners.

We all went back to the vehicle now and piled in. Hayne knew some rough trails he thought I could handle, and we had all agreed to try to find a good deer for John Ebeling.

"You're the glassing fiend," Hayne said to me. "When you see a place you like, just stop."

We moved along slowly. As we rounded the base of a mountain, I saw a distant spot that reminded me of a Wyoming mule-deer hunt of some years ago when I had first begun to learn the value of carefully studying the slopes. Above us the heights past the first ridge were strewn with rocks and scattered with clumps of low cedar. Mule deer, I had learned, often lie in the spot of shade offered by such clumps and are impossible to see there.

But a Wyoming hunter had taught me that if you glass meticulously you can sometimes pick up the shine of a nose. In the dry air the deer lick their noses often. That was one of the best tips I've ever had.

We all walked over the first ridge and studied the distant slope. We were about to give it up when Ebeling said, "I'm not sure what I'm looking for, but something shines up there."

He got me zeroed in on the spot. Sure enough, he'd found a deer. A buck. I could make out antlers but could not tell how good they were. The buck was a very long shot away.

"Let me try my spotting scope," Casey said. He set it up and studied the deer. West-Texas mule deer do not have the massive horns of mountain mulies, so you have to judge them differently.

"It's a very respectable buck," Casey said at last.

A deep rocky draw with sheer sides appeared to bar a stalk. Ebeling cranked his Bausch & Lomb 2½X-to-8X scope up to the top power and had a look.

"I've got a good shoulder shot," he said. "But it sure is a long one."

He was shooting a 6 mm. Remington, and I had advised him to use the load I do, the 80-grain softpoint. Many hunters feel that this load is too light. I disagree. On long shots especially it is deadly when well placed. And it is very accurate and flat-shooting over long distances.

John seemed to fiddle around interminably trying to get a proper rest.

"Quit shaking," Casey needled.

We kept our glasses trained. Finally the little 6 mm. barked.

"Great!" Hayne yelled.

There was no movement up where the deer lay. Ebeling had anchored it. Now he was up and running around, doing an excited dance, and yelling. How, he wondered, were we going to get to the deer and bring it down?

"Ebeling, you stay right here and coach us," Casey said. "I think we can climb around the head of the draw and come in over the top. You can motion us to the right bush."

I didn't say so, but I felt vindicated in regard to my glassing hangup. We never would have seen that deer without the extremely careful study. Though this is slow hunting and much time passes without any drama, it pays off and furnishes unique thrills.

I decided to go up with Casey and Hayne. As we climbed I thought of the many times I had sat on a mountainside looking for some other type of game. Sheep hunters spend most of a hunt glassing. So do goat hunters. Once, a guide and I sat for two hours on a mountain in Wyoming's Gros Ventre River country, looking far off to another ridge, seeking a bear. Finally we found two, both of them asleep among rocks. They had been there all the time.

Presently we could see Ebeling far below, waving his arms. But we had already spotted the deer, a very good buck. The long drag was mostly downhill, and by changing off we had a fairly easy time of it. Finally we loaded the buck atop the wagon while Ebeling gave us numerous cautions about not marring his trophy.

We rested a bit and talked deer hunting. One of my favorite spots to glass, I told the others, is a high point—any high point, whether timbered or jutting out from a hill of bald rocks or sloping down from a high rim. The big bucks select such places, usually in shade or at least with backup cover. They can see far off in front. And the lie-up spot gives them an escape route. If danger approaches, the buck simply ducks out along the other side of his point.

"Bucks can easily be trapped in such places," I said. "A hunter takes a stand on one side, at the base of the triangle, and a companion moves in noisily along the other side. The deer runs right to the hunter."

Hayne chuckled.

"It sounds real good," he said, "but maybe a little too pat."

We eased along, looking for likely terrain. Presently we spotted a high rocky rim atop the third ridge in from the trail. It fell off on a steep slant to a point that overlooked an enormous sweep of country. We paused and looked it over. A buck lying on the point could see almost full-circle—the valleys on both sides of his ridge and the valley at the end, where the point slanted.

We glassed the point casually, then hiked over the first two ridges, sat down, and studied it in earnest. Hayne swept his binoculars meticulously over the scene. Suddenly his glasses paused.

"I've found a deer," he said, "but it's nothing I'd shoot."

Casey was glassing too.

"I don't see your little one," he said after a moment, "but there's a pretty fair antler sticking up behind a rock a little way off the end of the point."

Hayne studied the scene. Finally he put down his glasses.

"Let's go," he said. He picked up his .270 custom Mauser, adjusted the 3X-to-9X Redfield scope, and slung the gun over his shoulder.

"No," I said. "Let's move clear back out of sight as if we were leaving, then circle back along the rim the deer is on."

We planned our maneuver. Casey was to climb up and cross over and move toward the point to push the deer around to the opposite side. I elected to go with him and take photographs. Hayne would simply move up the ridge and take a stand behind a rock near the rim.

As Casey and I crossed the rocky spine and moved toward the point from that side, a small forkhorn gave us a real start. It bounded up almost in our faces and then went clattering away down the ridge in plain sight. I swung my telephoto and caught the buck with all four feet off the ground.

"You can bet the big one won't act like that," Casey said.

He had barely finished the sentence when from back toward Hayne's position the massive *caroomph* of a rifle shot echoed against the rocks. The shot was followed by a distant yell, but we couldn't make out the words.

We scrambled up atop the rim and looked. Hayne was moving down the slope, and it was obvious that his buck was down. I raced ahead, stumbling over rocks, and yelled at Jim to hold up. I wanted to get a picture of him coming in on his deer.

"It worked like a charm," he said enthusiastically. "When the buck heard you fellows it sneaked off the point and headed back on this side of the rim. If I had waited it would almost have trotted over me."

"Just for that performance, Jim," Casey said, "I'll gut it for you."

Hayne didn't argue. He sat on a nearby rock and watched.

Of course, things don't always work out so neatly. And I certainly don't mean to imply that mule deer can't be hunted by other methods. I've killed many bucks between dawn and eight or nine o'clock in the morning, and between four p.m. and dark, as they moved out to feed. Seldom, however, do mule deer—especially the good bucks—move around much in daylight except during those hours.

Also, though prowling slowly in cover is a good way to hunt, the plain fact is that trophy bucks are very sensitive to their surroundings. Mule deer, especially those in mountainous or hilly terrain, sneak away if they catch wisps of man scent carried by whimsical air currents, hear a minor sound, or see some slight movement that is too close. But a wise old buck won't move a muscle if danger is sighted, scented, or heard at glassing distance. He does not want to give his position away.

Deer, like all animals, have what might be called an approach quotient. In other words, they will allow danger to come just so near and no nearer. This distance differs among species and varies with the type of terrain. In dense cover a deer, knowing it is unseen, may allow a closer approach.

In my experience, however, most large bucks do not habitually lie up in snug quarters, though they certainly favor the roughest and least-accessible areas. Hiding, to them, means being in a spot where they are protected by cover behind them but still can see over a wide area. A deer situated so that it can see can also be seen—perhaps not easily or plainly, but that's where the long and careful search with glasses comes in.

Bucks in heavily timbered mountain areas often lie-up just inside the timber on the point of a knoll that overlooks a valley or a mountain park. If there's a breeze, the deer will usually be facing it.

A deer lying in such a place seldom can be closely approached. A hunter prowling in the timber will invariably spook the deer before he sees it. But the deer can be seen from the open side — with a glass.

I'm sure most hunters know that the naked eye can see only to the "wall" of the woods, even at rather close range. The light-gathering power of good binoculars lets you peer almost magically a surprising distance into the deep forest shadows.

Weather has a definite effect upon where deer lie. On warm days, and even on days that may seem chilly to you, fat deer seek shade. They lie in pockets on the shady side of the rocks. On colder days that are not really bitter, they commonly take up lookouts in more open, even well-sunlit spots; but the animals themselves are almost always in shade or dappled shadows.

A very severe wind, especially a frigid one, is not relished by deer. They do not like to move in it or to lie facing it. Instead, they gather on the protected sides of ridges, but on some of these days not even careful glassing can locate them. They get deep into the draws and the timber and wait it out.

Of course, heavy snows will move mountain deer to lower levels, but that's another story.

The next morning I set out with Casey to help him find a deer. After some careful glassing I spotted one peering out of some thick gray brush on a hillside.

"I can't see it plainly," I said, "but I think it's a good one."

The only way we could get a shot was to move in on the deer and hope for a jump shot. Gun ready, Casey sneaked ahead. I followed with my camera.

We jumped the deer all right — at close quarters. But it was a dumb little youngster that just stood and stared, then moved off through the cover. Casey gave me and my theory quite a ribbing.

Later in the day Ebeling found Casey a nice buck. John was all hepped up now on "looking for shiny noses," and sure enough, that's how he found this one. But the buck was too skittish: before Casey could get set to shoot, it bounded up and disappeared over the ridgetop.

Casey's big thrill, however, was yet to come. And to me it was the high point of the hunt.

Casey had become thoroughly intrigued with using his spotting scope, and he carried it as he and I left the others and hiked into fairly open ridges and hills. We found some interesting rims and draws back in there. John lay down and carefully looked over some of them. After long study he turned to me.

"Believe it or not," he said, "I've found a whole herd of deer

The mistake, says Dalrymple, is glassing the slopes only superficially and indiscriminately. This buck knows he's been spotted.

up toward the top of the ridge. I can't tell, though, whether there's anything that we would want to shoot."

"Well," I replied, "let's move up and see if we can't make them show themselves."

We cached the spotting scope. John was carrying a .25/06 that he had made up from a Model 70 Winchester .257. On it he had mounted a Supra 4X-to-10X scope.

We approached the top of the ridge. Suddenly deer were bounding from beds all around us. John's gun was up and swinging. There was the confusion of animals racing over the ridge. Some whirled, startled and puzzled, to look back. Casey began to chuckle. Facing him and skylined on the crest were three deer—a little spike buck and two does.

"Gad!" he said. "That was close. I expected a big one, and I damned near shot."

I was some yards behind John, about where the deer had been bedded among yuccas. As John spoke I heard a rattle of stones and a crackle of low brush a few feet from me. I jumped as if I'd been shot at. A big buck that had stayed down as John passed had burst out almost into my face. It hurtled off to my right in a wild race to put distance between us.

Instinctively I raised my camera almost as if it were a gun—which I was wishing now that it was.

"Shoot that buck!" I yelled.

But from where Casey stood, wheeling and flinging up his rifle, he could not see the deer. It had gained sanctuary in a small draw and was racing toward the ridgetop and the safety of the other side.

"Run!" I yelled at Casey. "That way."

He sprinted toward the draw, got to the edge, and looked up-ward. At the top the draw petered out. The buck hove into view, really moving. I watched Casey bring up the rifle, steady it, and fire, all in one smooth motion. The deer, caught behind the left shoulder, did a complete cartwheel and fell. In three more bounds it would have cleared the ridgetop. The whole sequence was as dramatic as any I've ever seen.

After that incident, collecting my buck was almost an anticlimax. Casey and I drove back into the hills and then took off for the waterhole where he and Hayne had seen the big buck the previous day. I carried a Model 70 Winchester .243 with a 3X-to-9X Redfield scope, plus my binoculars.

I could hardly expect to see the big fellow in the same spot again, but nearby was a slope with a rimrock that looked awfully good to me.

I hunched beside a tall cholla cactus and kept trying to make out a deer somewhere up there. Finally Casey, behind me, said, "This is getting a little ridiculous. It works too perfectly. I think I've found that big deer."

Things happened fast then. I saw a deer get up and start to trot along under the rim. I dropped my glass and grabbed my rifle. The deer paused broadside. I rested my left elbow on my knee, steadied, and started to squeeze.

"No, no! Not that one!" Casey said almost frantically.

But it was too late. The shot was off, the report reverberating from rimrock. The deer dropped. I stood up, confused, and looked where Casey was looking. A buck that appeared twice as good as the one I'd shot was bounding away.

My buck turned out to be respectable, but I had the gnawing exasperation of knowing that a bigger one had been right there for the taking.

We dressed out the buck. Dusk caught us before we got it out to the trail. When I'd caught my breath, I couldn't resist shooting a picture of huge Santiago Peak, landmark of the Big Bend country, glowing far to the south as if molten.

As I was thinking about how much this rugged mule-deer range had taught me, Casey interrupted my reverie.

"That *little* buck of yours!" he said with mock contempt. "This morning you were haranguing me: 'Look longer and you'll find more.' Maybe you ought to heed that advice too."

We laughed. It was a telling point indeed.

Maine's Biggest Buck

Horace R. Hinkley

I saw the buck alive only the one time, and he was dead a minute after I caught sight of him. The last thing I suspected right then was that I'd never hear the end of him as long as I lived. But even in that first brief glimpse, with him coming through the brush like a runaway express train, I found it hard to believe my eyes. I hadn't dreamed that such a whitetail could be found anywhere in the Maine woods, and I had hunted there for more than forty years.

It was a wet morning in early November of 1955. My wife Olive and I were hunting northwest of the town of Bingham, on the Kennebec River below Moosehead Lake and about sixty miles up-state from Augusta, where we lived at the time.

I was fifty-nine then, working as a lumber grader at a planing

This chapter originally appeared in the August 1969 issue of *Outdoor Life* under the title "Mystery of the Hinkley Deer."

mill in Augusta. Now, at seventy-three, I am retired, and Olive and I live at Embden, on the Kennebec south of Bingham.

I've lived in Maine all my life, and I started to hunt deer when I was sixteen. At the time of this hunt I could look back over thirty-six falls without recalling one when either my wife or I failed to get a deer. And in many of those years both of us had scored.

My job didn't include vacations with pay, and we lumber workers didn't get paid for any time lost to stormy weather. So I didn't feel that I could afford to take a week off for deer hunting. But on holidays and whenever it rained or snowed, I headed for the woods.

I came home from work on the first Friday night of November that year, after two days of storm (I had put in my time piling lumber), and decided from the looks of the weather that Saturday was going to be a day of layoff. Olive and I would go hunting.

My son Philip, thirty-three then, and his wife Madeline drove into the yard after supper. They had come from their home in South Portland. Philip didn't have to work the next day either, and they had brought their guns and hunting togs along. We set the alarm for three a.m. and turned in.

Saturday morning was wet and dark, with misty rain still falling—exactly the conditions I like for deer hunting. At such times a man can move through the thickest cover with almost no noise.

We ate a good solid breakfast—bacon, eggs, toast, doughnuts, and coffee—headed north, and reached Bingham just at break of day. Fine rain was still coming down, and everything looked good.

We'd start in the country west of Fletcher Mountain. Very few of the mountains there are higher than 4,000 feet; most of them are under 3,000. I suppose Western hunters would call them hills. But they're mountains to us. Mostly they go up in terraces and the slopes are laced with small brooks. You climb, come out on a flat bench, then climb again.

Now and then you can catch a deer feeding on the flats in the early morning or shortly before dusk, but when they bed down for the day it's usually in a thicket or on some high spot, often near the very top.

We split up, Philip and Madeline going one way, Olive and I another. My wife and I found an old tote road bordered with cuttings, and we hunted along it for an hour. There was plenty of deer sign, but none of it was fresh, and we turned onto a truck road that would take us down to the valley and across to the opposite range.

We had walked only a short distance when a jeep came along. The driver was a foreman for one of the local lumbering operations, and he knew the area. He told us that he had been cruising the valley for hardwood and had found a place only a day or two before

Maine's Department of Game recognizes this 355-pound dressed buck as the state record. Hinkley, shown here, feels Boone and Crockett records should include a weight class also. "After all, you can't eat the antlers," he says.

that had lots of fresh deer sign. He offered to take us as close to that spot as he could get with the jeep.

He followed a rutted tote road until it ended beside a brook, pulled up, and wished us luck. Just before he drove off he added an interesting bit of information.

"There's a buster of a buck in here," he said. "Our woodcutters see him every now and then, and they claim he looks like an elk. But he's so smart and careful they've named him Old Eagle Eye."

"That's the deer I'm looking for," I joshed. "We'll have him out of the woods before dark."

"I hope you do," the foreman said, grinning. He turned the jeep

161

and started back down the tote road, and Olive and I walked into the woods. I didn't give his story about the big buck a great deal of thought. I'd heard quite a few rumors of that sort in my years of hunting, and most of them weren't worth putting much stock in.

The mountains rose steeply on each side at this point, and the brook that ran down the valley was swift and noisy, swollen by rain. Olive and I followed it, moving quietly. Most of the timber was fairly open, but here and there we came to thickets of what Maine people call winter beech. It's a scrubby and bushy type that keeps its leaves all winter. They turn brown but hang on until the swelling buds push them off in the spring.

Where it's thick, winter beech is more difficult to hunt in than a fir thicket, for the dead leaves make the going very noisy. Olive and I came to a belt of it that reached nearly all the way across the valley. We stopped at the edge and took stands a few yards apart. It was now around nine a.m., a very good time to catch a buck crossing from one mountain to another.

I had been standing for about twenty minutes when a twig snapped and through the brown leaves I spotted part of an antler. I couldn't see the deer, and the antler disappeared before I could line my sights on the place where he should be. I told myself that the buck had seen me and was sneaking off.

It's always a letdown when a deer outsmarts you that way. But the wind was in my favor, and I knew he hadn't scented me, so I stayed where I was, moving not a muscle and hoping for the best. After a few minutes I heard another twig break. He hadn't moved out, after all. Then brush cracked, and I heard other deer moving on both sides of him.

There was no chance for a stalk. I knew that if I tried one I'd jump the whole bunch before I could get close enough to see them. All I could do was wait.

I had hunted deer too long to get buck fever now, but a situation of that kind, where a man can hear game he can't see in a place he can't work up on it, is pretty strong medicine. I admit my heart was pounding.

Next I saw an antler shine again and made out a brownish-gray back. The deer went out of sight, and then I caught another glimpse but not enough to judge his size. That happened two or three times, and I realized that he was moving away.

If I wanted that buck, it was now or never. The next time I caught a patch of brown, I tried a quick shot. It was a clean miss.

The deer crashed off, and everything got quiet. For five minutes I didn't hear another sound. Then the silence was broken by the loud thump of Olive's .38/40.

After a few seconds, she called, "Come over here, Ransom. I've shot a big buck."

For some reason, maybe because I knew that more deer were in that thicket, I didn't answer or start toward her. In a minute I heard a loud crashing and saw this enormous buck coming straight for me.

If a deer can sneak along at a dead run, that's what this one was doing. Though he was going flat out, he wasn't bounding but instead was keeping his body close to the ground and his neck outstretched. I had never seen a buck do that before, not while running.

I got one good look at him where the brush thinned out, enough to realize that I had never laid eyes on such a deer. Then, fifty yards off, he swung a little to my left. I was going to have a perfect shot.

My rifle was one that very few of today's hunters have ever heard of, a Winchester Model 1886 in .33 caliber. In Maine we used to call it a moose gun because of its knockdown power. It hasn't been made for many years. I bought mine used when I was in my early twenties. The thing I liked best about it was the heavy bullet, 200 grains, just right for punching through brush and then flooring a deer for keeps.

I used to guide and do other work at hunting camps, and I've had to trail many wounded deer. Almost every time, failure to kill quickly was caused partly by a light bullet. Any time I hit a buck with the 200-grain load from that .33, if he traveled more than 400 yards I could bet he had suffered only a slight wound. And even that happened only a few times.

(I have always believed that once a hunter gets accustomed to the feel of a rifle, he'd better hang onto it. But the barrel of my old Winchester played out a few years ago, and I couldn't get a replacement, so I went to a Remington Model 742 in .30/06 caliber.)

The rear sight on the old .33 was a Lyman peep, and I had taken out the small center ring that morning for better sighting there in the rain and poor light. I brought the rifle up and waited for the buck to break out of the thick brush. He was about thirty-five yards away when I put the front bead where his neck and shoulder came together and let him have it.

He piled up in a heap. I levered in another cartridge and kept him covered. He struggled to his feet and made one lunge, making a strange noise that was half hoarse bleat, half roar. But before I could get off a second shot he went down again and it was all over. He didn't even kick.

I walked up to him and saw that he was just as the woodcutters had said. Except for his rack he looked more like an elk than a deer. Only then did I answer Olive's hail.

"You come over here," I called. "If you think you've got a big buck, I'll show you his grandfather."

I dressed the two deer, but it was useless to think about getting them out of the woods without help. We followed the brook back to the tote road and walked three more miles to our car. We got there just before noon, and Olive waited while I went to look for Philip. I couldn't find him, but it wasn't far to where my brother Ralph lived in the town of Concord, so we drove to Ralph's place.

We ate dinner and started after the two deer with his jeep, leaving word for Philip to follow us. Ralph drove the jeep as far as where the foreman had dropped us off earlier, and he and I went the rest of the way on foot.

When we got to the kills we took time to look things over, and while we were following deer tracks through the wet leaves Ralph jumped a nice six-pointer and downed it with one shot. Now we had three deer to drag out.

We dressed his and took it down along the brook to the jeep. We found a fairly good trail, mostly downgrade, and the deer was freshly killed and not too heavy, so that wasn't a bad chore. Next we went back after Olive's, and that was more like work.

Then we tackled the big one. We cut a short maple pole and tied it to his antlers, but it was all the two of us could do to lift his head and neck off the ground, let alone drag him. We strained and heaved, panted and puffed, moved him a few yards, and gave up.

I went back to the jeep in the hope that Philip had arrived. Sure enough, he was just coming up the tote road.

He had astonishing news. His wife had killed a nice spikehorn, and he had taken a ten-pointer that would dress out at over 200 pounds. He'd shot it almost within sight of their car while they were dragging Madeline's out. Both of those deer were now out of the woods.

Talk about luck! In less than a day five members of the Hinkley family had filled. That would go down as the best year of deer hunting we'd ever had.

Philip and I went back to Ralph, and the three of us tackled the giant buck. It was about as hard work as I have ever done. We'd skid him a few yards, rest, grunt and tug, and make a few yards more. It was pitch-dark when we finally reached the jeep.

We wrestled the buck aboard, loaded Olive's and Ralph's deer on top, and headed for Ralph's place. There we put our bucks on our two cars and started for Augusta. On Sunday we skinned out Philip's and Madeline's and cut them up for the freezer, but we didn't have time to work on mine.

Since 1949 our state has had a Biggest Bucks in Maine Club. I'd shot a few deer that probably would have qualified me for membership, but I had never bothered to enter them. And it didn't occur to me at first to enter this one.

I went to work at the mill Monday morning, and somebody asked me, the first thing, if I got my deer. When I said yes, the next question was, "How big?"

"A three-hundred pounder," I replied.

I don't think anyone believed me, but nothing more was said. That night, however, just about the whole crew came to look at him, and everybody agreed that he was the biggest buck they had ever seen. All doubt about the 300 pounds seemed to vanish.

A deer that big is bound to attract a lot of attention. I had so much company that night I didn't get him skinned, and the next day he was the main topic of conversation at the mill. I could see that one man still doubted the weight.

"We've got to find some scales and weigh that buck," I overheard him say during the afternoon, "or Hinkley will claim the rest of his life that he shot a three-hundred-pound deer."

He found scales that night, but their limit was 260 pounds, and they didn't even come close. After the man left I told my wife, "There's been so much said that I'd like to know myself just how much this deer weighs."

A neighbor told me that Forrest Brown, a state sealer of weights and measures at Vassalboro, north of my place, had scales that would handle the buck. On Tuesday evening, three days after I'd killed the deer, I went to see Brown. That same night, he brought portable beam scales, state certified, to my place and we put the buck on them. The scales read 355 pounds.

While we were weighing the buck my milkman, Fred Brewer, and one of his drivers, Alvin Greeley, came along. They checked the weight and offered to stand as witnesses. As things turned out, that was lucky for me.

Brown suggested that I register my trophy with the Biggest Bucks Club, so I called Roy Gray, a local game-warden supervisor, and he contacted Bob Elliot, then with the Maine Department of Game and now the state's director of Vacation Travel Promotion.

Elliot passed the word to the Kennebec Journal. The next day's paper ran a front-page picture and story, the buck's fame grew, and a stream of visitors began to arrive for a look at him.

The first thing Elliot undertook was to calculate the buck's live weight. The established procedure is to add thirty percent to the dressed weight, a formula based on long study, including records of 112 deer from New York and 131 from Michigan.

But because in dressing my deer I had removed the heart, and also because the buck had lost a lot of blood in the chest cavity, Bob added twenty pounds to the dressed weight before he applied the standard formula.

He came up with a live-weight figure of 488 pounds! That may have been high, but certainly the buck had weighed well above 450. And in any case, based on his dressed weight of 355 alone, he went into the records as the biggest deer ever killed in Maine.

State game men even raised the question at first of the possibility that he was a deer-elk cross, but that theory was quickly ruled out.

Had I shot the heaviest whitetail ever recorded in North America as well as the heaviest in my home state? On the basis of all available evidence it seemed likely that I had, and Maine officials thought so.

"We believe this is the heaviest whitetail ever shot anywhere," Bob Elliot wrote me.

Reliable weight records of big deer are not too common, partly because all scoring is now done according to antlers. In that category my buck didn't stack up as extraordinary. His maximum spread was 21 inches, the outside curve on both antlers measured 24½ inches, and there were sixteen points, of which twelve were over an inch long. The rack was never scored by the Boone and Crockett Club method, but I had killed deer with better racks.

To this day, however, I have not learned of another whitetail that could match mine in weight. Ernest Thompson Seton, a leading wildlife authority of past years, cited as the biggest whitetails that he knew of a Vermont buck that weighed 370 pounds before it was dressed; one from New York that dressed at 299; a third, also from New York, with an estimated live weight of 400; and one from Michigan that dressed 354. That still leaves mine the front-runner.

I have heard a rumor that a buck killed in the Rainy River country of Ontario in 1938 dressed out at 358, three pounds more than mine, but there seems to be no official record of it.

My story should end there, but it doesn't. An astonishing development was yet to come.

In the next couple of evenings at least two hundred people came to see the deer, among them a Maine game biologist, Jack Maasen. He made careful measurements that showed the kind of whopper I had killed. The neck girth was 28 inches, body girth behind the forelegs 47, greatest girth over the shoulders 56, and length from hind toe to tip of horns 9½ feet.

I still hadn't had a chance to skin the buck, and the meat was starting to show signs of spoiling. Maasen wanted him mounted life-size for exhibition, but the Game Department had no funds for that, and neither did I. I hunt for venison as well as sport, so I decided to send the deer to a freezer plant for processing. Maasen offered to take him in, to save my losing time from my job.

The processing would cost eight cents a pound. There was a lot of fat and tainted meat that I didn't want to pay for, so I got up early that morning and trimmed away fat, kidneys, diaphragm, lungs, windpipe, and a great amount of spoiled meat. When I finished I had more than a bushel of scraps.

Then the roof fell in. On Friday, six days after the deer was shot, the freezer plant put him on scales in the presence of a group of witnesses, and he then weighed almost 100 pounds less than I had reported. I was notified that Maasen had entered him in the Biggest Bucks Club at the reduced weight, after shrinkage and trimming, and the deer now stood a long way from the top of the Maine record list. The matter would be dropped and forgotten.

I was heartsick and dazed, and I was also baffled. I knew that the deer had been weighed honestly on certified scales, and I had truthful witnesses to prove it. Was it possible for him to lose as much as 100 pounds from trimming? Was that what had happened, or had some incredible blunder been made? I resigned myself to the fact that I'd probably never be able to prove it. The whole thing seemed likely to remain a mystery so far as the public was concerned.

Then one morning I picked up a Bangor newspaper, and a headline on the front page stared up at me: "Big Buck Loses Weight Fast."

I boiled over. Not only was Maine being cheated out of a valid record, but I felt that I was being held up to ridicule. I wasn't going to stand for that. I swore I'd vindicate myself if it took a year.

It took a little longer than that.

I went first to Forrest Brown. He rechecked his scales with official weights and found that they were absolutely accurate.

"I'll take oath that the weight of your deer was correct," he told me. He did too, giving me a certified statement in his capacity as sealer of weights and measures. And Fred Brewer and Alvin Greeley, the milkmen, signed that statement as witnesses.

Next Richard Esty, a local meat cutter who had advised me how much of the deer to trim away, gave me a letter in which he said, "The parts that I advised you to remove would very easily shrink the weight 75 to 100 pounds."

Bud Leavitt, outdoor writer for the Bangor News, came out flatly on my side. Even the freezer plant came through with a letter to Bob Elliot saying, "The deer arrived here several days after being shot, with all fat, kidneys, etc., removed, and, as do all deer, it had dried out considerably."

In the meantime I was getting letters from as far away as New Jersey, Indiana, and even California, from people who had seen a picture of the deer and on the basis of the picture accepted my claim at face value. They believed that I had an all-time record.

I pressed my claim with the Game Department without letup, and Roy Gray, the supervisor of game wardens who had first brought the buck to the department's attention, sided with me, saying that in his opinion the weight at the plant with the carcass trimmed had no bearing on the original record.

In late November of 1956, a few days over a year after the controversy first erupted, it was settled completely in my favor.

"We have decided to ignore the second weighing and accept the original figure of Forrest Brown as official," Bob Elliot notified me. "We believe you acted in good faith, and although the buck was not weighed by a game warden, Mr. Brown was an official sealer of weights and measures. We accept your belief that the meat trimmed away between the two weighings was enough to account for the difference."

The mystery of the Hinkley deer—if mystery it ever was—had been officially solved. That monster whitetail would stand in the records now for keeps, at the dressed weight that I had originally claimed.

So far as I know, that leaves a Maine deer at the head of the list, the heaviest ever shot anywhere. That was what I really wanted all along.

Northwestern Whitetail Trophy

Jack O'Connor

T he Northern variety of the whitetail deer in its various forms
is the most widely distributed big-game animal in the United States.
Found from Maine to Oregon, it furnishes more sport to hunters
than any other big-game animal and is responsible for the sale of
more rifles and ammunition for the manufacturers and more telescope sights for the scope makers. And, because sportsmen buy
licenses to hunt it, the money it brings in keeps most game departments functioning.

But until recently the Northern whitetail was to me as strange a
trophy as the greater kudu, the desert bighorn, and the ibex are to
most hunters. I have hunted all of these fine animals and others
just as exotic, but the Northern whitetail had always eluded me.

This chapter originally appeared in the February 1972 issue of *Outdoor Life* under
the title "Salmon River Whitetail."

Of all the varieties of Northern whitetails the one least known is the one found in the Northwest. The more plentiful mule deer and the elk sell the out-of-state licenses and get the publicity. In fact, many hunters do not even realize that some of the largest whitetail deer in North America and some of the best trophies come from the Northwestern states of Idaho, Washington, Montana, and Oregon, and from the Canadian province of British Columbia. These Northwestern whitetails are probably just about as heavy as the famous whitetails of Maine, and their heads compare favorably with those of whitetails shot anywhere. The Number 4 listing in the 1964 edition of *Records of North American Big Game* is a white-tail shot in Flathead County, Montana, in 1963, and I have seen handsome and very large antlers nailed to barns and garages and poorly mounted on walls of backwoods bars and country stores. Mostly these big whitetails are taken not by trophy hunters but by backwoodsmen and farmers who are after meat. These white-tails of the Northwest are classified Odocoileus virginianus ochrourus.

I grew up in the country of the Northern whitetail's little South-western cousin in the Sonora, Arizona, or Coues whitetail. I have hunted these fine deer in Arizona, in Sonora, and in the Big Bend of Texas, and I have taken many handsome bucks of this diminu-tive species. Such small skill as I have at hitting running game I owe to the Arizona jackrabbit and the Arizona whitetail. I have also shot the small but quite different Texas whitetail found around San Antonio. But a good Northern whitetail was one of the few major North American trophies I did not have.

I had never laid eyes on a Northern whitetail until I moved from Arizona to Idaho more than twenty years ago, and then it took me about three years to see one. I'll never forget the first one I saw. I was hunting pheasants with a wonderful Brittany spaniel named Mike. He had been cruising through a field of rich golden wheat stubble when he went on point at the edge of a grassy swale. I thought he had pinned a cock pheasant, but when I got up to him he looked at me out of the corner of his eyes and wore the sneaky expression he assumed when he was doing something he knew he should not do.

I picked up a stone to flush whatever it was, and threw it at the spot in the grass where Mike's nose was pointed. Out burst a little whitetail doe. Most dogs are convinced that they have been born to be deer and rabbit hounds, but Mike almost fell backward in surprise.

Another time Mike hauled up on the edge of a brushy draw on solid point. I walked in, kicked the brush. A pair of cackling roosters came barreling out. I shot, dropped one of them, was about to take the other when a big whitetail buck sailed out of the brush and headed across the stubble toward a patch of woods. For the rest of the bird season, which mostly at the time ran concurrently with the deer season, I carried a couple of rifled slugs in my pants pocket so that if I jumped another whitetail I could jerk out a shot shell and slam a shell loaded with a slug into the chamber. But the news must have got around; I never saw a buck.

Memories of long experience flash through O'Connor's mind as the camera records the end of an elusive mission—his 10-point Northern whitetail.

A farmer I knew told me he just about had a big whitetail buck tied up for me. He said that the old boy lived in a canyon that bounded one of his wheatfields. That buck fed on wheat all summer and in the fall feasted on the sweet, stunted little apples that fell in an abandoned orchard in one corner of his place.

So I spent about ten days hunting him off and on during the season. His tracks were everywhere—in the orchard, in the wheat stubble, along the deer and cattle trails among the brush and trees, and on the bank of the little trout stream that ran through the bottom of the canyon.

Keeping the wind in my favor, I still-hunted cautiously and quietly along the trails, taking a few steps, stopping, listening, watching. Once I heard something moving quietly off through thick brush, and I found his bed below a ledge in a warm spot where the sun had melted the frost off the grass. Another time I heard a crash below me and caught a glimpse of his white flag flying. I sat for hours with my back to a tree waiting for him to show up. He didn't.

"I can't understand why you can't see that buck," my farmer friend said. "I seen him yesterday when I was looking for a stray cow, and Bill Jones seen him from his pickup when he was coming back from getting the mail four or five days ago. Said he wasn't a danged bit wild; stood there looking at him. He could have hit him with a slingshot."

Another year, while scouting for good pheasant areas in eastern Washington, I found a pretty little valley full of trees and brush and with a clear brook wandering through it. It lay between two grassy hillsides that ran down from rolling wheatfields. The valley was full of pheasants. The hillsides supported several coveys of Huns. Quail roosted in the trees. And the valley also contained a herd of whitetails. I saw a doe, a fawn, one small buck, and also the tracks of a big buck.

I made up my mind to be in a strategic spot in the valley as soon as it was light enough to shoot on opening day. So when the day came I parked my station wagon along the road half a mile from the valley and left my Model 21 Winchester 12 gauge and my puzzled, whining Brittany spaniel locked up. Wearing a pair of binoculars around my neck and carrying a light 7 x 57, I walked through a wheatfield toward the head of the valley. I was almost at the spot I had in mind when I heard the crash of rifle fire. A startled doe streaked by me. Running along the grassy hillside and up into the wheat stubble were the dim forms of about a dozen deer flaunting white tails. I sat down and got them in the field of the binoculars. All were does and fawns. Then something caught my attention just under the skyline about a quarter of a mile away. I put the glasses on whatever it was. It was a big buck sneaking along. When he topped out I saw heavy antlers.

About twenty shots had been fired, but now the last deer was out of sight. I could hear voices coming from the valley. It was quite light now. I walked a little farther. Then I saw four men gathered around a small and very dead buck. One was gutting him. I talked to the men a few minutes. Before long they departed in triumph, each holding a leg of the buck. I went back to my car and stowed the rifle and the binoculars. Then I let my joyful dog out and set off to see if I could have any luck on birds.

In Arizona and Sonora the Coues deer are found high. In southern Arizona they are seldom lower than the altitude where the evergreen oaks the Mexicans call encinos grow—about 4,000 to 4,500 feet. The desert variety of mule deer are out in the mesquite and cactus of the flats and the low rolling hills. Out on the flat Sonoran desert west of the railroad that runs south from Nogales, Arizona, the mule deer are on the perfectly flat sandy aboreal desert where they range among the mesquites, ironwoods, and chollas. Low hills and little ranges rise from the desert floor, and on all of them are (or used to be) whitetails. Sometimes the whitetails are in easily navigable foothills of the tall, rocky, desert-sheep mountains.

But in the Northwest, at least in areas with which I am familiar, whitetails are found lower than the mule deer, on the brushy hillsides near wheatfields, and in the wooded riverbottoms back in the elk mountains. They are bold but furtive, and they'll live all summer in a farmer's woodlot.

Some of them grow to be very large. I once knew a man who ran a meat locker in Lewiston, Idaho, my home town. He told me that the heaviest buck ever weighed at his plant was a whitetail. As I now remember he said its field-dressed weight was around 335 pounds. I have heard of Northwest whitetails in Washington as well as Idaho that were about as heavy. I have never seen a deer of any sort that I thought would dress out at anything like 300 pounds, but now and then one undoubtedly turns out to be that heavy.

I started closing in on my first Northwestern whitetail in the fall of 1969 when my wife and I drove to the ranch of our friend Dave Christensen on the Salmon River downstream from Riggins, Idaho. Dave operates an elk hunting camp on Moose Creek in the Selway Wilderness Area and lives most of the year on the beautiful Salmon River ranch. When I first knew the elk-hunting camp it was Moose Creek Lodge, a luxurious bit of civilization out in the wilderness. A hunter could go out after elk all day and return at night to a drink around a fireplace, a good meal served with silver and linen, a hot shower, and a sound sleep on an inner-spring mattress. But the area was declared a wilderness. The federal government bought the lodge and burned it down. Now in the fall Dave's dudes fly in to a U.S. Forest Service landing strip a few miles away and hunt elk from a comfortable tent camp near the spot where the lodge used to be. I have shot five, six, and seven-point elk out of Moose Creek. Dave and his father, Ken, took the money they got from the sale of the lodge and their land and put it into the Salmon River ranch.

As my wife and I drove in that November day in '69 we saw a whitetail buck in a field a mile or so from the ranchhouse. Not long afterward we saw some whitetail does and fawns.

"You must have a lot of whitetails around here," I said when Dave came out to meet us.

"Plenty," he told me. "The whitetails are mostly low down along the creek and in the brushy draws that run into it. The mule deer are higher."

The season around Dave's place was closed then, so my wife and I had to forgo the whitetails. We hunted mule deer in another management area about twenty miles away. But we made a promise to take a run at the whitetails.

Along in August, 1971, Dave called me.

"You haven't forgotten our date to hunt whitetails?" he asked. "No? Well, the season opens October second. Drive down the afternoon of the first and we'll have at them."

My son Bradford, who is outdoor editor of the Seattle Times and who is a long-time pal of Dave Christensen and his wife Ann, flew from Seattle and joined us on the drive to the ranch.

One of Dave's successful elk hunters from Moose Creek had come down to the Salmon to try for a deer, and three other hunters who were on their way into Moose Creek for elk were camped down the creek a mile or so from the ranchhouse.

The strategy was simple. Eleanor, Bradford, and I, accompanied by a guide named Stan Rock, would climb about 1,000 feet above the ranch near the head of a canyon that carried a little stream that ran into Dave's creek. After giving us time to get into position, Dave would walk up the canyon on a deer-and-cattle trail that ran along the bottom. There were whitetails and mule deer in those canyons, and with luck we should get some shooting.

It was dark and chilly when we started out, and the sun was not up when we arrived near the head of the canyon. We were high on a grassy ridge. The canyon dropped sharply below us, and the bottom was a tangle of trees and brush. The far side of the canyon

The author and wife Eleanor study the rugged canyon from which the prize buck ultimately was harvested.

was steep, mostly rocks with a few low bushes and sparse grass.

Eleanor had gone on to the brink of the canyon. Bradford was twenty feet or so to her left. I was in the process of filling up the magazine of an old pet .270 I had used from northern British Columbia to Botswana and Iran. It is a pre-1964 Winchester Model 70 Featherweight stocked in plain but hard French walnut by Al Biesen of Spokane and fitted with a Leupold 4X scope on the now-obsolete Tilden mount. It has the original Winchester barrel with the original Featherweight contour. The only thing Biesen did to the metal was to put the release lever for the hinged floorplate in the forward portion of the trigger guard and checker the bolt knob.

This is a terrific rifle. I bought it from the Erb Hardware Company of Lewiston, Idaho. Year after year it holds its point of impact. Carry it in a saddle scabbard, jounce it around in a hunting car on safari, ship it a few thousand miles by air, let it get rained on for hours in a Scotch deer forest, shoot it at sea-level or at 10,000 feet, in the crackling heat of the Kalahari desert or under the glaciers in the sub-arctic Stone sheep country of British Columbia and it always lays them in the same place. It is also one of those rare light sporters that will group into a minute of angle — if I am using good bullets and do my part.

I had just finished slipping the last cartridge into the chamber and putting on the safety when Eleanor, who has eyes like an eagle, said, "Deer . . . two deer. The lower one's a buck."

Two deer were scooting up the far side of the canyon about 225 to 250 yards away. Both were waving big white tails. I could dimly make out antlers on the lower one.

The sight of those flaunting flags across the canyon made me shed twenty-five years. Once again I was back in my favorite Calelo Hills along the Mexican border of southern Arizona, where I had some small reputation among the local yeomanry of being a fair hand on running whitetails. I sat down quickly, put the intersection of the crosswires just to the left of the buck's head for lead, and squeezed the trigger. So far as results went, it was almost as spectacular as a brain shot on an elephant. The buck fell, started rolling, and tumbled clear out of sight into the brush and timber at the bottom of the canyon.

"Some shot!" said Bradford.

The buck was a big one. It had long brow points and four points on each beam—a four-pointer Western count, a 10-pointer Eastern count. He had been hit rather far back through the lungs. Down there in that narrow canyon it was so dark that the exposure meter said half a second at f/2 would be about right. Since we had no flash, good pictures under those conditions were impossible. Later someone would come out from the ranch with a packhorse and get him.

By now the sun was up and bright, and while the others went along around the head of the canyon where I had shot the buck and to the head of the next, I stayed behind admiring the scenery. Far below, the little creek glistened through the timber along its banks and as it twisted through the meadows. The meadows were still green, the pines dark and somber, but along the creek cottonwoods and willows were shimmering gold, and patches of crimson sumac blazed on the hillsides.

Up in the high country at the head of the creek, ridges where the Salmon River elk ran, an early storm had frosted the dark timber with snow. Far below against the green of a pasture I saw some moving black dots. The glasses showed me I was looking at a feeding flock of wild turkeys.

Clear down in the bottom of the main canyon I heard a fusillade of shots. I made a mental note that they were probably fired by the Californians who were going to try for deer before they went in to Moose Creek for elk. I hurried to catch up with the other O'Connors, who were out of sight over a ridge.

I heard two quick shots. Then I saw Eleanor and Bradford, rifles in hand, sitting on the hillside looking down.

"Get anything?" I asked.

"Buck mule deer, sort of a collaboration," Bradford said.

"The heck it was," Eleanor said. "I shot behind it and then Bradford dumped it. See? It's lying down there on the road."

The glasses showed me a young buck mule deer close to 300 yards away.

When we returned to the ranchhouse we found that the Californians had taken three whitetail bucks out of a herd of eight. The largest had heavy antlers with three points and a brow tine on each side. Though their measurements were the same as those of my deer, this buck appeared to be heavier. The next buck was somewhat smaller than mine and the third was a youngster.

Soon a packhorse came in with my buck. He and the largest buck shot by the Californians measured 18 inches in a straight line from the top of the shoulder to the bottom of the brisket. Both were fat and in fine condition. We had no means of weighing them, but I have weighed many mule deer with the same measurements and they have weighed between 185 and 195 pounds. These two whitetail bucks in weight and measurements were every bit as large as typical large four-point mule-deer bucks.

I was interested in comparing them to Arizona whitetails I had hunted so long. They were just about twice as large, since an average large, mature Arizona whitetail will weigh from 90 to 110 pounds. As is true among Arizona whitetails, the top of the tails of the old bucks is a grizzled brown whereas the upper portion of the tails of the young bucks is bright orange. Oddly, the tails of these big bucks looked to be the same size as those of their Southern cousins.

The beams of my buck's antlers were a bit over 23 inches long, and the inside spread was 18 inches. I have never shot an Arizona whitetail with beams anything like that long, but I did take one once that had a 20-inch spread. Though the Northwestern whitetail is twice as heavy as his Southwestern cousin, his antlers aren't twice as large.

The coats of the big deer were a bit more brownish and less grayish than those of Coues as I remember them. The young Northwest whitetails have much more grizzled coats than those worn by young Arizona whitetails. These are quite blueish.

Sad to say, my underprivileged wife didn't get another shot. We drove up a precarious ranch road late that afternoon and early next morning when the deer should have been moving. We hunted the heads of several canyons and glassed the points and ridges, but all we saw were does and fawns. The bucks had got the message.

Wyoming Hunt with Bill Rae

Charles Elliott

The first creatures we saw in the brightening light of dawn were two doe deer. They stopped to look back at us, and we gave them a cursory glance through our binoculars. This being the amorous season for mule deer, an old buck was probably close by, and we strained for a glimpse of antlers among the scraggly tops of the sagebrush.

"He's bound to be around," our guide Jim Gay whispered, though a whisper was hardly necessary. The does were 200 yards upwind in a frigid, gusty gale. Unhurriedly, the deer walked into an aspen thicket and out of our sight.

"It could be that somebody's already collected papa," Jim mused.

We climbed into our guide's big four-wheel-drive wagon and spun up a rocky two-rutted trail that circled the aspen patch and

This chapter originally appeared in the November 1968 issue of *Outdoor Life* under the title "Frontierland Mulies."

angled toward a saddle on the massive mountain. My eyeteeth were being jolted loose when the road — if it could be called a road — ended in a mass of boulders. There was no alternative except to turn back. Just as we started downhill, I touched Jim on the shoulder.

"There's a deer watching us from just under the rim of the ridge," I told him. "Better take a look through the glasses."

"It seems bigger than those we first spotted," Bill Rae observed from the front seat.

"It is," Jim agreed, looking through his glasses, "and beyond are several more does, standing and looking downhill toward the aspen patch. There are animals in here that we haven't seen." We got out to look around.

Minutes passed. We covered every foot of the slope with our binoculars while the does stood motionless, their attention divided between us and the hillside below.

"A bunch of deer are coming up the draw," Bill said suddenly.

"Looks like a pretty good buck bringing up the rear," Jim said a bit breathlessly as he stared through his glasses at the deer.

As Bill and Jim spilled out of the truck, I put my glasses on the buck. His spread was only reasonably wide, but the antlers were high enough to be exciting. The tines on both sides were long, and they shone in the early-morning light.

"A rack that tall," I said, "has to be a good one."

The buck came toward us at an angle but stayed beyond and below the rocky backbone of the ridge so that we could see only his rack and head. Bill put his rifle scope on the deer and kept him covered, but the buck and his does swung sharply left and walked behind a clump of trees.

We'd had only one quick look at the buck, but both Jim and I were struck by the height of the rack and the length of the points. Then the buck stepped outside the shelter of the tree trunks. No does were in the way. The first golden shaft of sunlight came over the mountain, spotlighting the little park, the clump of trees, the boulders, and the buck standing with his head held high. The sight mesmerized us all.

"Shoot!" Jim barked at Bill.

Bill Rae is editor-in-chief of *Outdoor Life,* and I'm one of the magazine's field editors. We were hunting in a corner of Wyoming that had long fascinated us. In all our safaris to the state during a third of a century, however, we had never seen that stretch of country except from a distance. On the Game and Fish Commission's deer-area maps, it is known as the Steamboat Area (named after Steamboat Mountain) or Area Number 28.

It is a fascinating region in an incredible land. Below South

Pass, where California-bound and Oregon Trail wagons topped the Continental Divide more than 100 years ago, the Divide and the 42nd parallel of latitude cross at a historic spot. A monument has been erected there to mark the place where three territorial acquisitions of the United States touched: the Northwest "Oregon" Territory, the Louisiana Purchase, and land that was then part of Mexico.

Below South Pass the Continental Divide splits into two rims. Before the rims meet again below the city of Rawlins, they enclose a region of some 4,000 square miles known as the Great Divide Basin. The basin is said to have been the floor of an ancient inland sea. Now the streams born within the basin die in the thirsty sands.

Down the middle of the Great Divide Basin stretches a vast area of sand dunes, much like a corner of the great Gobi Desert. The mountain slopes bordering these dunes are crowded with high sage, some of the bushes as tall as small trees. When we hunted the slopes, Jim had to stand on top of his truck to glass over the sage and into the draws.

That brush is checkered by deer trails. Deer moving through it are not easily spotted, and those lying down are all but invisible.

Our hunting friend Ray Risser had told us that because of the thick deer cover and the vastness of the region, Steamboat Mountain has produced some big racks.

"The high sage is full of deer," Ray told us. "The only problem is getting to them. I was down here on opening day, when it was crowded—by Western standards, that is—with local hunters. I was standing on top of a big ridge that slopes down to the sand dunes. Some guy's car was stuck in the sand near a sagebrush road, and a fellow with a tractor came in to pull it out. Where he came from in this huge uninhabited place, I couldn't even guess. He took a direct line through the sage with the tractor. Small deer, average deer, and big bucks flushed ahead of him and went in all directions.

"The place was full of hunters, too, and it sounded like a Georgia dove shoot. I didn't hear how many deer were killed. I never did get close enough to one that was big enough for me."

That morning before daylight, we had met Ray and his hunting partner, Gerald Mason, both from Pinedale. Ray had hunted with Bill, Jim, and me on our last Wyoming try for trophy bucks.

Ray had agreed to show us what he knew of the Steamboat Mountain region. He owns the Triangle-R Lodge at Pinedale and is a licensed outfitter who uses guides and jeeps. Ray told us that his hunters had already accounted for eighty-five bucks so far in the season.

Ray Risser is himself a dedicated trophy hunter. Even after a couple of months of hunting with his clientele, he was out with Gerald simply for the pleasure of the hunt.

Ray was sitting on the mountain about a mile away, glassing the deer in the draw below us, when Jim and Bill decided that the buck was big enough.

Bill had his faithful old .30/06 Winchester Model 70, which has taken game from Utah to the Yukon. When the buck strolled partly into the clear, he squeezed off a shot. The buck went down but bounced back to its feet and began to run downhill, trying to make the protection of the distant ridge.

Bill got off another shot just before the deer steamed around the corner of the ridge some 200 yards away. The buck went out of sight.

"Looks like we've got a wounded buck on our hands," Jim said, shaking his head. "We'll have to stay with him now until we finish him off."

"I don't think so," said Bill, who had run out ahead of us about fifteen yards and shot offhand. "He pitched down like an arrow right after he crossed the ridge line."

Bill climbed the opposite hillside, and I trotted down the sage-brush road beyond the aspen patch. This put us both in position to see the buck if it moved on the hillside. Jim walked in to pick up the blood trail, if any.

When I looked back from the aspens, Bill waved and made signs to indicate that Jim had found the buck — stone-dead. Bill's last shot had cut off the top of its heart. When I got back to the men, both looked disappointed, and then I saw why. The rack was tall and evenly matched, but it was only a three-pointer (Western count).

"The only thing to keep this one out of the books, Jim said, "is the number of points. This is the biggest three-by-three I've ever seen. From the quick first look we got, I was sure it was a five-by-five."

We gutted the deer and dragged it down to the road. Ray and Gerald came up just as we got there. Ray looked at the buck's teeth and found them worn down enough to indicate that the mulie had been around for a long time.

We hunted throughout this last legal day in the Steamboat Area, glassing herd after herd of deer, but we did not see a buck as large as the one Bill had taken. The wind was very cold and strong, and cloud masses were building up to the west.

"Looks like we'll be heading into a real storm tomorrow," Jim predicted.

Next morning, clouds of snow slanted down out of an opaque

The now retired editor-in-chief of Outdoor Life, *Bill Rae, shown left, discusses his big three-pointer (Western count) with guide Jim Gay.*

void. We put off changing our address until the storm slackened somewhat around noon. Then we drove to Kemmerer, eighty-five miles west of Rock Springs.

We found Kemmerer to be a quaint Western town surrounded by the several routes of the old California Trail. Compared with other portions of Wyoming, Kemmerer is away from the heavily traveled tourist routes and has retained much of its original charm and many picturesque reminders of the Old West.

To the north of town lay deer areas 30, 32, 32A — some of the last mule-deer country open that late in the season. In evidence were hunting cars from California, Utah, Colorado, and Idaho, as well as some from several counties in Wyoming.

Jim Gay says that the next five days brought the toughest hunting weather that he has ever experienced. Next morning, when we climbed the high ridge between the west and middle branches of Beaver Creek, we had some indication of what we were in for. The snow was six or eight inches deep. But Jim's big four-wheel-drive rig had heavy-duty tire chains, and he experienced no difficulty in getting us up the sharp grades and along the sawtooth backbone, from which we could glass the hillsides and aspen hollows on both sides.

182

The hunting party encountered 50-mile an hour winds that lashed snow into clouds and forced them off this 9000-foot ridge.

"When I was here a month ago," Jim said, "the big bucks were high in the timber. We'll check them out there before we go lower."

We had planned to spend the day on this 9,000-foot ridge, and we might have filled out with a good head there. But the 10° temperature and the wind decided otherwise. Almost before we realized what was happening, it rocked us with gusts that must have hit fifty miles per hour.

"If we don't want to spend the winter here," our guide told us after our third trip away from the vehicle, "we'd better get off this ridge. If this wind keeps up, 10-foot drifts will pile up over the road between here and the bottom of the valley."

Snow was already beginning to drift over the jeep trail. Even with the heavy chains, we attacked some drifts two or three times before breaking through. To make matters worse, snow froze on the brake drums, and then there was no way to slow the heavy truck except by shifting all the way down into grandma gear.

At noon in one of the back valleys, we ran into Ray Arzy, the local game warden. He and Jim Gay are old friends.

"We've got more deer in Area Thirty than I've ever seen anywhere," the warden told us. "Nearly every hunter fills his license with some sort of buck. We have only one trouble. Hunting pressure isn't nearly heavy enough."

During the next few days, we saw the accuracy of Ray's appraisal. Never have I swapped curiosity with so many mule deer in so short a time. Apparently the animals had been driven out of the high country by the icy winds and deepening snows. They seemed to be concentrated in the aspen and evergreen thickets between their high summer range and their winter range in the sagebrush.

At Ray Arzy's suggestion, we moved into Fontanelle Basin,

183

which lies to the east of Commissary Ridge. On the range of hills that bulwarks South Fontanelle Creek lie a number of ranches. Snow was pelting at an oblique angle out of leaden skies when we drove up to one of the ranch houses. The rancher was stomping in from his corral, his hat and coat gray with snow.

"Come in and warm your face and hands," he invited cordially, "and have a cup of coffee."

We followed him into the kitchen and sat around an old-fashioned cooking range.

"I'm Joe Krall," he said. "Forgive this mess. I batch here, and I haven't had time today to straighten things up."

While we absorbed the heat, Jim asked about deer hunting.

"I have to keep my place posted," Joe said. "A lot of hunters come into this basin, and some are a mite careless with their rifles. I give a fellow permission to hunt if I think he knows what he's doing."

Joe told us that he is a licensed outfitter and guide and that each fall he accommodates deer hunters.

"Your best hunting in this country," he said, "is from the top-side of a horse. That way, you can get farther back where the big bucks are."

I had a sudden inspiration and knew that it had struck Bill at the same instant.

"What are our chances of hiring you and your horses for a day?" I asked.

Joe scratched the back of his head thoughtfully.

"Well," he said, "I have some lost sheep to find and some stock to feed, but I guess they'd forgive me if I put it off for a little while."

I looked around to get Jim Gay's approval, but he wasn't in the room. As I suspected, we found him outside with his spotting scope set up in the icy wind. Jim's the kind of guide who never stops hunting.

"There's a big buck in the aspens on the lee side of the mountain," he informed us. "He looks big enough to be the one we want."

Bill and I got one look before a snow squall moved in on the 40-mile-per-hour wind and blotted out the mountain. The buck, which had a wide, high rack, was so far up on the mountain that horses seemed our best means of approach.

Joe Krall and a couple of his ranch hands saddled horses for us, and we followed an old trail that led through the edge of a spruce-and-aspen forest. Joe suggested that we divide forces at the first knoll. Jim and Bill cut through the timber, while the rancher and

I continued up the hill. I was slowly congealing in the saddle when Joe pulled his horse to a stop in the middle of a rocky park.

"In this storm I don't know whether he's the right one or not," Joe said, "but there's a big buck standing up there between those two boulders."

My binoculars were hanging around the rancher's neck, so I slid off my horse and put my variable 2½-to-8X scope on the deer. He was almost completely obscured by flying snow, but his rack did look big.

The uphill shot was a long one. I sat down in the snow, braced myself as firmly as possible against the wind, held the crosshairs on the top of the buck's back, and squeezed off a shot.

"He went down," Joe said calmly.

When I picked up the buck through my scope again he was on his feet climbing the hill, much farther away. Just as I got the crosshairs of my .300 Kennon Magnum on the deer, Joe yelled and startled me.

"There's the big buck off to the right. He's getting out pretty fast!" Joe was no longer calm.

Racing through my mind was the fact that I already had a wounded buck on my hands. I did not want to kill or wound another, so I just sat on my haunches in the snow and watched both bucks go into the timber under the crest of the ridge.

When Bill and Jim heard the shot, they rejoined us, and we climbed the rooftop slope afoot. With frozen ground under the snow, the mountainside was treacherous, and I climbed with my buttocks and belly as much as with my feet.

We found a small patch of crimson where the buck had gone down and a spot of blood every fifteen feet going uphill. With the wind-and-snow squall beating at us, Jim and I trailed the deer through a higher patch of aspens and out toward the crest of the ridge. Where the fading trail turned upward toward the skyline, we gave up.

"He can't be hit too hard," Jim observed, "or he'd be coming downhill and bleeding a lot more. You probably scratched a muscle."

Joe could give us only one morning, so, on our own, we hunted the big buck afoot for two more icy days. The snow now came almost to our knees. We glassed innumerable does and passed up a dozen bucks that ranged from forkhorns to small five-by-fives, but the picture of the big buck kept coming back to me, and I wasn't even tempted.

More hunting cars moved into the valley, and Joe had a number of friends and guests spread out over his ranch, so we moved to another location, one with less hunting pressure. We made a long circle up La Barge Creek to get to the head of Fontanelle Creek. There was no sign of other hunters.

We had stopped the truck in a snowdrift to glass the high mesas around us when I spotted a herd of elk on a ridge that broke over into Bear Trap Gulch.

Elk weren't much on our minds. They weren't legal everywhere, and while we saw some in areas where they were legal, and while Bill had an elk license, he was interested only in a bull bigger than the good one he had shot in Wyoming's Thorofare some years ago. I didn't have an elk license.

"Look to the right," Jim said, his glasses up. "Two bucks are browsing in the aspens."

"Neither of them is as large as the one at Joe's," Bill commented.

"No," Jim agreed, "but the old fellow on the right is carrying a keeper rack."

"Let's try for him," I suggested. "These seasons have a way of closing right in your face."

Our problem was to plan a route that would take us within reasonable range without our spooking the elk, which might in turn spook the deer. This meant keeping under cover and staying downwind of the animals while we climbed the slope.

Jim backtracked along the road to the edge of timber. We parked the wagon out of sight and set out on the long, steep approach through the edge of the trees. The six or more inches of snow on the frozen ground was treacherous, and snow-hidden logs and rocks made every step uncertain.

Uncertain is really an inadequate word. In some places we slid back three steps for every step forward. But the walking sticks we fashioned out of dead limbs helped.

It took us an hour to reach the rim of an open mesa. From there we could see the aspen grove in which we had spotted the deer. We studied the grove through the glasses until my eyes ached. Not an animal was in sight anywhere.

"The tracks in the snow," Jim said, "indicate that the deer went downhill to the left. They could be out of sight in that little pocket beyond this flat. Let's ease up and take a look."

At this point, Bill remained out of sight in the trees to watch the hillside while Jim and I made a slow, crouching climb to the flat part of the mesa. About the third time Jim stopped to straighten up and look, he quickly crouched again.

"No wonder we couldn't see that bigger buck," he whispered. "He's lying down on that ridge. Only his antlers show above the sage."

I think I have a good game eye, but it took me a minute with the glasses to distinguish the points of the rack from the sprigs of sagebrush. When I finally did see the antlers, however, they stood up big against the skyline. Jim and I backed downhill into the timber, where Bill waited.

"That old boy sure picked himself a spot," Bill told us. "You could get to him without being seen through that patch of timber above us, but the wind would be right on your backs. If we go the other way, we'll be in the open."

"We know what the wind will do," Jim said, "so we'd better gamble on the open route."

We retreated farther downhill in order to stay under the brow of the mesa rim that paralleled the ridge on which the buck was lying. Our next look at him was from more than 600 yards away. Off to our right stood two large spruce trees. By putting these between us and the buck, we were able to get 200 yards closer.

"We've got to get a mite closer and higher," Jim whispered, "but it'll sure be taking a chance. Suppose you cover him from here, Charlie, and I'll try to reach that small tree on the hillside. If my move doesn't disturb him, you can climb to me while I watch."

I kept my eyes on the tip of the rack while Jim sneaked through the snow-covered sage for 100 yards or a little more. He got into a sitting position, raised his glasses, and then motioned for me to join him. I made the tough crawl through the snow and reached the guide with my tongue hanging out.

"Better sit down and get your breath," he suggested. "It's still a long shot, and you need to be relaxed."

I noticed that the walking stick Jim had used on the slope was forked, so I set it up at an angle in front of me as a rest for my rifle. I was looking through the scope at the antler tips when two does ran up the hillside between us and the buck. The buck stood up, his rack high and wide against the skyline. He was looking straight at us.

"Broadside would be the best shot," Jim said sotto voce, "but if you want to try him head-on, hold for his nose."

My crosshairs were already on the buck's nose, so I squeezed the trigger. It seemed to take a long time for that bullet to reach the buck, but he went out of sight, and the smack of lead against flesh came back to us.

"You stay here and keep him covered," Jim said, "while I climb to him. If he stands up, shoot him again."

Bill, who had watched the whole show from behind us, came up.

"If you had shot him much farther away," he said, "the critter would have been out of legal territory."

Jim Gay, left, congratulates the author on his 275-yard shot, which Bill Rae jokingly reckoned had been squeezed off at "the right point in the circle."

Jim took a photograph of Bill and me to show the distance from which the shot had been made. Then he waved us up to him. He pointed out where the buck had been hit—about an inch to the right of its nose. The Nosler bullet had broken the buck's neck.

"You pulled the trigger at just the right point in the circle," Bill said, laughing.

I readily admitted that the shot—made at 275 yards (Jim paced it off) as I sat on my haunches in the snow, out of breath, and with an icy wind in my face—was a lucky one, even though I had used the forked stick as a rest.

We were half a mile above the valley floor, but the ridge was so steep and the snow so deep that dragging the buck out was easy. In a couple of places, Jim sat on the buck's back, held up the antlers so that he could steer and steady himself, and rode the deer downhill as though on a sled.

We had our bucks, so we took a busman's holiday and went to help Ray Risser fill his license. We went back to deer-rich La Barge

Creek, which is the northern boundary of Area 30. After turning up into the hills, we stopped to glass a mountainside. Ray found a foraging doe through his binoculars. Then the entire hillside on the other side of the creek seemed to come alive with animals.

My own license was filled, but that didn't keep me from getting excited when Jim spotted a heavy-antlered buck lying in a sage-brush patch with just its rack showing.

"The distance is about three hundred and fifty yards," Jim said, "and it's too long a shot unless he stands up. You can't throw a rock that far, and a rifle shot might spook him. You want to wait him out, or go find another one?"

"This one's big enough to wait for," Ray said, unlimbering his .30/06 sporterized Mauser.

Unexpectedly, the buck got to its feet and made a pass at a doe strolling nearby. Against the sage and snow, its rack looked even larger than it had when we could see only the antlers and top of its head through the glasses.

Ray steadied himself across the hood of the truck and touched off a shot. The buck staggered but did not go down.

"He's limping," Jim said grimly. "You'd better try again."

Ray shot again, but we could not see where his bullet hit. The herd started up the mountain, the buck with it, and some of the does went into the trees.

"You'd better get him," Jim said tensely. "If he gets into the timber, tracking him down might take all day."

Jim was looking through his spotting scope and saw Ray's third bullet kick up snow just under the buck.

"Raise your sights seven feet," the guide instructed.

"I'm holding so high now that I'm lobbing 'em in," Ray said.

Though I was watching through the glasses, I didn't believe the shot I saw. The deer dropped, slid 100 feet down the slope, and disappeared in the sagebrush.

"This," Bill said, "must certainly be the farthest kill on record!"

No one in our group had the temerity to estimate the distance, and yours truly is too old to be sticking his neck out. Even if I tone the distance down a bit, you still wouldn't believe it.

That buck's rack wasn't large enough to make the record book, but it was a beauty, and Ray's performance was a great climax to one of the best mule deer hunts Bill, Jim, and I ever had in Wyoming.

The Rifle on the Horse

Jack O'Connor

Those who carry rifles around on horses feel as strongly about the proper way to do it as many feel about politics. An outfitter friend of mine and I have just about quit speaking because we disagree on the subject. Since we are both reasonably intelligent, the reason we don't see eye to eye is that his horseback hunting has been done largely in open country that has good trails, whereas much of mine has been done where man and horse often have had to plow through brush in a land of no trails.

I started riding around on a horse with a rifle scabbard hung on it many years ago. I have tried various types of scabbards and I have hung them in various places. Some have worked out quite well. Others haven't. It pays anyone planning to make a pack trip or to hunt on horseback in the Western United States or Canada to

This chapter originally appeared in the August 1965 issue of *Outdoor Life*.

give a little thought to acquiring a reasonably suitable saddle scabbard and to where he is going to hang it when he gets it. Outfitters sometimes furnish saddle scabbards, but they are seldom right for scope-sighted rifles.

A great many notions as to what saddle scabbards should be like come from those for the flat, light Winchester Model 94 carbines with their 20-inch barrels and for the similar Marlin Model 336 carbines and the Savage carbines like the obsolete Savage Model 99-T and current Model 99-E.

The scabbard for the scope-sighted rifle should be of leather heavy enough to give the rifle considerable protection from bumps, snug enough so that the rifle does not rattle around in it, and loose enough so that the rifle can be quickly inserted and quickly withdrawn. In addition, it should cover the rifle well past the point of the comb. If it does not, riding through brush and thorns will quickly take the finish off a buttstock and often score the wood so deeply that refinishing is almost impossible.

A scope-sighted, bolt-action rifle is a fine precision instrument for big-game hunting, but it is a pretty unwieldy gimmick to hang on a horse. The scope makes it bulky and awkward to carry and the bolt knob is a lethal projection which has a tendency to gouge into the horse's hide if the rifle is carried on the right side butt forward or on the left side butt to the rear. For years, I carried a .270 on a Mauser action that had a "butterknife" bolt handle, and it was flat and handy in a scabbard. Before World War II many German sporters had these flat bolt handles and the Mannlicher-Schoenauer rifles and carbines still do. They are a bit clumsy for rapid fire, but in the years I hunted with the flat-bolt .270, I cannot remember being slowed up much by it.

Rifles with short barrels are convenient to carry on horseback. The Remington Model 600 with its 18½-inch barrel is a handy little musket, and so is the Winchester Model 94 carbine and the similar Marlin Model 336. Each has a 20-inch barrel. However, these light, short-barreled weapons are frightfully muzzle light and hard to shoot accurately, particularly from the offhand position. Furthermore, if such short-barreled jobs are chambered for modern cartridges using slow-burning powders, velocity loss is pretty serious and muzzle blast would give pause to a worker in a boiler factory. At one time, Winchester made a Model 94 with a 16-inch barrel. The muzzle blast was grim. I cannot muster any enthusiasm for a saddle rifle with a barrel less than 20 inches. I think a 26-inch barrel is too long for the saddle, but a 24-inch barrel endurable. For the dude hunter, a 22-inch barrel is about right. With a barrel of that length, muzzle blast isn't increased a great deal and velocity loss is not serious. In addition, a rifle with a 22-inch barrel balances and handles nicely.

As I write this, the majority of American factory big-game rifles are standard with 22-inch barrels. The Remington Model 600 has an 18½-inch barrel and the Model 700 in such calibers as .280, 6 mm., and .270 was made for a time with a 20-inch barrel, but Remington added a couple of inches to all these barrels in 1965. A rifle for one of the various magnums should never be made with a barrel of less than 24 inches. If the barrel is chopped off more than that, muzzle blast and velocity loss become serious problems.

The rifle carried by the rancher who is in the hills most of the time and demands nothing more of it than to knock off a piece of meat occasionally or smoke up a coyote can well wear iron sights and be light and short of barrel. If he misses a coyote or doesn't bring in the fat little forkhorn, he will see another coyote and another fat forkhorn tomorrow or the day after. The rifle for the once-a-year hunter should be a better piece of ordnance, a scope-sighted rifle capable of catching good aim and knocking off a trophy buck or ram at 300 yards if the need arises.

For the trophy hunter, the saddle rifle and the mountain rifle are about the same thing — a rifle with a 22-inch barrel, mounted with about a 4X scope, and chambered for an accurate, flat-shooting cartridge. If nothing larger than deer, sheep, or black bear is on the menu, a cartridge like the .243 Winchester, the 6 mm. Remington, or the old .257 is perfectly all right. If, on the other hand, the hunter is likely to run into elk, caribou, moose, white goats, or grizzlies, he should have a musket with more bullet weight and somewhat more soup — the .280, .270, .284, .30/06, 7 X 57, or something of the sort. Rifle and scope should weigh in the neighborhood of eight pounds.

I am a bolt-action man myself. For one thing, I cut my teeth on the old Model 1903 bolt-action Springfield. For another, I am a handloader, and the bolt-action is more satisfactory for handloads than actions of other types. If the horseback hunter wants to use a lever-action rifle for a reasonably potent cartridge, there is no reason why he should not. The Savage Model 99 in .308, .300 Savage, or .284 makes a good solid saddle rifle when equipped with a 4X scope. So does the Winchester Model 88 in the same calibers. Suitable autoloaders are the Remington Model 742 or the Winchester Model 100 in .308, .30/06, or .280, or .284. The levers, pumps, and autoloaders are somewhat thinner than the bolt-action rifles.

All of these actions are faster than the bolt, but for open-country hunting I have never seen much need for firing a fusillade. However, many love firepower, and if they find busting a few extra

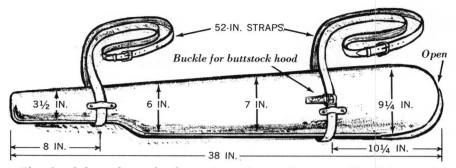

The sketch here shows the dimensions of a satisfactory scabbard designed for a scope-sighted rifle with a 22-inch barrel. The rifle is inserted with the scope up so no weight rests on it.

caps agrees with their constitutions I am all for them.

When scope-sighted rifles first began to come into wide use thirty years or so ago, there were simply no saddle scabbards on the market for them. My first satisfactory scope-sighted rifle was a Griffin & Howe .30/06 Springfield with a 22-inch barrel and mounted with a 2¾X Hensoldt scope on a Griffin & Howe mount so high that I could see through the Lyman 48 receiver sight underneath. I couldn't get a scabbard to fit the outfit, so I used to carry the scope in a little case hung on my belt when I hunted on horseback. I never had time to put the scope on when I was hunting on horseback and some frightened buck was putting geography behind him. The only times I knocked off game while using the scope was when I was hunting on foot.

I eventually soured on this miserable business of mounting a scope above the receiver sight. I had a 7 X 57 with an old Noske 4X scope mounted low on the Noske side mount. This was a fine outfit. Later, I acquired the flat-bolt .270 Mauser I mentioned previously. But even with these low-mounted outfits, I still could not get a store-bought scabbard to fit.

Another horseback hunter and I, with the aid of a Mexican saddlemaker, worked out the saddle scabbard shown in the accompanying sketch. As shown, the scabbard will fit a bolt-action rifle

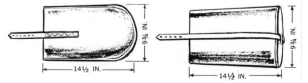

These buttstock hoods are designed for the scabbard at the top of the page.

with the scope mounted low. It can be made by any competent saddlemaker. However, since saddlemakers do not work with micrometers, it is wise to leave the rifle with the maker so he can make sure it fits the scabbard.

There is much that can be said in favor of this scabbard. It is not difficult to make, nor is it frightfully expensive. It holds the rifle securely, and yet it is easy to yank the rifle out. It is so designed that it does not bind the scope and it does a better job than most of protecting the buttstock from scratches and gouges. If it is made of heavy saddle-skirting leather and, combined with a cap or hood, it can double fairly well as a rifle case. Crozier & Son, Lewiston, Idaho, will make the scabbard shown in the sketch for $17 and for $21 will add a hood to protect the buttstock.

About twenty years ago, the late Cap Hardy, a famous Los Angeles leather worker and former exhibition shooter, borrowed one of the scabbards from me and made an elaborate variation which doubles nicely as a carrying case. The scabbard itself is made of very heavy, stiff leather which protects the rifle beyond the point of the comb.

It has a soft leather hood which can be zipped shut, tied back to give quick access to the butt of the rifle, or even removed by unzipping. The George Lawrence Company of Portland, Oregon, used my old scabbard as the inspiration for one which I allegedly designed and which is called the "O'Connor scabbard." I did not design it, but the scabbard has most of the good features of my old one. It has a stiff leather cap which buckles on and which converts it into a carrying case.

One type of saddle scabbard on the market has a sort of flap which snaps around the rifle at the pistol grip. This gismo is of some value in keeping the rifle from falling out of the scabbard,

The buckle on this Lawrence scabbard fastens the buttstock hood.

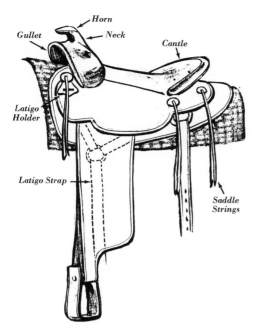

Horn
Gullet
Neck
Cantle
Latigo Holder
Latigo Strap
Saddle Strings

The scabbard is tied to the saddle by fastening straps through the gullet or latigo holder and then to the rear saddle strings.

but it leaves the buttstock sticking out like a sore thumb. If the hunter has to ride through areas of thick brush, particularly thorny brush, he will find that a scabbard of this sort does not protect the buttstock of his rifle. Furthermore, unless the snap is on the outside, it is very clumsy to use and the scabbard must always be carried on one particular side. This limits its usefulness.

The location of the scabbard on the horse depends on many things. Most important is how fast the hunter wants to get his rifle out and go into action. If he is simply using his horse to carry him and his rifle to where he wants to hunt, the position makes no particular difference. But if he wants to get off his horse, grab his musket, and lay down a barrage, that's another story.

In some areas, hunting can be done almost entirely from horseback. The hunter rides in such a way that he will move deer and see them when they move. He rides along ridges so he can see into canyons on each side. He rides along the sides of canyons and around the heads of draws. To be hunted successfully in this manner, country must be pretty open and it must be cut up and hilly. Generally, heavy brush country and flat country cannot be hunted on horseback.

I have shot many mule deer in the hills and canyons of Arizona when I was hunting on horseback. I have likewise shot a great many Coues (Arizona) whitetails in Arizona and Sonora the same way. Generally, such shots are at running animals and are at fair ranges—from 200 to 300 yards. For this work, I like what is generally called the southwest position for the scabbard. For this, I put the scabbard on the horse with the butt to the rear on the left side and the butt pointing up at an angle of about 45 degrees. This slant is important for two reasons. For one thing, it keeps the rifle from sliding out of the scabbard when the horse is going sharply uphill. For another, this position puts the forward portion of the scabbard low so it does not cramp the left leg. Another advantage is that since the open portion of the scabbard is at the rear, the scabbard does not fill up with leaves, twigs, and miscellaneous crud as it does when the open mouth of the scabbard points forward.

With his scabbard in that position, the rider gets off his horse on the left side, drops the reins (since Western horses are trained to stand when the reins are down), grabs the rifle by the small of the stock, yanks it out, sits down, and goes into action. If his horse gets nervous and spooks, the animal goes forward and the hunter keeps the rifle in his right hand and does not lose it.

Some say they like to carry their rifles on the left side with the butt forward along the horse's neck. I do not like this position. For one thing, the scabbard fills up with leaves and twigs if the hunter must ride through brush. For another, the horse is often spooked if the excited hunter makes a sudden grab for the butt of his rifle. Then, if the horse takes off, the hunter will lose his hold on his rifle even if he has grabbed it. This position is okay for transporting a rifle from one place to another, but I do not like it for actual horseback hunting.

With the scabbard in the southwest position, the rider dismounts on the left side and yanks the rifle out by the butt.

When the scabbard is in the trail position, the muzzle is low. This prevents cramping the hunter's knee during long rides.

Another fast position that was formerly quite popular was to sling the scabbard high on the right side, butt to the rear and projecting above the horse's rump. Then the hunter grabbed the butt with his right hand as he dismounted on the left side. This position is feasible only with a short-barreled carbine like the old Model 94 Winchester.

Most Southwestern horses and good cow horses all over the West have a high proportion of hot blood in them and, as a consequence, their backs are shaped to carry saddles. The position of the saddle scabbard or the rider's getting on and off doesn't tend to pull the saddle over on one side or another.

In the Canadian Rockies from the American border to the Yukon, most of the horses are from cold-blooded work stock, and their backs are shaped like sausages. Keeping a saddle on an even keel on these goats is a chore. On such a horse, I like to carry my rifle in what I call the trail position. This is on the right side, butt to the front and at an angle of about 45 degrees. The rifle is then carried about even with the front cinch. Its weight doesn't have much tendency to pull the saddle over, but such tendency as it does have about balances the sudden pulls when the horseman mounts from the left side. This is no place for the man who wants to carry his rifle so he can jump off, grab it, and shoot, but it is right for a Rocky Mountain pack trip. I can see no point whatsoever in carrying a rifle on the right side with the butt to the rear, as I have seen

197

some do. Slung that way, the rifle and scabbard pull the rifle over to the right. The rifle is slow to get to, and if the excited hunter goes charging around Black Beauty's fanny from the left side to the right to grab his musket he is likely to get kicked.

Now and then some innocent citizen comes around to my house to borrow a saddle scabbard. When he returns it, the straps are almost always on backward and it is plain to see that he has been carrying his rifle upside down with all the weight on the scope. Why anyone should want to carry his rifle so that it bounces around on the scope has always baffled me, but many do.

The rifle carried in the scabbard should have the weight resting on the muzzle and on the bottom of the rifle. Weight should never rest on either glass or iron sights. The scabbard should be roomy enough so that the scope and rifle do not wedge into the scabbard. I learned these things the hard way. Once I hunted on horseback with a .30/06 fitted with a scope on a side mount with aluminum arms. The scabbard was too narrow and none of the weight rested on the muzzle. Most of the weight was on the end of the scope tube and every step the horse took wedged the scope more solidly into the scabbard. Since the wedging action bent the aluminum arms of the bracket mount and made the scope point down, this made the barrel point up in relation to the scope. I shot over a couple of nice bucks, and then when I found out what was happening I managed to kill one at 200 yards by holding a foot under the line of his chest.

Another good tip is to remove the sling from the rifle and carry it in the saddlebags if it is to be needed, or to take great pains to tuck the sling inside the scabbard. If it dangles out, it may catch on a limb and yank the rifle out.

Anyone hanging a rifle scabbard on a horse should remember that his mount is only slightly less powerful than a bulldozer. Unless whatever is tied on Old Dobbin is anchored securely, it is likely to get yanked off. If a sizable branch gets between horse and scabbard, the straps may be torn off. Hunters are always tying binocular cases, camera cases, and whatnot to their saddles. I have seen at least three pairs of binoculars lost because they were tied to the saddle or hung over the horn. A chap I knew lost a $600 movie camera he had tied to his saddle. Once I led a horse down a steep hill through thick brush. One of my saddlebags was ripped open, and I lost a $300 miniature camera and a $400 movie camera. However, I backtracked and found the stuff.

When the rifle is carried butt forward, the top carrying strap is put in the latigo holder or through the fork of the saddle. This is a strong place, but there is always a chance that a limb could get between horse and scabbard. When the rifle is carried butt to the rear, the top strap is tied to the saddle with the rear saddle strings and the bottom strap goes through the fork.

Another point is to sling the rifle and scabbard so that the bump they cause is low enough not to twist the knee. A knee strained by a scabbard during a long ride can be just as painful as one strained by riding with the stirrups too short.

Anyone ordering a scabbard for horseback hunts out from a ranch has no need for a cap to cover the buttstock. If he wants to get into action fast, it gets in his way. If he is afraid of a sudden rain, he can cover butt and scope with an old boot sock. On a long pack trip, during which the rider may travel in rain and snow and almost never have to get to his rifle instantly, some sort of a gimmick to cover the butt with leather is a good idea. Then, if the scabbard itself is of good, hard, molded leather, it can serve as a carrying case on trains or planes. Even so, it is a good idea to ask permission to take rifles and scabbards into the cabin of a plane. Some baggage handlers get a bit careless with rifles at times, and a scope-sighted rifle that gets tossed around may come out of adjustment.

Scabbards are better when not lined with fleece. Genuine lamb fleece attracts moisture and is likely to promote rust. The synthetic fleece I have seen goes to pieces when it gets wet. Furthermore, fleece is not needed since a rifle does not wear in a scabbard that fits properly.

Anyone who takes a long pack trip should take along a pair of screwdrivers, one with the blade ground to fit the guard screws of the rifle and the other ground to fit the smaller screws in the scope mount. Jouncing a scope-mounted rifle around on a horse is not the best way to keep it sighted in. The scope can get so loose it rattles, particularly if the mount and scope screws have some oil in the threads. Every time the rifle is cleaned, all screws should be checked to see if they are tight.

The best type of scope mount for the saddle rifle is the popular bridge type, and the farther apart the rings are the better the scope is supported. Base screws particularly should be dipped in shellac or Loctite before they are tightened. Then the jolting from the horse will not loosen them.

A companion piece for the saddle scabbard is a pair of saddlebags tied on behind the cantle by the rear saddle strings. Satisfactory ones, more or less on the order of the old cavalry saddle bags, can be bought at some sporting-goods stores and saddle shops for around $15. In them the hunter can carry his lunch, camera, and extra film. The bags are just about a necessity. Not all outfitters furnish them. A saddle slicker or a warm jacket can be tied on behind the cantle of the saddle with the saddle strings.

Buck Fever

Ben East

One of the strangest experiences that can happen to a hunter is buck fever. It's a very queer affliction, and I have yet to hear a really good explanation of it. It can result from excitement, fear, a trance-like concentration on getting game, even from fascination, or from a combination of all of them.

It befalls beginners, and also men who have hunted for many years. Some are afflicted with it when they first go after big game, no matter how long they have hunted rabbits and squirrels. After a time or two they may get over it. Then, on the other hand, there are hunters who suffer attacks every time they get close to a deer, elk, moose or bear, no matter how long they hunt.

You could hear a million buck-fever stories around the hunting

Though this chapter recounts attacks of "buck fever" during hunts for a variety of big game, its implications for the deer hunter are evident. This is the first printing of these accounts.

camps of the United States and Canada any fall, and most of them would be true.

Of all the hunters I have known, my old friend Ted Updike knows most about this unexplained malady. Ted is a former bush trapper in northern Saskatchewan, past seventy now, retired from the trapline a number of years ago and living at the hamlet of Love, on the edge of the roadless bush two hundred and fifty miles north of Regina.

He has hunted since he was a boy, always for food rather than for sport or trophies. Deer, moose, elk and caribou have supplied his winter meat most of his life, and he has done as much hunting, and is as good at it as any man I have ever met.

He has also had a great deal to do with buck fever, not in himself but in partners and hunters he was guiding.

His own firsthand experience with it was limited to one occasion, when he was a boy of twelve, starting to hunt with a battered old .22 single-shot. And then it wasn't really buck fever; it was crane fever, Ted told me with a chuckle. But the effects were the same.

He crawled over a low ridge on the grain prairies north of Regina one fall morning and found himself staring at a flock of twelve or fifteen sandhill cranes, feeding only fifty feet away. He was so startled and excited at the sight of those tall, stately birds so close by, and so fascinated by their size and beauty, that he forgot the .22 in his hands, forgot that his brother and he were hunting meat for the table, forgot everything except the cranes themselves. He lay motionless and rigid. But if he had buck fever the birds didn't. They leaped into the air and were out of range before the boy recovered his senses. Since that long-ago day Ted Updike has never again suffered buck fever.

That experience was fairly typical. It's most likely to happen when a hunter is getting started, and afterward he may not even remember what took place.

Ted tells a story of a hard case that he saw in the 1930's. He was trapping that winter on Caribou and White Gull creeks, tributaries of the Torch River, in the bush about forty miles north of Love, where he now lives.

A year or so earlier he had gotten acquainted with a wheat farmer by the name of Guy Gibson, living southwest of Saskatoon. Just before he headed into the bush for the winter, Gibson asked to join him for a few days for a caribou hunt, after snow came. Ted replied that he'd enjoy the company, and gave directions as to how to get to the nearest of the four trapline cabins he'd be using that winter.

Gibson arrived while Updike was out on his trapline, and put in the time hunting until Ted got back. Then they headed out together with their gear on a small hand toboggan, to look for a shootable caribou.

They were crossing a valley that was covered for the most part with willows and alders when a regal looking bull broke out of the brush behind them, coming at the caribou gait that Ted calls a running walk. It eats distance surprisingly fast.

This bull was coming at an angle that, if he kept his course, would bring him past the two men no more than thirty yards away. Whether he kept his course would depend on their not moving. Updike knew that so long as they stayed motionless the caribou would see them as no more than a couple of broken tree stubs. In that remote country, in all likelihood they were the first men he had ever encountered, and caribou eyesight for objects that don't move is notoriously poor.

Gibson was walking in the lead. Ted tapped him on the shoulder and said in a low voice, "Here comes your caribou." Guy did the right thing. He turned, raised his rifle very slowly, and held it steady on the bull. When the animal came broadside to them the hunter had it dead to rights, at a range so close he could have hit it with a slingshot. But to Updike's amazement, he didn't shoot.

For what seemed like several seconds, as the caribou trotted past, he held a bead on it. Then he lowered his rifle, turned to face Ted, and blurted, "Are you sure that's a caribou?" It wasn't more than fifty yards from him at that instant, in muskeg as open as a hay meadow.

"Sure it's a caribou. Shoot!" Ted cried.

His own rifle, a .25/20 Winchester, was tied on top of the load on the toboggan. All he could do was stand and wait. Gibson took aim again. The bull was past them now, angling away across a ridge that ended where thick spruce swamp bordered the muskeg. Once more Updike waited for the shot. Instead he heard again the astonishing query, "You're sure?"

He barked his reply. His partner kept his rifle on the animal until it went out of sight in the spruce. Then he wheeled around, shoved the gun, a brand new Savage Model 99 in .300 caliber, into Ted's hands and muttered, "You shoot."

Updike stared at him, baffled, and after a minute Gibson said slowly, "I lost my chance, Ted. Get him for me, will you?"

The country along that part of Caribou Creek was mostly muskeg, with a scattering of jackpine ridges and tongues of spruce swamp. If the caribou kept going the way it was headed it would come out of the spruce in a flat area where there was nothing in the way but a few willow thickets and stunted trees. If Updike could get there in time he could still get a shot.

He ran two hundred yards at the best speed he was capable of and broke into the open completely winded, to see the bull crossing full tilt seventy-five yards in front of him. By that time it knew something was after it and was clearing out.

There was a patch of willows in the way, and Ted's first shot missed. The second one connected. It hit in the shoulder and the caribou went down front-end-first, plowing into the snow. Momentum carried its rear end around, and when it got back on its feet it was facing the way it had come. Ted took two more shots to floor the bull for keeps. About that time Guy came panting up with the .25/20.

He didn't say much. He had flubbed an opportunity the like of which a hunter seldom experiences, passing up a chance he had come two hundred miles for and looked forward to for many months. Updike never asked him why.

"I don't think he knew," Ted told me. "The victim of buck fever is rarely able to account for his actions. I probably understood as much about it as he did. It was his first chance at a caribou, and that was all it took."

Ted suspected that particular case of buck fever was aggravated by an unusual factor, too. When he shot the caribou he found that the barrel whip and recoil of the .300 were the worst he had ever experienced with any rifle. He knew there had to be a reason, for he had handled quite a few Savage Model 99's, had owned one for a couple of years, and had always considered them very well balanced and pleasant to shoot.

"What have you got in those shells?" he asked Gibson. "Nitro glycerin?"

Guy looked a little sheepish, and related the story. When he bought the rifle he told the salesman he wanted a gun that would kill coyotes at long range. In turn he got advice that was all right in theory but didn't work out well in practice. The salesman sold him a reloading kit and told him to handload with plenty of powder and 110-grain bullets. Updike never learned whether the salesman overdid the dose of powder or whether Guy made a mistake.

"But I'm sure of one thing," Ted said. "If he had ever hit a coyote with one of those loads there wouldn't have been enough left to skin. I have always thought that this acute attack of caribou fever may have been due in part to subconscious dread of the recoil and whip of that rifle. If you didn't hang on tight it would jump out of your hands. I steered him to factory loads and so far as I ever heard that ended his troubles."

Not that it takes gun-shyness to bring on buck fever, not by any means. Ted told me another story, about a moose hunter whom his trapline partner, Ches Rea, guided one fall. It was the man's first hunt for big game of any kind. When he arrived in the area and asked about a guide, somebody sent him to Rea.

There were plenty of moose at that time in the bush just beyond the clearings north of the Saskatchewan River, where Ches and Updike had homesteads, so Ches loaded a packsack with everything two men would need for a couple of days in the bush, let his client carry part of the bedding, and they headed for a big area of willow flats a few miles away.

Everything was new to the hunter, and it was all something he had dreamed about for years. He had a new and expensive rifle, the best of outdoor clothing, and while they sat by their fire under a big spruce and chatted that night he explained how long he had wanted to camp under the stars and cook his meals over an open fire.

They left their makeshift camp as soon as it was light enough for shooting the next morning. Luck was with them: In the first willows they came to they found a good bull moose feeding, and with a little careful circling downwind they were able to get a clear look at it; broadside at fifty yards.

"There's your shot," Ches said quietly. "Right behind the shoulder." The hunter took deliberate aim, then levered the shell out of his rifle unfired. A second later he did the same thing over again. He racked three or four hulls through the gun without pulling the trigger, and at that point Ches took over. He was a man who didn't like to kill game for anybody, except maybe a hungry homesteader. But under the circumstances he couldn't bear to see his hunter go home empty-handed, so he threw up his own rifle and put a slug into the moose in the right place.

It ran, and as it disappeared in the willows the hunter exclaimed in a crestfallen tone, "I must have made a poor shot. He got away."

Ches led him to the blood trail, and a hundred yards ahead in the brush they found the moose dead. Ches turned to his client, poker-faced, and said, "That was good shooting. Congratulations."

They shook hands, dressed the moose, hiked out and hired a man with a team to haul it to the railway. The elated hunter left for home with stars in his eyes, blissfully and totally unaware that he had not fired a shot.

Updike's son Merv had a similar and equally incredible experience with a stricken hunter in the fall of 1959. The two were hunting along the Torch River about six miles above where it flows into the Saskatchewan. They were a quarter mile apart when, in response to Merv's calling, a big bull moose crashed out of the willows on the far side of the Torch and started walking back and forth at the water's edge, grunting and grumbling. Merv didn't want to kill him on the opposite bank, since the river was too deep to wade, and anyway, he wanted his partner in on the kill. So he backed away carefully and went to find Ralph.

When they got back the bull was still there and still spoiling for a fight. But he wouldn't come across the Torch and finally they decided to kill him where he was, hike the six miles to the Saskatchewan, get a canoe and come back.

They sat down on the bank, and Merv shot first. The bullet from his .303 British Enfield rocked the bull but didn't knock it down, and before Merv could shoot again he felt something strike his boot.

He looked down, and it was an unfired shell that his partner had levered out of his Savage. It took a couple more shots from Merv's Enfield to finish the moose, and by that time all five of Ralph's shells were lying on the ground unfired. And Ralph was not a beginner, either.

"It took a neighbor of mine to show me, years ago, just how hard buck fever can nail a man, no matter how long he has hunted," Ted says. "I'll call the neighbor Bill. That is not his name, but he still lives not far from me, we know the same people, and he would be embarrassed if I identified him."

Ted was trapping by himself that winter, running a long line and using a dog team. Money was scarce on the fringe of the settlements, and everybody relied mostly on wild game for a meat supply. Toward the end of the winter, when the main fur harvest was over, Updike made a trip home with his dogs for provisions, and Bill asked if he could go back into the bush with him, accompany him around his trapline, and try to kill a caribou.

They had known each other for years. Bill was an experienced hunter and had killed plenty of deer and moose, but this would be his first caribou hunt. Caribou were not plentiful that year in the country where Ted was trapping, but he saw them often enough that he didn't run out of meat for himself or his dogs and he didn't think Bill would have any trouble downing one. He welcomed a few days of company to break the monotony of the long winter alone, so he told Bill to come along, and promised he'd haul out with his dog team any meat that was shot.

They stayed the next three nights in trapline cabins, small, low-roofed, built of logs and chinked with moss, heated with a little tin stove, and lighted by the crude elk-tallow lamps that trappers called witches. They were made by cutting a milk can in half around the middle to form a shallow container, leaving a tab of tin on one side to nail them up by. Ted got the tallow for his by rendering down elk fat. He used it for cooking and in place of butter, too, as well as for lighting.

For a lamp he filled one of the tins with the melted fat, putting in a narrow strip of cloth for a wick and letting it hang down over the side. Lighted, the tallow burned with a pretty fair light, and the heat kept enough of it melted to feed the wick.

That kind of life was all new to Bill, and he stayed as excited as a kid at Christmas. The routine of coming in to one of the cabins just before dark, unhitching and feeding the dogs, unloading the toboggan, getting a fire going in the little stove and lighting a couple of witches, and then cooking supper, was completely fascinating to him. But by the third night Ted could also see that he was becoming aware of the isolation, of the fact that there was no other human within twenty or thirty miles, that the bush was a big and wild and lonely place.

"I have always thought that it was the solitude and unfamiliar surroundings that helped to key him up and accounted in part for what happened the third morning," Ted says in relating the story.

It was a windless day, quiet with the eerie silence of the winter wilderness, no sound except the soft swish of snowshoes and the occasional odd little groan of the toboggan as it eased over a hummock of moss.

A few miles from the cabin where they had spent the night they came to an area of muskeg, open except for a few scattered tamaracks, broken by long ridges bordered by scrubby spruce.

The snow was about two feet deep and there had been a fresh fall a day or two before. They began to see caribou tracks, and as often as they crossed one of the ridges Ted halted the dogs in the fringe of spruce and took a careful look ahead before they showed themselves. Finally he spotted what he was looking for, a solitary bull caribou about two hundred yards out in the muskeg. He stepped back beside the lead dog and motioned Bill up.

The bull was a beautiful sight, with a pure white neck and a tall rack of antlers standing up from his head like bleached tree skeletons. Bill stood and looked at him for a long time but made no move to lift his rifle.

It was a long shot but not an impossible one, and he had come a long way for this opportunity. Finally Ted said, "Well, aren't you going to try for him?" He got no answer, and when he looked more closely he saw that his partner was literally in a trance.

Ted was carrying an old .44/40 Winchester carbine on the trapline that winter. He liked it for bush hunting, and it was a killer if you put your shots in the right place, but it was no gun to use on the caribou at two hundred yards. Bill's rifle was a Savage Model 99 in .303 caliber.

"If you're not going to shoot, give me your gun," Ted said, and reached for it.

Bill did not answer, but he would not surrender the rifle. He hung onto it and actually struggled to keep it away from Updike, with his eyes fixed on the caribou all the while. Ted decided to bring him out of his daze. He picked up the old .44 and blasted a shot into the snow in front of the bull.

Many times in caribou country, when one or two of the animals are standing by themselves, maybe feeding a little but showing no disposition to move along, there are others lying down nearby, usually hidden in willows or long grass. The one that's on its feet apparently is doing sentry duty against wolves and other enemies.

That was the case this time. At the blast of the .44 seven or eight more caribou exploded out of the willows in a cloud of snow. The two men didn't even get a clear look at them until they were out of range, and of course the lone bull ran with them.

At least the action had the desired effect on Bill. It jolted him back to life, and he got off three fast shots as the caribou angled away. But at that range and with targets moving in full flight, he didn't hit anything. Those were the only caribou they saw on the hunt, too.

That was one time when Ted asked a buck fever victim what accounted for his actions, but Bill could give no explanation. He said he just seemed to freeze, but he did not know why nor did he remember his refusal to let Updike have his rifle.

Bill never had buck fever again, either. In fact, in later years when he was after elk or deer with a party of friends and a drive was made, he was the man who was put on a stand to do the shooting. The rest knew they could count on his steady nerves and good eye. He still has an excellent reputation as a deer hunter.

The kind of animal that's being hunted, and the circumstances of the encounter, often seem to have a lot to do with bringing on an attack of buck fever. I know a man who in twenty years of deer hunting had never known a touch of it, not even when he killed his first buck. Then he fired four standing shots at a deer at sixty yards, missing because thick brush deflected his bullets, and when the deer didn't move or flinch, probably because it had not located the direction from which the shots were coming, the hunter blew his cool completely.

It was an eerie experience, he explained afterward, like shooting blanks, and at the end he was so badly rattled that when the buck finally lit out he didn't even use the last shell in his rifle. He just stood and watched it run, shaking like a half-drowned puppy.

I know hunters who have downed deer for years but hit the panic button the first time they came across a moose at shooting range.

Apparently a bull moose that may weigh as much as one thousand pounds is just too much for them. One man told Ted that when he killed his first moose he ran to it, cut its throat, and then grabbed up his rifle and fired a shot in the air. He had no idea why.

Moose, elk and caribou have accounted for some classic cases, but it doesn't necessarily take a big animal to bring on an attack. Plenty of hunters have been thrown into a tizzy by a whitetail buck that wouldn't have weighed 150 pounds.

Bears are especially likely to bring on a full-blown case of the fever, I suppose for understandable reasons. Many hunters who have had no dealing with them stand in great awe of any bear, to begin with. There is cause to feel that way, too. All bears are unpredictable and potentially dangerous, and a cornered or wounded one can be pure poison. So it's not too surprising that when a full grown bear, even a black, steps into view fifty yards away many hunters tighten up as tight as a bowstring.

A friend of mine tells a story of an eighteen-year-old beginner, on his first deer hunt, who found an ideal place for a stand, where a heavily used runway crossed an abandoned logging road in thick swamp. The logging road branched at that point and the runway was only a hundred feet from the fork. By sitting with his back against a convenient spruce, the young hunter would be screened by low branches and could watch both forks of the trail. He reasoned that if he sat there long enough a buck was sure to come along.

What came along instead was a black bear that, if the subsequent description was anywhere near right, must have weighed at least three hundred and fifty pounds.

The boy's first warning was the sound of twigs breaking in the brush beside the right fork of the road. Before he could get his rifle up the bear stepped into the open about thirty yards away. The rifle stayed where it was.

The hunter sat there, paralyzed, with a .348 lever-action Winchester in his lap, and didn't move a muscle. So far as he could recall, he didn't even breathe, although his heart was racing. The bear stood in the old road for a minute, looking both ways, then walked into the brush on the far side. The boy traced its course through the cedar tangles by the noise it made, but before it reached the other fork he knew he wasn't going to shoot.

Again the bear showed itself in plain sight. It even turned and walked a few steps in his direction. Then it moseyed on its way and the encounter was finished. The Winchester had never been lifted.

"I just couldn't shoot," that young hunter said when he got back to camp hours later, still shaken and pale. "I turned cold and stiff all over and I was a little sick at my stomach, too."

What accounts for a nervous reaction as violent as that? For one thing, I believe that the close presence of a big animal, exciting enough in itself and frequently under circumstances loaded with suspense, is made even more earth-shaking by the hunter's knowledge that he is supposed to kill it. That is what he is there for, but there seems to be some instinctive and overpowering reaction that demolishes his self-control.

I have talked to more than one victim of buck fever who said he was sure he wouldn't be plagued by it if he were merely looking at a moose or elk or deer, or even if he were hunting with a camera instead of a gun. It's the idea of shooting it and knowing it will go down that is the final straw, the factor that sends the hunter to an uncontrollable pitch of excitement—and that often prevents shooting altogether.

Maybe a psychiatrist could explain that, but I can't. I doubt that anybody really knows the reason for buck fever. Some of the things that bring it on are clear enough, but exactly what happens in the mind and nerves and muscles of the victim is still a mystery so far as I am concerned.

I have never known of a case where a hunter, confronting a wounded or enraged animal at close range, was frozen by the fever and hurt or killed in consequence, but I'm convinced it happens.

Ted Updike has had such meetings, and so have friends of his and his son Merv, with both moose and bears. They have all faced situations where a well placed shot, fired in a split second, was all that stood between them and deadly danger.

If at any of those times buck fever had hindered them even for seconds they'd have had the animal in their laps.

An experience that befell a fellow trapper and friend of Ted's, Willie Sager, supplies a good illustration.

Willie rounded a bend in his trapline trail one morning and was looking a big black bear in the face at sixty feet. Neither he nor the bear hesitated.

The black, which must have heard him coming and waited deliberately to waylay him, ripped out a blood-chilling roar and came in a headlong charge. Willie, who had been a wilderness trapper for many years and always toted a .30/30 everywhere he went in the bush, whipped the rifle up and cut loose. It took three shots to pile the bear in a heap, just twelve feet from where the trapper was standing.

That was certainly a case where a man couldn't have afforded even a touch of the strange affliction called buck fever.

The Fable
of the Sacred Doe

Ben East

A deer population that is hunted, under proper regulations, fares far better than one that is not hunted at all. And often the proper regulations have to include the killing of does as well as bucks.

The classic case was recorded on the Kaibab Plateau, on the north rim of Grand Canyon in Arizona, fifty years ago. In 1906 President Theodore Roosevelt, one of the country's pioneer conservationists and a lifelong hunter, set aside that area as the Kaibab National Game Refuge.

The action won widespread approval. The move to protect and conserve wildlife was in its infancy; the sorry examples of the buffalo slaughter and the extinction of the passenger pigeon were in the minds of many men; and a move to safeguard the beautiful

This chapter was written especially for this book.

These two starving whitetails are close to the end. They are too weak to run away from this game biologist.

Kaibab country and its herd of mule deer was plainly a step in the right direction. But at Kaibab the safeguards were excessive.

No hunting was allowed in the refuge, and in four years more than 600 mountain lions and numerous smaller predators were destroyed. By 1910 the deer herd had climbed to 4,000. It didn't stop there. By 1924 it numbered 100,000 and its food supply was exhausted. In the next two winters 60,000 Kaibab deer died of starvation, and the range still shows the effects of the damage done by that swollen wildlife population.

Annual hunting seasons, including the regulated harvest of the necessary number of does, could have prevented both the wildlife disaster and the environmental damage that happened half a century ago, but the lesson is still worth remembering.

Yet, despite all the irrefutable evidence, the shooting of doe deer under any circumstances is something many sportsmen find almost impossible to accept. And in that attitude is rooted the most troublesome headache that has plagued state game departments in almost every part of the country for the last forty years.

"We can manage deer all right," I have been told by wildlife authorities more times than I can remember. "It's people that cause the trouble."

Game researchers and administrators know how to maintain deer populations at the peak levels that food and cover conditions will permit. They have the formulas, based on decades of study and experience, to supply their hunters with maximum annual harvests of both trophies and venison, with no danger of depleting the breeding stock.

But often, when they have tried to put those formulas to work, sincere but misguided sportsmen have risen up in alarm and indignation, stirred emotional public resentment, and blocked the deer-management program. On the other hand, it has to be said that in some cases the game officials have invited resentment by the arbitrary and even arrogant manner in which they have put such programs into effect.

Deer are among the most prolific of big-game animals. Given adequate cover, sufficient food, favorable weather conditions and protection from poaching and predators, they are capable of building up their numbers at a rate that is hard to believe.

Take, for example, the case of the George Reserve, a 1,200-acre outdoor laboratory of hardwood, brush, swamp, marsh and unused farm land formerly operated by the University of Michigan, about twenty-five miles from the campus at Ann Arbor.

Enclosed within a deerproof fence, this reserve was stocked with two whitetail bucks and four does in March of 1928. In December, 1933, a drive yielded an actual count of 160 deer. In the next twelve years, under a controlled hunting program, the herd yielded 564, an average of 47 a year, divided about equally between bucks and does, and a breeding stock of 74 remained.

Along with this tremendous capacity to increase, deer inevitably have the ability to eat themselves out of house and home very quickly, and that makes management programs essential. State after state supplies overwhelming proof.

But in the beginning, as one state after another confronted the problem of too many deer for the available food supply and tried to thin the herd by allowing the hunting of antlerless animals, there was bitter opposition among sportsmen and angry charges that the deer were about to be exterminated.

In its December 1963 issue, *Outdoor Life* ran an article of mine,

When deer congregate, as in this New York orchard, natural food is scarce. Thinning the herd by allowing antlerless hunting prevents major damage and mass starvation, according to researchers.

titled "The Deer War," in which I detailed the progress and problems of deer management around the country.

In gathering material for that report I contacted twenty-five leading deer states. All but five had run afoul of heated opposition to doe shooting at one time or another, and were still having serious difficulties.

What is the situation today? To get the answer to that, in March of 1974 I checked a number of those same states. In general, public acceptance of doe hunting is much better than it used to be, and game authorities also have learned a great deal about the necessity to take public attitudes into account in carrying out the needed management programs.

Pennsylvania was one of the early states to confront an overpopulation of deer, and the figures there tell a dramatic story.

Alarmed sportsmen hamstrung the first big-scale antlerless season in 1928 with a series of court injunctions in many counties, in spite of glaring evidence of wholesale winter starvation and severe damage to farm crops. At that time, hunters were taking 10,000 to 14,000 bucks a year. (The 1907 kill had been only 200.)

Despite the opposition, 27,000 antlerless deer were killed in 1928, with the buck season closed, and sportsmen screamed the herd had been wiped out. But it yielded 23,000 bucks in 1929 and 20,000 in 1930. A year later, with both bucks and does legal, the kill soared to 25,000 bucks and 70,000 antlerless. And still there were too many deer for the land to support.

A still bigger kill came in 1938, with the season closed on antlered bucks once more, when hunters gathered in 171,000. At that point, the legislature stepped in with a law giving any county the right to veto antlerless seasons, a provision that stayed on the books

213

until 1951. The 1939 kill was 49,000 bucks and 14,500 antlerless, and in 1940 it shot up to 41,000 bucks and 145,000 antlerless.

In the twenty-two years from 1940 through 1962 Pennsylvania's "wiped out" herd yielded 780,000 bucks, an average of 35,000 a year, and, despite the handicap of the local-option county law, the antlerless kill had gone as high as 84,000 one year.

Today Pennsylvania has had seventeen consecutive antlerless hunting seasons, under a permit system. The number of permits issued in a year has gone as high as 482,500 and has never dropped below 202,000.

At the end of the seventeen-year period the state went into the 1973 hunting season with an estimated population of 570,000 white-tails. With 352,000 antlerless permits out, the buck kill was 70,000, the antlerless harvest 56,000. Hardly a record of extermination.

Opposition to antlerless hunting has virtually disappeared, and the Pennsylvania Game Commission even gets complaints that it is not issuing as many permits as it should.

Some idea of the size of the deer herd can be gained from the fact that the known road kill in 1972 and again in 1973 reached the staggering total of 26,000 animals annually. Some starvation losses still occur in hard winters. They mounted to 16,000 in the winter of 1969, in the fourteen-county area that state game men call their big-woods country.

I asked Dale Sheffer, chief of the Pennsylvania Division of Game Management, what accounted for his agency's apparent victory in the long deer war.

First, he said, state game protectors did all they could to sell the idea that antlerless harvests were necessary. Seminars were held all over the state and every effort was made to interest the non-hunting public as well as sportsmen's organizations.

Finally, Sheffer concluded with a chuckle, "Nothing succeeds like success."

The experience of many states in the last dozen years is closely parallel to that of Pennsylvania.

Take Oregon, for example. The doe-shooting rhubarb there erupted almost out of a clear sky in 1962. The deer kill had climbed steadily from 1948, and hunter success was growing better and better. Antlerless seasons were opened for the first time in 1952. That year 188,250 hunters took 77,659 deer, a score of 41 percent. Nine years later, after almost a decade of modern management practices that included generous seasons and the taking of both bucks and does, the 1961 season was the best on record. The harvest was a whopping 158,000 deer, taken by 265,000 hunters, a success score of 60 percent.

There had always been some individuals unalterably opposed to anything but a buck season, but Oregon game officials had every reason to believe that most of their hunters had accepted the modern way of handling a deer herd.

Then in 1962 the kill dropped by 26,000, and despite the fact that 50 percent of the hunters scored, a cold deer war suddenly turned hot.

A sportsmen's group was organized for the express purpose of battling game commission policies, branch chapters sprang up in several counties, public indignation meetings were held, and newspapers screamed, "Angry Hunters Protest Vanishing Deer Herds."

But the Oregon Wildlife Federation and the Oregon Division of the Izaak Walton League climbed into the game commission's corner, and a bill in the legislature that would have banned all killing of antlerless deer died in committee after months of wrangling.

Oregon still has antlerless seasons to control its blacktail deer population, and harvests on these animals stay high, but state game men have learned to trim their sails to suit the wind and there is very little opposition.

No permits for the taking of antlerless mule deer have been issued since 1971. The muley population is declining, as a result of changes of habitat, weather factors and predation. A state game official told me frankly that it makes no sense politically to harvest does when a deer herd is going downhill.

In the early days, Wisconsin game men fought a battle every time they opened a season of deer of either sex. Now, after years of controversy, they have finally discovered a workable formula for winning public support for their program of deer management. It represents a sensible compromise between what the game biologists may think desirable and what sportsmen will tolerate.

The goal of state game officials is a kill of 75,000 to 100,000 a year, depending on the size and condition of the herd. The buck kill in recent years has held steady at about 50,000 annually; the antlerless kill has gone up and down according to the number of permits issued.

The regulations each year are set after a meeting attended by delegates representing the Wisconsin Conservation Congress (the state's major sportsmen's organization) and biologists and game managers from the Department of Natural Resources.

The meeting, held when all possible information on the deer herd is in, may open with the DNR people advocating a quota of 25,000 antlerless permits. Sportsmen delegates may counter with a proposal for half that many. Neither side gets its own way completely. A friendly compromise is hammered out, and because hunters have had a hand in framing the regulations, in general they support the final decision. The angry deer wars of the past appear to be ended in Wisconsin.

California is another state that has had major controversies over doe shooting. Now it has settled on one basic rule: A game department must have public support.

Plagued by a series of poor seasons (1973 was the poorest ever), California has been cutting down on its antlerless hunts.

"We are striving to regain the trust and confidence of sportsmen and the general public," a wildlife management official told me.

When this report was written, California was in the process of drafting a new deer management program, utilizing the suggestions of some 800 employees of the Fish and Game Commission, including all field men. The program will provide for close cooperation with the U. S. Forest Service and the Bureau of Land Management, the two federal agencies that own much of the big-game lands in the state. It will provide for equally close cooperation with the sportsmen.

"We expect to use antlerless hunts where they are needed," says E. G. Hunt, chief of wildlife management, "but first we will convince the public of the need."

New York has been using a party permit system to achieve harvests of antlerless deer since 1960, and the program has been a success in the central and western sections of the state.

In the Catskill and Adirondack mountains, however (more than 21,000 square miles of deer range), forest cutting is prohibited by law in the forest preserves, and there are large areas of poor deer habitat. The hands of the Division of Fish and Wildlife are tied by legislation, and opposition to antlerless harvests has blocked all efforts at management of the deer population in these areas in recent years.

"There are indications that public attitudes are changing in the direction of support for antlerless hunting," a New York deer biologist told me. "However, we still have much public relations work ahead of us before we can reinstitute antlerless hunts in the areas where they are most needed."

Many states say that weather has more to do with the size of their deer herd than hunting. Minnesota is a case in point.

For years that state hunted under any-deer rules and things went along fine. Then starting in 1965, came a series of six extremely hard winters, including two that were the worst on record. The whitetail population nosedived, and in 1970 the game department sent shock waves through hunting circles by limiting the season to two days.

The plan was not a rousing success. In those two frantic days 200,000 hunters fanned out in the Minnesota deer woods. The result was a kill heavier than was desired and a hunt of poor quality. In 1971 the department took the drastic action of closing the season outright.

It was reopened in 1972, an entirely new ball game. To spread out and reduce hunting pressure, a thirty-day framework of open seasons was set. During the first fifteen of those thirty days the individual hunter could choose three consecutive days and buy a license for those three only. During the second half of the season he could have his choice of five consecutive days.

The plan is still in effect. The greatly curtailed hunting period shocked Minnesota hunters into an awareness of the state's sudden deer crisis, and also served to stave off bills in the legislature that would have kept the season closed indefinitely.

Until 1973 Minnesota kept its any-deer rule. That year, because of the large numbers of hunters in the woods in 1972, part of the hunt was any-deer. But in the poorer areas hunting was limited to bucks-only, as an experiment.

Deer now average fifteen to the square mile in the better range, about ten in the bucks-only zone. And Roger Holmes, state supervisor of game, believes that 80 percent of Minnesota hunters approve the present management policy.

I doubt that any state has had a more unhappy experience with its deer-management program than Michigan, where I live and have done the bulk of my hunting.

Up to a dozen years ago the Michigan story was a typical one. Between 1900 and 1910, following the logging era, fires that burned millions of acres, and decades of market hunting, the state's deer herd was at a very low point. By 1921, fires were being controlled, cutover lands were growing up, and a buck law was passed to help bring the herd back. A statewide conservation movement was getting under way at that same time, and the new law took deep root.

By 1925, Michigan's best areas were getting close to the hunter's dream of a deer behind every bush. Then something went wrong. Browsed-out yards began to show up; starved deer were found at the end of every hard winter; and game men realized that a major headache was shaping up. In the next twenty-five years, Michigan's bare-cupboard areas, where deer had eaten themselves out of food, soared from 100 to 16,000 square miles, and losses grew to staggering size. In a year when hunters killed 70,000 bucks, for example, starvation victims and illegally-shot does and fawns were estimated to total more than 100,000.

Meantime, the deer war was on. Game experts, striving to bring

These Oregon deer died of starvation at the site where a private club had attempted to help them through the winter by feeding them alfalfa. Unfortunately, such feeding usually fails.

the overgrown herd into balance with its food supply, began to press for doe shooting. But a majority of hunters, convinced that the buck law had saved the herd and only the buck law could preserve it, fought the proposal tooth and nail.

The ice was broken in 1941, when legislators who had visited deer yards in spring and counted dead deer sparked a law permitting parties of four or more hunters to take a doe or fawn for camp use. The resulting kill totaled 17,000, and deer-country residents were outraged. Newspapers even predicted it would be 10 years before Michigan would have any deer hunting again. The law was repealed.

The next major break came in 1952, when a three-day, any-deer season was opened in the northern half of the lower peninsula, following regular buck season. Hunters took 66,500 bucks and 94,500 antlerless, by far the biggest kill ever recorded in the state. The roof fell in. Many sportsmen sincerely believed the herd had been destroyed. The Conservation Department received a flood of furious letters, including one signed in doe blood, and scores of protest meetings were held. The outcry forced the department to back down. Doe shooting was put on a permit basis the next year, and the antlerless kill fell to 26,000. The next year it was only 7,500, and in 1955 Michigan went to bucks-only for a year.

After that there were good years and bad. When the kill was high something like six hunters out of ten favored the program of the Conservation Department, now called the Department of Natural Resources. When bad weather or other factors sent hunter success plummeting (in 1960, in the face of continuous rain, the harvest totaled less than 72,000, the poorest season in years) six out of ten demanded doe protection. It was plain that the deer war had not been won.

Early in the 1960's opposition began to harden into outrage and bitter hostility, especially in the Upper Peninsula, which had long provided the state's best hunting.

As the herd declined, the storm grew. Biologists blamed failing habitat and hard winters; sportsmen charged doe killing. County boards of supervisors passed ordinances to ban doe shooting but the courts ruled them invalid. Members of the legislature brought injunction suits to stop the antlerless seasons, but the suits failed.

On the eve of summer adjournment in 1973 the legislature rammed through a bill limiting the Upper Peninsula to bucks-only hunting and stripping the DNR of all authority to set regulations.

Gene Gazley, DNR director, fanned the fire by calling on Governor William Milliken to veto the bill. The Governor acceded to the request. And 18,000 antlerless permits were issued for the Upper Peninsula, in the face of ugly threats that doe hunters would be refused gasoline, restaurant meals and motel accommodations.

Early in 1974 the legislature struck back where it hurt most. It refused a DNR request for a hike in fishing license fees, and the agency was left $1,000,000 short in operating funds for the next year.

At that point the game authorities finally capitulated. Gazley announced that antlerless hunting was at an end in the Upper Peninsula for the foreseeable future. Will the badly depleted herd now make a comeback? No one can say.

Doe shooting will continue in the southern farming counties of the state, where road kills total more than 2,000 in six months and where damage to farm crops and orchards is a problem. And a limited number of antlerless permits will also be issued for those northern counties of the Lower Peninsula where game men believe the deer herd is still too big for the range to support in winter.

What many sportsmen do not realize is that not only the numbers of deer but their size and quality drop fast when food is limited.

In the farmlands of southern Michigan, where food is abundant, nineteen out of twenty bucks carry racks or forkhorns when they are only eighteen months old, and many at that age are eight-point trophies good enough to hang over any hunter's fireplace. In the browse-short areas farther north, only six eighteen-month-old bucks in twenty are better than spikehorns, and it's not rare to find even 2½-year-olds with spikes less than three inches long. It may seem strange, but if hunters want trophy bucks they must sometimes put up with doe shooting.

Scarcity of food is just as hard on the does, too, and results in a poor fawn crop. Michigan has learned that ten does, not starved but poorly fed, will produce an average of thirteen fawns a year, while the same number in a prime food area produce twenty.

What are the reasons behind the stubborn resistance to doe shooting, regardless of sound evidence that a deer herd has grown too big for its food supply? Why does that resistance die so hard? Why do so many sportsmen, willing to hunt most kinds of game without quibbling about sex, balk at the mere suggestion of killing a female deer? Why will they accept almost every other concept of game management but refuse to believe that there can be too many deer on a range?

Probably mostly because of a sentimental belief that does are in a category by themselves, on a pedestal, too good for shooting. It's a tradition that comes down from the years when buck laws were applauded as a means of restoring shot-out herds and the man who killed a doe was a poacher beneath contempt. Under today's conditions, that's a badly outworn tradition.

Game authorities call it, "The Fable of the Sacred Doe." And coupled with it is the honest fear that any doe shooting will doom a herd, despite all the proof to the contrary.

Dr. Ira Gabrielson, one of the country's foremost conservationists a generation ago, once told me that he thought the buck-law tradition was more to blame than any other factor.

"The idea was oversold," he said. "Many states preached that it was immoral to kill a doe, and sportsmen believed them."

"I'm convinced mentally but not emotionally," was the way

This splendid California mule buck died of starvation.

California Dept. of Fish and Game photo

one Michigan newspaper editor put it after a spirited public hearing. Another editor said bluntly, "I'd be almost as reluctant to shoot a doe as I would my own mother."

On the other hand, Tom Kimball, executive vice-president of the National Wildlife Federation, lays the blame chiefly on the game authorities themselves. Far too often they have failed to do an adequate job of selling their programs to the public, he thinks.

The basic problem is simple enough for any hunter to understand. Just as one hundred acres of pasture can support only a certain number of cattle or sheep, so a square mile of deer range can furnish food for only so many deer. The number will depend on the kind and abundance of food available, but, in every case, a given area has a fixed carrying capacity. When that is exceeded, trouble is inevitable. State after state has demonstrated that fact with staggering starvation losses. And to make matters worse, the surplus animals over-browse the range before they finally perish, so that year by year the range can carry fewer and fewer deer.

As a Texas biologist points out, the rancher who removed only a certain share of his male livestock each year and left all the females to reproduce until they died of old age would soon be bankrupt. The same rule can apply to a deer herd.

Maybe the most encouraging thing about the whole problem is the fact that although deer wars still flare and there are occasional setbacks, game departments, with few exceptions, say the situation is getting better.

The lessons of the whole angry affair are obvious. The Fable of the Sacred Doe is no more than a fable. Under certain circumstances the hunting of female deer is essential to keep a herd in balance with its food supply and prevent long-lasting damage to the range.

But it is equally necessary for game authorities to take public attitudes into account, to avoid flying in the face of overwhelming and honest, even if misguided, opposition. Authorities should sell deer-management programs before they are put into effect. They should remember, too, what Oregon officials say: When a herd is going downhill, it is hardly wise to arouse the anger of sportsmen with doe seasons.

Finding Wounded Deer

Ray Beck

The fellow on the big pudding stone raised his rifle and shot. Once. Twice. Three times. Because of the young hemlocks, I couldn't see the deer he was shooting at, but I figured it would be coming my way. I eased the hammer back and waited. In a couple of seconds a frightened doe rushed by the rock I was standing on, never even noticing me. I waited, thinking a buck might be following, but none appeared.

I was as sure that doe didn't have antlers as though I had just given her a shampoo, but I knew there was no use chewing the guy out about shooting at her. He'd insist that he saw horns, and I couldn't prove otherwise.

Later, after the hunter left, I back-tracked the doe to see if I could

This chapter originally appeared in the September 1956 issue of *Outdoor Life* under the title "How to Find Wounded Deer."

find any hair or blood spots showing she'd been hit. About 200 yards from the stone from which the stranger fired I found a six-point buck with a hole in its ribs. More back-tracking showed it had come nearly 100 yards after being shot through the heart.

Locating an unknown hunter in the Allegheny National Forest of Pennsylvania in deer season was out of the question, so a soldier in our party who had to start back to camp the following day put his tag on the buck and took it home. It wasn't the way he wanted to get his deer, but ninety pounds of venison wasn't to be turned down in those meat-shy days of 1944.

If the fellow who shot that buck is still hunting, I hope he's learned by now that it pays to investigate.

It would be hard to estimate how many fatally wounded deer are lost each season. In this and similar cases, the hunter never realizes he connected. In others, he believes the wound superficial and doesn't try to trail the deer. Most common of all is the hunter who defeats himself by driving the wounded animal too hard.

When the deer you shoot at keeps going, the first thing you want to know is whether you hit it at all. That's easy. Deer hair is brittle, and a bullet anywhere but the lower legs will knock off a lot of hair. Don't let the absence of blood fool you. The wound may not bleed for five or ten seconds, or the animal may bleed internally.

Like most condensed pieces of wisdom, the saying that a wounded deer always pulls its flag down, isn't always true. A wounded deer usually runs with its tail down, but the tail doesn't work automatically like lights on a pinball machine. A frightened deer may not feel the bullet for a few seconds. This is especially true when there's no shock of bones being struck, and when the bullet fails to expand properly. A deer hit in the legs will often run with its tail up, and occasionally a badly terrified one will run with its tail down when it hasn't been hit at all.

The deer's response to your shot gives you a pretty good clue as to where the bullet went. If the animal jumps straight into the air, you probably shot too low. A few hairs suggest that you just creased its belly. No hair means that you missed entirely but came very close—or else you shot so low the bullet threw dirt up and stung the deer. If there's considerable hair and some blood along the trail, you've paunched the animal low down.

In 1954 my nephew shot at a standing buck which reared up, turned around, and went back the way it had come. Later in the day the deer was killed, and we found that his bullet had cut a crease through the chest hair without breaking the skin.

A deer that drops at the crack of the gun, then regains its feet and bounds away apparently unhurt was probably creased across

A deer rearing with the shot may be grazed in the front or lower part of his body—or just stung by flying dirt.

When the tracks of a wounded deer show drag marks, the deer is wounded in the dragging leg.

Hit in the paunch, a deer hunches up, usually drops his tail, and then heads for cover.

Many hunters have been surprised to find that their trophy kill was only stunned by a creasing slug.

the back. There will be plenty of hair but little or no blood, and the deer is practically uninjured. A deer which goes down and then regains its feet with difficulty is most likely paunched.

If your deer drops at the crack of the gun as though struck by lightning, you probably made a perfect shot. But don't waste any time getting to it. Every season "dead" deer come to life and get away. A bullet striking an antler, creasing the skull, or nicking a vertebra will knock a deer cold, but when the deer comes to it's unhampered by the minor wound. Hunters used to capture wild horses by knocking them out with a bullet high in the neck.

If the deer you shoot at gives no indication of being hit, yet quantities of loose hair say otherwise, you have a problem on your hands. Not all deer flinch when hit. So did you hit it solidly or only crease it?

A lot of old-timers advocate waiting an hour to give such a deer time to calm down if it's just frightened, or to lie down and stiffen if it's wounded. A better plan is to follow the trail a quarter of a mile or so. The deer ordinarily won't stop within that distance unless it's too weak to go farther. If it keeps going, you should have a pretty fair idea of the extent of its injuries by its tracks and blood spots, if any. Then you can lay your plans accordingly, and decide what course of action to follow.

A keen student of animal behavior can predict very accurately what deer wounded in different ways will do. After deer season in 1939 Bill Best and I were hunting foxes in the Allegheny National Forest east of Marienville, Pennsylvania. It's a country of big rocks, bracken, and quaking aspens, but halfway up this particular mountainside is a five-acre patch of scrub hemlocks.

Pointing toward these evergreens, Bill said, "I'll bet a dollar there's a dead deer in there, and I'll bet another dollar I can tell you where it was hit."

I figured I was a pretty good woodsman, but I couldn't see anything to indicate a dead deer in a patch of brush half a mile away. Even so, how could anybody tell where it had been shot? We hadn't hunted that section, so I knew Bill hadn't found the deer previously. I also knew I was going to lose two dollars.

"Okay!" I said, "We'll settle the stakes when we sell the furs. Now where was it hit?"

"Gut-shot," Bill said.

The deer wasn't hard to find. The foxes had the snow tramped down all around it, but they were too suspicious to come closer than ten or twelve feet. As Bill had predicted, there was a hole back of the ribs. Near the other end of the brush patch was another doe with a bullet hole in practically the same place.

Bill said, "I guess I'll have to explain it to you so you can get your mind back on fox hunting. A gut-shot deer wants to hide. It will leave the rest of the herd, get into the thickest cover it can find, and lie down. Soon it's too weak and stiff to get up, and it dies there. But if it's kept on its feet, it can go for miles. That's why you should give a gut-shot deer time to lie down before you follow it. Those hemlocks are the only good cover within two or three miles, so any gut-shot deer in this area would be there."

"I can see that," I admitted, "but deer get shot in the legs too. How did you know we wouldn't find one in there with broken legs?"

"That's easy," he told me. "A deer with a broken hind leg can travel down hill easier, and it ends up down along the creek without the strength to climb. Deer with a broken hind leg usually die, but deer with a broken front leg get along pretty well so long as they don't have to go downhill. Any deer around here with a broken front leg will be sticking to level ridgetops or flat bottoms, not hanging along the sides of a mountain where it's likely to upset if it tries to run. Any more questions?"

"Yes," I said. "How did you know there were any deer here at all?"

"Oh, that was easiest of all," he grinned. "We're about three miles from the road, and in doe season there are a lot of hunters, and there's the creek. A deer can cross the creek, but a man would have to make a five-mile detour. So when a wounded deer gets on this side of the stream nobody chases it any more."

A paunched deer which slows to a walk within a quarter of a mile has probably been hit in the liver or kidneys and won't go much farther. The old-timers used to say that if a wounded deer wasn't chased it would walk twice as far as it had run and then lie down. The rule is fairly accurate for paunched animals, providing there's a place to hide within that distance.

A deer hit in the liver or kidneys with anything in the .30/30 class or heavier will be dead or unable to regain its feet in an hour. Shot through the stomach or entrails, it will take three times as long to stiffen up.

If you paunch a deer in late afternoon, let it go till morning. Even if there's no snow, you'll probably find it without much trouble by searching the thickets and windfalls in the direction the animal headed. It won't travel far if it isn't chased.

Where the woods are full of hunters, however, it's sometimes a matter of following the deer right away or having some other hunter cut in ahead of you. The best method under these conditions is to follow the deer till it enters a thicket, then circle around to the other side to see if it came out. If it's still in the thicket, begin at the side opposite where the deer entered, and work back, taking plenty of time, and being as quiet as possible. The deer will be watching its back trail, and it won't be as alert as an uninjured one, so you have a fair chance of seeing it first. If some other hunter follows the tracks into the brush, he's quite likely to drive the deer to you.

When a party of hunters are working together, one should take the trail while the others spread out on each side, staying just close enough to keep track of the man doing the trailing. Since the deer will most likely double back to where it can watch its trail, the flankers have a better chance than the man on the track. As you approach promising thickets, at least one man should circle ahead to be in a position to get a shot if the deer runs.

If it heads for a river or creek you can't cross, stop and wait. Unless it's driven, a wounded animal is reluctant to enter the water.

I'll never forget the time a kid in our party put a shotgun slug behind the ribs of a buck along the Clarion River, a few miles below the power dam. The buck was hit hard, and if left alone he'd probably have crawled into the nearest thicket and died. But it was the kid's first deer, and he chased that buck like a greyhound after a rabbit. This foolish zeal drove the deer into the river. It fell dead on the opposite shore.

To reach that buck, we first drove to a bridge — six miles over a bumpy dirt road where the axle dragged most of the way. Having crossed the river, we hiked to the deer and then dragged it two miles uphill through laurel brush so thick a man could hardly walk.

It was after dark by the time we got the buck to the car. Then we got hung up trying to drive back another way, which turned out to be worse. We had to back-track and didn't get home till nearly midnight.

If that deer had just been left alone for an hour it would have died on our side of the river.

Deer with broken legs are less common than paunched animals, but you actually see a lot more of them. The reason is that a deer with a broken leg continues to travel about, while paunched animals crawl into a thicket and die where their remains are very seldom found.

Tracks will indicate if a leg is broken, and which one. A deer with a broken hind leg has lost a lot of its driving power, and while you can't run it down, it tires rapidly. Before long it will turn downhill. It gets along pretty well going down, but it can't climb efficiently and ordinarily won't try.

To get a deer wounded in this way, station a couple of your party where they can watch the bottom of the valley, then drive the deer toward them. Most likely it will move down the valley, keeping the levelest course possible. If it does try to climb, it will move so slowly and awkwardly that somebody should get a shot. If a deer with a broken hind leg escapes because of a blizzard or darkness, it can usually be located the next day by searching the bottoms of near-by valleys and ravines. Always do your utmost to recover a deer with a broken hind leg, as very few survive.

A broken front leg, however, is not so serious. The first deer I ever shot had a completely healed break in one front leg. It was easily keeping up with the rest of the herd at the time I shot it.

A deer with a bullet-broken front leg can run uphill or on the level nearly as well as any, but it has trouble running downhill. The best way to get a deer with a broken front leg is for one of the party to follow it while the others wait at stands chosen to take advantage of the animal's reluctance to run downhill. If this strategy fails, chances are you'll never catch up with the deer. Unless there's a tracking snow, an extended hunt for a deer with a broken front leg is usually hopeless.

Sometimes a deer is wounded in the brisket, or the fleshy parts of the legs without breaking any bones. Such wounds aren't serious, but they may bleed enough to mark the track plainly. One of the party should follow it while the others wait at likely locations. If the deer escapes, it will most likely recover.

A deer wounded in the fleshy part of a leg will use the leg, but not lift it as high as the other. If one leg is being dragged through the snow after each step, you can figure there's a hampering flesh wound on that leg.

We can't possibly recover every wounded animal, but spending a little time and effort could cut the losses considerably. There's no excuse for such shameful sights as I saw in the spring of 1952 while trout fishing—seven dead deer within a mile, in the brush along Little Salmon Creek.

An outdoor column in a local paper had recently told of large numbers of deer starving in the Allegheny National Forest, so I examined these seven with that in mind. Two of them—one an old gummer doe whose teeth were too worn to chew browse—apparently starved. But three had been paunch-shot, and two had broken hind legs.

By using the systems we've just discussed, hunters could have recovered these five wounded deer, converting them into venison instead of leaving them as carrion in the woods.

Field-dressing and Care

Clyde Ormond

What you do within the first half hour or so after you've downed a deer will largely determine whether you get home with sweet, edible venison or something hardly fit to eat.

Immediately after a deer is dead, several natural factors or agents begin to act adversely upon the flesh and, if not opposed, will quickly spoil the meat. These are (1) animal heat, (2) taints from body fluids and fermentations, (3) blowflies, (4) scavenger birds and animals, and (5) time. All these "enemies" of good meat may be thwarted with simple care, while performing two fundamental procedures—"hog-dressing" the animal cleanly and quickly and then immediately hanging it off the ground to cool, with appropriate protection against blowflies and predators.

The first vital "step" in ensuring good venison is to avoid gut-

This chapter was written especially for this book.

229

shooting the animal. A bullet-punctured abdomen spills out intestinal fluids and nauseating paunch contents; and the taint resulting from their contact with flesh is almost impossible to remove.

Once the deer is dead, lay it on its back and prop it in position by wedging rocks or wood chunks along its sides. Then, careful to avoid getting musky taint on your hands, remove the metatarsal glands found on both sexes inside and outside the hind legs below the hocks. (This is a precaution against later tainting your hands and then the meat.) For removal, cut the skin around each "fluffy" appearing gland and then skin it off.

With a doe, next cut around both anus and genitals as deep as possible into the rear orifice of the pelvic bone without puncturing organs or intestinal walls. Then tie off natural openings with a string or hem of a handkerchief. This important step prevents urine or excreta from escaping and possibly running onto the meat.

With a buck, first slice off the testes. Then tie off the penis an inch or so from the front. Cut the skin around the base of the penis so as to leave a thin strip running toward the anus. With this skin attached, carefully cut the penis away—back to where it enters the pelvic bone at the rear. At the junction with the bone, carefully separate, or "peel" the tissues away from the bone with the tip of the knife. Then, as with a doe, girdle-cut and tie off the anus.

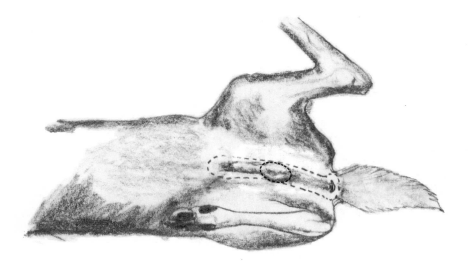

This drawing shows the initial cutting patterns for field-dressing a buck.

Now, with buck or doe, you can cut away the abdomen from pelvis to rib cage. This is done by lifting the abdominal muscles at the forward end of the pelvis, and carefully making a small slit lengthwise. To do this, form a "V" with the index and second finger of your free hand and insert your fingers, "V" forward, wedging the muscles and hide away from the "insides" to facilitate cutting with the point of the knife. This way you don't puncture the intestines. The abdominal cut ends at the rib cage. When you wish to quarter the animal, it is possible to split the ribs with an ax and continue the cut all the way to the throat. This is necessary only with huge deer in backcountry and will spoil the cape in the event you later want to mount your trophy.

Next, by depressing the exposed stomach, and pressing it sidewise, you can see the diaphragm, which separates the chest and abdominal cavities. Cutting the diaphragm away from the ribs is a bit tricky, since there is limited space in which to work with the knife. For best going, do one side completely before starting the other.

With the diaphragm girdled all around, the chest cavity is opened. Next, reach up into the opened chest and then into the neck to grasp both the gullet and windpipe. Pull down on them as hard as possible, eliminating slack, and with the knife in the other hand sever them.

With the gullet and windpipe still in your grasp, pull sharply back. This action will strip the lungs and heart away from the backbone. Continue this stripping motion, next pulling the intestines and stomach downward and out of the animal. You'll have to perform a small amount of judicious cutting to separate the tissues holding the remaining "insides" to the backbone. But most of this separating can be done simply by pulling.

With the insides "rolled" out of the animal all the way to the pelvis, there remains only one important step to complete dressing —that of removing the colon and genitals from inside the bony pelvis. If you initially cut around the anus deeply enough, most of the remaining separation may be done with your fingers. To do this insert the index and second finger alongside the colon (lower end of large intestine) at the top of the pelvis until you feel the connecting tissues. Then simply pull these string-like tissues free all around the colon.

Occasionally, you may have to cut around the anus at the rear end and work the stubborn tissues free with your fingers. With this done, a pull forward on the colon at the front of the pelvis will "strip out" both colon and genitals—still attached to the other viscera. Wipe or dip any remaining blood out of the carcass.

With this, you've "hog-dressed" your deer. All you needed was a little know-how, a piece of string, and a sharp knife of medium size and thin-blade.

If you down a huge buck in rugged backcountry, you may have to quarter the animal and pack it out on a packboard. But for the average hunter and normal conditions, hog-dressing and transporting the whole animal are standard.

When in heavily hunted areas, when in mild weather, or when there is only a short distance to camp, many hunters will immediately drag, haul, pack, or otherwise transport their freshly-dressed deer to camp. This is not advisable.

Moving freshly killed meat fevers it, and allows remaining body juices and blood to work into it, causing taint. This is especially true during warm or mild hunting weather. It is far better to hang the dressed deer on the spot and allow it to cool for several hours — overnight if necessary — before getting it to camp. Also, it's wise to move scavenger-attracting offal away from the carcass.

Hanging your dressed deer is the second, basic phase in field care. Body heat is one of the biggest causes of meat spoilage. This heat will ruin fresh meat in a matter of hours. Dressing the animal eliminates a great deal of the heat. Hanging the deer will drain off remaining body juices and blood, and, with air circulating all around, will speed the job of cooling. In order to cool out, the entire carcass must be completely off the ground.

To hang a deer it's best to have the help of a hunting partner. Tie a rope around the antlers or neck and toss the free end over a suitable limb. While one of you hoists upward on the carcass, the other pulls down on the rope. When the rump clears the ground, secure the rope.

The best position in which to hang a deer is not by the hind legs from a gambrel, as with domestic meat. A deer is best hung by the antlers or head. This position allows remaining blood and body juices to drain away. In case of rain or snow, the grain of the hair and position of the body will cause the water to drain away from, not into, the body cavity. More, a head-hung deer does not allow scavenger birds such as magpies, jays, and camp-robbers as much convenience in getting at the exposed meat.

If you are alone, there are several ways to hang a dressed deer, even a whopper, by yourself.

One simple aid is a tiny, light block-and-tackle. You can buy commercial models designed especially for the purpose, or you can make your own out of two light aluminum two-pulley blocks and thirty feet of light nylon rope. You can carry these in your rucksack, and they'll help you hoist the heaviest buck easily.

Another way of getting the dressed deer off the ground is to utilize a steep hillside in timbered country. Pull the dressed deer to the *uphill* side of a suitable tree. Tie the animal's head as high to the tree as you can lift it by the antlers or head. When the head is tied, swing the body around to the *downhill* side of the tree. You can gain up to three feet of height this way. If the rump still touches the ground, prop it up with branches. Or you can hold the rump off the ground by tying the feet with rope and staking them away from the tree.

Another good way to hang a heavy buck is based on principles behind the old-fashioned steelyard balance. Tie an eight-foot length of light rope (¼-inch hemp or nylon rope, testing 500 pounds) to the tip of a twelve-foot pole and then tie a four-foot length to the butt of the pole. Secure a third length of rope as high as you can reach on a tree, and tie the free end to the pole at a point four feet from the butt.

With the three ropes tied, drag the deer under the butt of the pole. Swing the butt downward until the pole rises almost vertically. Then raise the deer's head as high as possible before tying it with the length of rope at the butt.

Lastly, grasp the rope tied to the tip end of the pole (which is now high in the air) and pull downward as though tolling a church bell. As the tip comes downward, from about twelve feet, the leverage lifts the buck up off the ground. Since the mechanical advantage is approximately two to one, your weight can probably lift the heaviest deer. I once hung a 250-pound trophy mule deer in this

This rig allows a man to raise an animal twice his own weight.

This hunter raises a buck by pulling each pole in a foot or so in rotation.

fashion with little trouble. Once you have brought the tip of the pole to the ground, tie it to a bush or to a previously driven stake.

In timber country, such as the jack-pine country of the West, you can lift a heavy deer off the earth with a tripod. To do this, sharpen three nine-foot poles on the butt end. With the pole tips laid over the dressed deer's head, spread the poles equidistant apart, like spokes of a wheel.

Then lash the three tips together immediately over the animal's head. Next tie the head or antlers closely to the lashing of the pole tips. Standing over the head, lift as high upward as you can, raising the head and the pole tips. The average hunter can raise this assembly to a height of two or two-and-a-half feet.

At this point if the butt ends are sharp, all three poles will "stick" temporarily in the ground, and the tripod will support the head and neck. Then you can pull one pole butt at a time toward the deer a foot or so before thrusting the butt again into the earth. Then in rotation, repeat the procedure, gradually raising the tips of the tripod until the deer hangs free.

With any method of hanging, a carcass should be in the shade. Shade allows faster cooling, and helps discourage blowflies.

If you should kill a large deer in semi-open, brushy country, hanging is out of the question. But a brush pile will serve much the same purpose. Gather a high pile of brush and lay the animal, cavity upward, on top of the pile. A meager amount of brush won't do the job. The pile must be large enough and high enough so that the weight of the deer upon it won't depress it to a thickness of less than eighteen inches. The point is, air must circulate all around the animal, and this requires a lot of brush.

With the deer dressed and hung, you should perform one more vital step before leaving the animal to cool while you go to camp for help. You should protect the exposed flesh from blowflies, birds and animals.

If you carry three yards of common cheesecloth, you can cut off one yard of this to use for wiping blood, fluids or stuck-on hair from the body cavity. Then drape or tie the remaining two yards to cover the open cavity from the rib cage to the anal opening. Cheesecloth will stick to moist flesh if pressed against it, and will "hang" well on any bone chips.

Before placing the cheesecloth over the open cavity, on either a hung deer or a deer laid on a brush pile, you should spread the cavity open with a "spreader stick"—a fourteen-inch stick sharpened at each end, and stuck into the opposing abdominal walls midway up the cavity.

If you don't carry cheesecloth, it's best to insert the spreader-stick and then weave a few boughs loosely around it to discourage birds and blowflies. But be sure that your bough covering of the cavity isn't so thick that it prevents good air circulation.

There is one additional blowfly deterrent that will help you preserve your venison. That is a small can of black pepper. After dressing, wiping, and hanging the deer, you should pepper the exposed flesh thoroughly. Be especially sure to pepper the "wettest" areas before draping the cheesecloth. Blowflies are the worst in mild or hot weather and need moisture and warmth in which to work. Black pepper hastens the formation of a dry crust on the flesh and thus prevents blowfly damage.

Coyotes won't bother a hung deer for the first twenty-four hours, especially if you leave a "scare piece" such as an empty cartridge or your handkerchief right beside the hung animal. Coyotes hate man's scent.

After you bring the cooled carcass home or take it to cold storage, you should skin it and remove hairs from the meat. Then trim out all bloody areas or blood clots. Carefully trim away damaged tissues in areas around bullet wounds. And then give the entire carcass a meticulous "cleanup" by wiping away wet or bloody areas with a dry cloth.

Before you butcher the carcass, it should be hung in a room at around 40 degrees for at least a week. This allows the meat fibers to break down and become tender. When the outside of the carcass first shows signs of "slickness," it is ready for butchering and freezing.

Incidentally, one of the best uses for less desirable cuts and clean trimmings is deer salami.

This unusually fine typical whitetail scored 205, by Boone and Crockett Club standards. The world's record is 206⅝. Overall symmetry is broken only by unequal lengths of the brow tines and the acorn-shaped end of one point.

With only a few abnormal points, this typical mule deer scored 196²/₈ as compared to the world's record 226. Note the bullet hole through the left-most antler in the photo.

Measuring and Scoring Trophies

Wm. H. Nesbitt

I t's a huge buck—one of the largest of all time—and it's all yours! But just how large is it really? You can take a picture to show your friends, but even a photo will need some perspective to convey the relative size of the trophy. And, just how does your trophy stack up against all others ever taken? The answer is easy. You can measure your trophy by the Boone and Crockett Club system to arrive at a numerical score that can be compared to the all-time best listed in the records book. The Club's method is the only universally accepted system of measurement for native North American big game.

Down through the years, many systems of trophy evaluation have been proposed. Such proposals have favored body weight, body length, the number of points, horn characteristics, and combinations of such factors. But long use has proven the Boone and Crockett

This chapter was written especially for this book.

Club system of measurement of antlers, horns, or skulls to be a workable one. Under this system remeasurement of trophies can be done at any time to confirm or reestablish a ranking—this due to the enduring quality of the measured features. Remeasuring would not be possible if body weight or length were part of the system. Besides, weight and length measurement would be difficult to apply consistently, especially regarding heavy game taken deep in the wilderness that would require quartering and extended transport.

The current Boone and Crockett Club system of measurement evolved from several viewpoints over a period of years. The system was described by Grancel Fitz in 1963 in his book, *How to Measure and Score Big-game Trophies*. Fitz, a long-time friend of the Club and developer of a major viewpoint of trophy measuring, was commissioned by the Club to help establish the current system. The final format combined the best ideas of Fitz, Dr. James L. Clark and others who had long been interested in preserving big-game records for posterity.

Since its first formal recognition of outstanding trophies in 1932, the Boone and Crockett Club has held fourteen competitions for native North American big game. In 1973, the Club signed an agreement with the National Rifle Association of America to jointly sponsor future competitions under the name of the *North American Big Game Awards Program*. The word "Awards" was substituted for "Competitions" in order to better state the purpose of the program, that of awarding recognition to the outstanding native big game. The Fifteenth Awards, 1971-1973, was the first to be jointly held. The Club continues to set the standards for the programs, while the NRA performs the everyday administrative duties. Each awards program covers a three-year period of trophy registration. The finest trophies registered are eligible for medal and/or certificate awards. All accepted trophies are listed in the records book, *North American Big Game*.

Today, twenty-seven categories of huntable native big game occurring north of the south boundary of Mexico are eligible for the records book. None of them are endangered or protected from hunting. Of course, all trophies registered must be shown to have been taken in full compliance with all existing laws and in full compliance with the Club's tenets of fair chase. The "Fair Chase Statement," signed by the hunter before the trophy can be registered, states that the animal was not taken by air spotting followed by landing in the trophy's vicinity, by pursuing or herding with motor vehicle, or by using electronic communication or attractant devices. Certainly, the statement is not foolproof, but it does place the hunter on his honor in taking his trophy.

The joining of efforts by the two organizations is highly appropriate. Both have long advocated the benefits of selective trophy hunting. Both sponsor numerous wildlife and ecological research projects each year in universities across the nation and throughout the world. And both are deeply committed to the promotion of sportsmanship and fair chase in all types of hunting and to the continued support of sport hunting as a necessary and vital tool of modern game management.

The records book, *North American Big Game,* periodically summarizes the data of accepted entries. It is valuable and interesting reading for the hunter and serious student of big-game populations. The 1973 printing contains the listing of trophies above the 1968 minimum scores, complete through the Boone and Crockett Fourteenth Competition.

Hunters utilizing bow and arrow to hunt big game have a choice in listing their trophies. Such trophies are, of course, eligible for listing in *North American Big Game.* Additionally, they are eligible for the Pope and Young Club Awards and records. Patterned strongly after the Boone and Crockett Club system, the Pope and Young records use the same score charts but allow slightly lower minimum scores.

Most hunters are readily familiar with the two basic deer types of North America—whitetail and mule. Whitetails are characterized by their antler form of a distinct main beam, with the points branching from the beam. Mule deer show a Y-shaped or branching pattern in each beam, with no distinct main beam as in whitetails. In both, antlers are a secondary sex characteristic of the male. The occasional female with antlers can be likened to a bearded lady.

Two geographic races of the whitetail (*Odocoileus virginianus*) are recognized for records keeping. The common whitetail, with a live weight of up to several hundred pounds, is widely distributed from Mexico into the Canadian provinces. It is easily our best known and most popular big-game animal. Less known but very popular where it occurs is the Arizona whitetail or Coues deer (pronounced *cows*). This miniature whitetail is confined to Arizona, southern New Mexico and northwestern Mexico. It seldom exceeds 125 pounds live weight.

In similar fashion, the records book splits *Odocoileus hemionus* into mule deer and Columbian blacktails. Mule deer are slightly larger and have longer and wider ears. The blacktail, as its name implies, has dark hairs on top of the tail, while the mule deer shows white hairs on top down to the two-inch black tip. Both types show the familiar flag of the deer family, the white-haired underside of the tail.

This non-typical Coues deer scored 124⁴/₈. The record is 151⁴/₈.

Mule deer are distributed throughout the western half of the U.S., into Mexico, and north into the Canadian provinces. The Columbian blacktail is confined to the Pacific coastal area from Alaska to central California. Both mule and blacktail deer travel extensively between their summer and winter ranges, as much as one-hundred miles in the case of some mule deer herds. Blacktails may be considered for records purposes only if taken from geographic areas where no interbreeding occurs. This makes proper location of kill site important, especially where ranges overlap.

Thus, we have four classes of deer for records under the designation "typical." Again, these are the whitetail, Coues, mule, and Columbian blacktail. In "typical" designations, any abnormal antler points are subtracted from the total of normal points to arrive at the final numerical score. This procedure rewards symmetry and penalizes variation from the norm. Most deer taken each year fit readily into the typical category.

What is a normal point? That's not easy to define since a large part of the consideration of normalcy is tied up in the symmetry of the rack. Generally, normal points should be paired to corresponding points of nearly equal length on the opposite beam. Unpaired points and points growing from other than normal locations on the antler are considered abnormal. The basic consideration here is the

240

A non-typical mule deer can be difficult to measure. All normal points are tagged with one color of tape. Abnormal points are tagged with a contrasting color. This fellow scored 319⁴/₈. The record is 355²/₈.

overall effect of symmetry and what the individual point does to this effect. A point is any projection on the antler over one inch long, and longer than wide.

Although most deer taken by hunters have typical antlers, enough variation in point locations occurs in whitetail, Coues, and mule deer to merit "non-typical" categories for these species. In the non-typical categories, trophies are not penalized for a lack of symmetry. Measuring and scoring a non-typical deer is done exactly as for a typical one, except that the sum of the abnormal points is *added* to the total for normal points rather than subtracted.

You might wonder why there is no non-typical designation for Columbian blacktail. Although there is probably the same percentage of non-typical trophies here as in the other deer varieties, the current harvest is too small to show it. Increased harvest figures in the future could well produce the necessary evidence to call for the additional category.

A basic and important consideration to keep in mind is that a trophy may be measured as both typical and non-typical (in the three categories having a non-typical case), with the higher ranking score used to register the trophy.

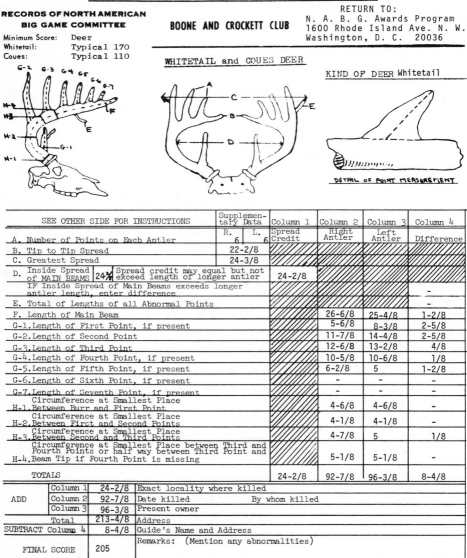

OFFICIAL SCORING SYSTEM FOR NORTH AMERICAN BIG GAME TROPHIES

RECORDS OF NORTH AMERICAN BIG GAME COMMITTEE

BOONE AND CROCKETT CLUB

RETURN TO:
N. A. B. G. Awards Program
1600 Rhode Island Ave. N. W.
Washington, D. C.   20036

Minimum Score: Deer
Whitetail: Typical 170
Coues: Typical 110

WHITETAIL and COUES DEER

KIND OF DEER Whitetail

DETAIL OF POINT MEASUREMENT

SEE OTHER SIDE FOR INSTRUCTIONS	Supplementary Data		Column 1	Column 2	Column 3	Column 4
	R.	L.	Spread Credit	Right Antler	Left Antler	Difference
A. Number of Points on Each Antler	6	6				
B. Tip to Tip Spread	22-2/8					
C. Greatest Spread	24-3/8					
D. Inside Spread of MAIN BEAMS 24-2/8 Spread credit may equal but not exceed length of longer antler			24-2/8			
IF Inside Spread of Main Beams exceeds longer antler length, enter difference						-
E. Total of Lengths of all Abnormal Points						-
F. Length of Main Beam				26-6/8	25-4/8	1-2/8
G-1. Length of First Point, if present				5-6/8	8-3/8	2-5/8
G-2. Length of Second Point				11-7/8	14-4/8	2-5/8
G-3. Length of Third Point				12-6/8	13-2/8	4/8
G-4. Length of Fourth Point, if present				10-5/8	10-6/8	1/8
G-5. Length of Fifth Point, if present				6-2/8	5	1-2/8
G-6. Length of Sixth Point, if present				-	-	-
G-7. Length of Seventh Point, if present				-	-	-
H-1. Circumference at Smallest Place Between Burr and First Point				4-6/8	4-6/8	-
H-2. Circumference at Smallest Place Between First and Second Points				4-1/8	4-1/8	-
H-3. Circumference at Smallest Place Between Second and Third Points				4-7/8	5	1/8
H-4. Circumference at Smallest Place between Third and Fourth Points or half way between Third Point and Beam Tip if Fourth Point is missing				5-1/8	5-1/8	-
TOTALS			24-2/8	92-7/8	96-3/8	8-4/8

ADD	Column 1	24-2/8	Exact locality where killed	
	Column 2	92-7/8	Date killed	By whom killed
	Column 3	96-3/8	Present owner	
	Total	213-4/8	Address	
SUBTRACT Column 4		8-4/8	Guide's Name and Address	
FINAL SCORE		205	Remarks: (Mention any abnormalities)	

This score chart has been filled-in for a hypothetical whitetail in the typical class. The final score of 205 would rank the trophy among the all-time best.

I certify that I have measured the above trophy on_____ 19 _____
at (address)_____ City _____ State _____
and that these measurements and data are, to the best of my knowledge and belief, made in accordance with the instructions given.

Witness: _____ Signature: _____

Boone and Crockett Official Measurer

INSTRUCTIONS

All measurements must be made with a flexible steel tape to the nearest one-eighth of an inch. Wherever it is necessary to change direction of measurement, mark a control point and swing tape at this point. To simplify addition, please enter fractional figures in eighths. Official measurements cannot be taken for at least sixty days after the animal was killed. Please submit photographs of trophy front and sides.

Supplementary Data measurements indicate conformation of the trophy, and none of the figures in Lines A, B and C are to be included in the score. Evaluation of conformation is a matter of personal preference. Excellent, but nontypical Whitetail Deer heads with many points shall be placed and judged in a separate class.

A. Number of Points on each Antler. To be counted a point, a projection must be at least one inch long AND its length must exceed the length of its base. All points are measured from tip of point to nearest edge of beam as illustrated. Beam tip is counted as a point but not measured as a point.

B. Tip to Tip Spread measured between tips of Main Beams.

C. Greatest Spread measured between perpendiculars at right angles to the center line of the skull at widest part whether across main beams or points.

D. Inside Spread of Main Beams measured at right angles to the center line of the skull at widest point between main beams. Enter this measurement again in "Spread Credit" column if it is less than or equal to the length of longer antler.

E. Total of lengths of all Abnormal Points. Abnormal points are generally considered to be those nontypical in shape or location.

F. Length of Main Beam measured from lowest outside edge of burr over outer curve to the most distant point of what is, or appears to be, the main beam. The point of beginning is that point on the burr where the center line along the outer curve of the beam intersects the burr.

G-1-2-3-4-5-6-7. Length of Normal Points. Normal points project from main beam. They are measured from nearest edge of main beam over outer curve to tip. To determine nearest edge (top edge) of beam, lay the tape along the outer curve of the beam so that the top edge of the tape coincides with the top edge of the beam on both sides of the point. Draw line along top edge of tape. This line will be base line from which point is measured.

H-1-2-3-4. Circumferences - If first point is missing, Take H-1 and H-2 at smallest place between burr and second point.

* * * * * * * * * *

TROPHIES OBTAINED ONLY BY FAIR CHASE MAY BE ENTERED
IN ANY BOONE AND CROCKETT CLUB BIG GAME COMPETITION

To make use of the following methods shall be deemed UNFAIR CHASE and unsportsmanlike, and any trophy obtained by use of such means is disqualified from entry in any Boone and Crockett Club big game competition:

    I. Spotting or herding game from the air, followed by landing in its vicinity for pursuit;
    II. Herding or pursuing game with motor-powered vehicles;
    III. Use of electronic communications for attracting, locating or observing game, or guiding the hunter to such game.

* * * * * * * * * *

I certify that the trophy scored on this chart was not taken in UNFAIR CHASE as defined above by the Boone and Crockett Club.

I certify that it was not spotted or herded by guide or hunter from the air followed by landing in its vicinity for pursuit, nor herded or pursued on the ground by motor-powered vehicles.

I further certify that no electronic communications were used to attract, locate, observe, or guide the hunter to such game; and that it was taken in full compliance with the local game laws or regulations of the state, province or territory.

Date _____ Hunter _____

This chart is reproduced by permission of the Boone and Crockett Club.

A sample score chart for typical whitetail and Coues deer is illustrated on the following pages. Score charts for the other deer categories are similar. Measurements recorded on the sample chart include the spread credit, main beam lengths, lengths of all normal points, the total of the lengths of all the abnormal points, and four circumferences of the main beam. Note that the numerical difference between corresponding points in Column 4 (Difference) is eventually subtracted from the total score to arrive at the final score. This is a measure of symmetry because it penalizes unmatched points and unequal lengths of corresponding points. As mentioned, all abnormal point lengths are summed and listed in Column 4. The penalty difference of the inside spread of main beams exceeding the longer antler length is also included in Column 4. An ideal typical whitetail would record all zeros in Column 4 as a reflection of perfect symmetry.

The idea of symmetry is secondary in the non-typical classes. As the name implies, non-typical specimens differ drastically from the idealized condition. Here, the total lengths of all abnormal points are added to the total score. The abnormal point total is shown in the final score so that it is readily apparent that the score is for a non-typical trophy. For example, a basic score of 180 with 26 as the total of abnormal points would be written, 180:26 = 206.

As shown on the sample chart, the first point (G-1) is the brow tine. This is the same in all categories of deer. Note that the brow tines are distinctly separated from the antler burrs of the skull base. Brow tines are never connected to the burr. A common mistake is to call the burr tines (when present) the first or G-1 points, thus misidentifying the whole point sequence. When burr tines do occur, they are abnormal points.

Measurement of points and the main beams is made on the outside of the antler with a flexible steel tape closely applied to the outer curve. To properly follow the curve, you may have to make pencil marks on the antler and then change the position of the tape. Remember to record all measurements in eighths of an inch.

With the rudiments of measurement in mind, it would be well to review several of the more common mistakes to avoid.

1. Mistaking burr tines for brow tines
2. Counting forked or branched points as normal (Point branches are abnormal.)
3. Measuring before the end of the 60-day drying period after death (This period allows for normal, maximum shrinkage of the antlers.)
4. Measuring with a stretchy cloth tape rather than the specified 1/4-inch-wide steel tape

5. Measuring point lengths to the bottom of the main beam rather than to the top edge

6. Counting split brow tines as normal (One tine per antler is normal, and additional branches are abnormal.)

7. Taking circumferences at other than the smallest diameter or at other than right angles to the main beam

8. Converting eighths of an inch incorrectly when adding or subtracting (Keep in mind that there are eight eighths in a whole: 4⁶/₈ subtracted from 10⁵/₈ leaves a remainder of 5⁷/₈.)

Okay. We've been over the basic theory of measuring a deer trophy. Now, with a flexible steel tape and a score chart, you should be able to make a reasonably accurate measurement of your trophy. A list of score charts with costs is available upon request from the Awards Program. Be sure to follow the instructions on the backside of the chart. Should measurement show your deer to be above or very near minimum, a list of official measurers for your area will be sent upon your request. You will need a signed measurement by an official measurer before the trophy can be entered in the Awards Program. Keep in mind that official measurers donate their time and efforts without payment; your appointment to have a trophy measured must be made at their convenience.

Orders for score charts, minimum scores, lists of official measurers, and all correspondence concerning the program and the records book, *North American Big Game,* should be addressed to:

> *North American Big Game Awards Program*
> *c/o Hunting Activities Department*
> *National Rifle Association of America*
> *1600 Rhode Island Ave. N. W.*
> *Washington, D. C. 20036*

As a closing thought, we might ponder the question "Why trophy hunting?" In general, the public today accepts the role of sport hunting in modern game management as a tool to reduce local populations. Trophy hunting, looking for and taking only the best, would seem to be on different ground. But millions of skilled hunters have gone beyond the stage of needing meat to qualify a hunt. Such a hunter broadens his aesthetic appreciation of the out-of-doors by watching the sleek does and youthful bucks but reserves his final stalk for the overage patriarch—the old buck whose scars and battered antlers provide a worthy record for the hunter's psyche. This hunter knows that it is truly the hunt that is important, and the sounds and sights of the hunt will live on in memory long after.

Saving the Trophy

Bud Ulrich

I 've practiced taxidermy for twenty years, and every winter, after
the hunting season is over and the last deer head has been taken from
my shop, I think about some of the sportsmen who came to me to
have their trophies mounted. They dragged bloodied and beaten
carcasses to my doorstep and expected me to work miracles. It
simply can't be done, so I had to turn them away disappointed.

Taxidermy is a creative art, but the taxidermist must receive from
the sportsman something to be creative with. The care the sportsman takes with his game is half the job in mounting a worthwhile
trophy.

Here are three simple rules to follow in helping your taxidermist
to recreate your trophy into a thing of beauty.

This chapter originally appeared in the October 1959 issue of *Outdoor Life* under
the title "Don't Spoil Your Trophy."

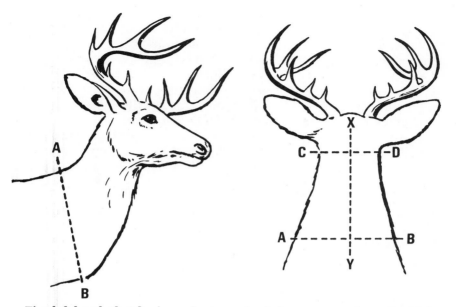

The **left-hand sketch** shows how much of the cape, or skin, should be saved for the taxidermist if the trophy is to be mounted. Cut A-B extends from just forward of the shoulders to the brisket, or breastbone. Saving any less than this will result in a short neck, which gives a trophy an unnatural look. Never cut the trophy's throat. The **right-hand sketch** shows cuts that should be made on the back of the head. After making cut A-B, shown on both sketches, proceed with X-Y, beginning midway between the antlers, and peel skin away to expose neck flesh and ear bases. Then start cut C-D, lightly at first, and deepen as more skin is peeled. When sawing through the neck bone close to the skull, be careful not to mar or puncture the skin.

Keep your trophy clean. Before it has dried out, wash blood from the fur with cold water. Blood that dries usually will stain fur and feathers permanently. Plug shot holes with moss and clay, or cloth, to keep blood and body fluids from doing their damaging work.

Keep your trophy fresh. Spoiling, which really means rotting, makes hair and feathers fall out and scales pop. For this reason, I won't handle a trophy that's gone very far beyond the eating state. A spoiling trophy can be mounted, but chances are it will last for only a couple of years. The best and easiest way to keep a trophy fresh is to freeze it. Freezing doesn't hurt fur, feathers, or scales.

Whether or not you freeze a game head, sever the head from the body as shown in the sketches. Most important thing is to allow enough cape for mounting purposes, for nothing looks worse than a short-necked mount. If you can't freeze your trophy, follow the steps shown in the sketches for fleshing out the head. Be sure to sever the neck bone carefully so as not to puncture the skin, and pour about five pounds of salt into the neck cavity, rubbing it into the base of the neck and into the ears, eyes, and mouth.

Little can be done for birds except to freeze them or get them to a taxidermist immediately. Their plumage is so fragile and susceptible to staining that only an expert should handle them.

If you can't freeze a trophy fish you'd like to have mounted, wrap it in burlap and keep it moist. Don't wrap the fish in newspaper, for the mucus on its body will stick to the paper and cause scales to pull off when the fish is handled. Avoid gutting the fish if you can; just get it to a taxidermist as quickly as possible. If the fish must be gutted to avoid undue spoilage, open the side that isn't going to show, pack the cavity with salt, and keep the fish moist and cool. Let the gills alone.

Don't mutilate your trophy. Never make a cut in a place which will be exposed in the final mounting. Don't cut off hair, break off feathers, or rough up scales. Don't slit a deer's throat, wring a pheasant's neck, or beat a muskie over the head. If you want the meat from your trophy, it's often a good idea, whenever possible, to let the taxidermist do the butchering.

If you'll abide by these simple rules your trophy will have a good chance to look lifelike when it's mounted. The rules add up to little more than your helping the taxidermist give you your money's worth by creating a trophy that will afford you many years of enjoyment.

Butchering the Easy Way

Robert S. Davidson

Photos by Phil Skiff

T he first time I ate George LaValley's venison at his home in
Idaho, I was astonished. The meat had none of the usual strong,
gamy flavor. George laughed at my surprise and told me how he
prepares big game for the freezer. He told me that he had learned the
method about fifteen years before from a hunting partner.

One of his basic principles is that the gamy flavor is concentrated
in the muscle sheaths or membranes. He removes every bit of that
material along with all the fat. The membranes and the fat seem to
deteriorate after a short time in the freezer, and can spoil the flavor
of the meat. His method also eliminates all of the bone, and that
saves freezer space.

Only a few tools are needed: a sharp butcher knife with a slightly
flexible blade, a carpenter's crosscut saw, and a meat grinder.

Most butchers split big game (and beef) by sawing the backbone
in half lengthwise along its entire extent. Then they remove roasts,

This chapter originally appeared in the November 1973 issue of *Outdoor Life* under
the title "Easy Way to Butcher Your Deer."

chops, and steaks by cutting each side across the grain of the meat. George takes off the major muscles of the animal lengthwise along their natural divisions and later cuts them into smaller pieces. His method avoids the lengthwise and much crosscut sawing of bone thereafter.

George prefers to freeze the major muscles whole and then cut them into smaller portions after they are thawed. The big pieces dry out less in the freezer than the small portions would. Properly wrapped in a double layer of freezer paper closed with freezer tape, packages of venison will keep for months. Of course, the deer or elk must be in good condition when you begin butchering, and that requires field dressing and cooling the animal promptly after the kill.

2. With a sharp knife, cut through the loin to the backbone, and then angle the knife through the flank along the forward curve of the haunch. (See the taped line.) Saw through the split backbone.

1. Remove all loose hair from the skinned deer. Then separate the hindquarters with a crosscut handsaw by splitting the backbone lengthwise. Stop the cut at the forward end of the hips.

3. Lift the haunch away from the carcass. This way, you avoid sawing the backbone in half along its entire length. To remove the other haunch, turn the deer over and repeat.

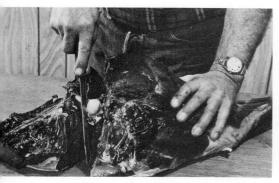

4. Place the inside of the haunch down. Cut the rump away from the thigh. This should separate the ball-and-socket joint. Turn the haunch over to complete the cut.

5. Strip the outside membranes off each piece of meat after it is cut free. All fat, dried crust, and bloodshot meat around the wounds also should be cut or scraped off.

6. With the inside of the leg up, use the knife to free the edge of the thinnest muscle. Then pull it off with your fingers.

7. Separate the major muscles of the thigh by pulling them apart with your fingers. This is easier than cutting.

9. With the knife, cut the tendons attaching each muscle to the bone and lift the meat free. Cut out the roots of the tendons and peel the membranes and fat off each major thigh muscle.

8. Muscles part easily, exposing interior membranes on each side of the separations. Peel the membranes off with the knife.

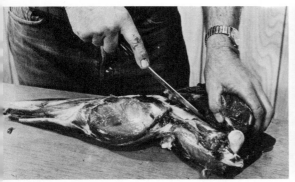

10. Since the interior muscle is firmly attached to the thighbone above the joint, use the knife to free the muscle. Cutting close to the bone minimizes the scraps.

11. Hold the meat flat on the table with one hand and bend the thighbone away from the meat. The joint will flex easily. Then cut it free at the tendon.

12. Cut the calf muscle away from the bone. Meat below the joint is stringy and is best used as deerburger or stew chunks. The rump is often used as a roast.

13. Strip the remaining membranes and fat from all cuts of meat. You can pull off some muscle sheaths with your fingers. You'll need a knife for others.

14. Here the major cuts from the hind leg are ready for cooking or freezing. It is best to freeze these pieces whole. Cut steaks after thawing the meat.

15. Place the remains of the carcass on the table as shown. Make two long cuts along the backstrap on one side.

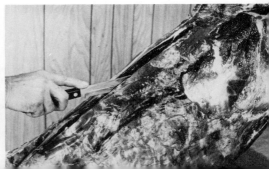

16. Free the forward end with a crossing cut just at the rear of the shoulder. Try to cut to the bone on the first pass with all cuts. Going over a cut usually creates scraps.

17. Lift the end of the backstrap with one hand, and cut it away from the ribs and backbone. The backstrap on a young deer is tender and makes good steaks.

18. Strip the membranes from the backstrap and other long pieces by pulling membranes against the knife, laid flat on the table. Repeat the whole process.

20. Separate the shank from the upper leg by sawing. Use a knife to cut the shank meat from the bone. Peel off the outside membrane. Then chunk and trim before grinding.

19. Turn the remaining carcass upside down on the table, and cut the foreleg off parallel to the body and close to the ribs. The knife should cut through easily.

21. Bone-out the upper leg carefully. Then peel the membranes off. This results in a flat piece that can be rolled up and tied with butcher's twine for pot roast.

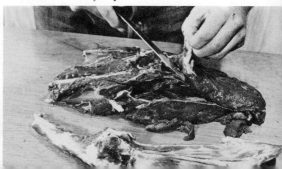

22. *Flank steak, which is the boneless muscle to the rear of the ribs, should be cut away on both sides. If the flank steak is tender and from a young deer, broil it.*

23. *Remember to cut out the tender muscles on each side of the spine inside the rib cage and along the loin. This tastes like backstrap and can be fried or broiled.*

24. *If the esophagus and windpipe weren't removed during field-dressing, cut them out. Make one long cut on the underside of the throat as shown.*

25. *Cut off the neck with a knife and saw. Trim off the membrane and fat, and remove the bone. The neck can be used as rolled pot roast or stew meat.*

26. *Cut off outside meat on the rib cage with a shaving motion of the knife. This meat can be cut into chunks or ground. For bone-in chops, saw off the ribs.*

27. Meat between the ribs makes tasty deerburger or soup stock. For ground meat, replace deer fat with fat from a beef loin. Deer fat spoils easily and sticks to the teeth.

28. Here the rib cage is ready to be discarded. This method of butchering eliminates most of the bone and saves freezer space.

Cooking Venison

Edna Wagner Piersol

Nothing riles me more than a raised eyebrow from a friend when I mention that I am preparing venison for my family's dinner. I immediately make a mental note to invite that uppity female to dinner very soon. I won't tell her until after she has begged for the recipe ("What exotic spices did you add to that beef to give it that fabulous taste?") that she has been eating venison with no exotic spices at all.

Maybe some women have a "thing" about venison because of the way it is killed. Well, given one visit to a stockyard slaughterhouse, these same women would never eat another filet mignon. A deer, on the other hand, is usually shot out in the fresh air while it is roaming free. We'd all be vegetarians if we worried about how all our meat is killed.

I'm the wife of a veteran hunter who has brought home his

This chapter originally appeared in the November 1969 issue of *Outdoor Life* under the title "How to Prepare Venison."

Venison pot roast like this will bring a stampede to the table.

seventh deer in as many seasons shot with bow and arrow, not to
mention the many he has felled with a rifle. So I make use of at least
seventy-five pounds of deer meat each year. I wouldn't give or throw
it away for anything. That's at least $75 saved in the food budget.
The kings of England had the right idea about the value of venison.
They had a death penalty for poaching.

Venison was accepted table fare in my home in Economy Township in western Pennsylvania when I was a little girl, but no one in
our family developed any very special recipes. They just adapted
beef recipes to venison. After I married my hunter, I did the same
thing. It's still a good plan, but I soon discovered that many of our
friends didn't enjoy the meat so much as we did. Some of the wives
wouldn't even cook the meat.

"If deer meat was good enough for kings," I thought, "surely I can
make it good enough for my friends." So I began experimenting
with gourmet venison dinners — with the following results.

There are three simple rules for preparing venison that make it a
gourmet treat:

1. *Always serve it piping hot onto heated plates, and keep the
seconds hot while they're waiting to be eaten.* This rule is the most
important. If venison becomes even slightly cooled, the fat turns
hard the way lamb tallow does and some of the taste of the meat
is lost.

2. *Keep it moist.* Venison always becomes a little dry while
roasting. Some of this dryness can be avoided by adding butter or
margarine in place of most of the fat, which should be trimmed off.
In the case of steaks and chops, *never overcook!* Serve them rare if
possible. If you must have them well-done, stop cooking the second

the juices stop flowing. Always spoon a little gravy over the meat on the serving platter, or pour on the pan juices.

3. *Always cook venison in something tart, such as wine, lemon juice, or sour cream.* This doesn't make the meat sour. It just enhances the flavor and also preserves the juices and tenderizes the meat.

Pot roast is the queen of recipes for the meat of kings, and this recipe has met the highest test.

Use a sheet of aluminum foil large enough to wrap the roast completely. If you must use two sheets, make sure the bottom one comes well up around the roast so that it catches all the juices. Place a 3- or 4-pound roast on the foil, sprinkle on top of it a package of dry onion-soup mix, and dot it with butter. Sprinkle ¼ cup wine over all (our family likes Cherry Kijafa wine, but a good red Burgundy will do).

Place the foil-wrapped roast in a pan, and cover the pan. Bake for 3 hours at 300°. By the way, if you want to be out all afternoon and still have dinner ready on time, you can roast at 200° for 6 hours.

Forty-five minutes before dinner, start boiling a large kettle of water. Cook a package of noodles as directed on their container. Just before dinner, drain them and stir 2 or 3 tablespoons of butter into them.

When the roasting time is up, the meat will be tender and falling apart and very brown. Place it on a hot platter. Pour juices from the foil into the pan. Rinse foil with ¼ cup wine so that all juices from the foil are caught, and pour into pan. Place foil over meat to keep it warm.

Add 1½ cups of water, and one small can of mushrooms plus their juice, to the juices in the pan. Now in a small bowl mix 3 tablespoons cornstarch with a little cold water. Heat juices to boil, and stir in cornstarch mixture. Keep stirring and boiling until gravy becomes thickened and shiny and smooth.

At this point slice the roast. Strangely, venison rarely is pretty enough to serve as a whole roast. It looks really good only when carved. Then the fine, close texture of the meat shows up and the surprising quantity in a small roast becomes evident.

After arranging the slices on the hot platter, spoon a little gravy over the meat (remember, never let venison get dry or cool). Put the rest of the gravy into a hot dish, to be served on the hot buttered noodles (into which you have also stirred 1 tablespoon of poppy seeds). Serve your favorite vegetable and salad.

Venison steaks have terrific possibilities. They can be dotted with butter and sprinkled with garlic powder, then broiled till done and placed on a hot platter. The juices from the pan are then rinsed with ¼ to ½ cup of Cherry Kijafa or Burgundy wine, and all liquid is poured over steaks on platter. Serve with baked potatoes, tossed salad, and more red Burgundy.

If you really want to get fancy with steaks, try Venison Stroganoff. Men, this might be a good way for you to impress your wife with your cooking.

For Stroganoff for four people, start by cutting about 2 pounds of steak into 1-inch cubes. Brown the cubes in 2 tablespoons butter. Stir in a package of dry onion-soup mix. Add 4 cups water, 2 tablespoons chopped parsley, ¼ teaspoon garlic powder, dash of pepper, and ¼ teaspoon oregano. Bring to a boil, turn heat very low, and cook gently about 1½ hours. When meat is tender, add ½ cup sour cream (dairy type). Do this by first taking a little hot sauce from the meat and stirring it into the sour cream, then stirring all back into the meat mixture. Blend ¼ cup cornstarch into a little cold water till smooth, and stir into meat mixture. Stir and cook until sauce thickens. Serve over cooked rice or noodles and along with a salad and vegetable. Fortunately there is enough here for second helpings.

When your deer comes from the butcher, there will be a few packages of chops. They look like small pork chops but are a dark, rich red. Fry them in butter over a fairly hot fire until barely done — rare, preferably. Either rinse the skillet with ½ cup wine and pour over chops, or make gravy using ½ cup wine (Burgundy or Cherry Kijafa) and 1½ cups water in drippings, thickening the gravy with flour mixed into cold water.

Notice that I said "when your deer comes from the butcher." That's where it should come from. Don't try to cut up the animal yourself. Take it to a meat packer, and let him cut and wrap it in serving packages ready for the freezer. Maybe he will even freeze it for you before you pick it up. Here in our section of Pennsylvania we pay about $15 for this service, and it is really worth it.

The heart and liver will have been removed in the woods when the hunter dressed the deer. My husband takes a plastic bag along to hold these parts. Don't take them to the butcher. They should come home with the hunter for a celebration dinner! Here's how to prepare it.

Wash liver in cold water, and cut into ⅜-inch-thick slices. Remove as much gristle and skin as possible. Refrigerate or freeze it for a few hours until ready to cook.

Meanwhile, soak heart in salt water overnight or all day. Drain heart for a few minutes, and rub the inside with salt. Stuff heart, using mixture of bread cubes, chopped celery, chopped onion, and ground sage moistened with a little warm milk, with some melted butter added. Amounts of these ingredients depend on size of heart. Close up with skewers as tightly as possible. Put heart in roasting pan, and pour over it ½ cup water and 3 table-spoons brandy. Bake in covered pan at 350° for 1½ to 2 hours or until tender. Add more water if necessary, and baste now and then. Bake potatoes in the oven at the same time. Prepare your favorite salad and vegetables for the dinner.

About 45 minutes before dinnertime, melt ¼ cup butter in a skillet. Dip slices of liver into juice of ½ lemon. If deer is an older one, sprinkle meat tenderizer on liver. Slice 2 large onions into skillet, and saute for about 10 minutes or until tender but not brown. Put onion slices into a warmed dish, and quickly saute liver slices until barely done. Serve rare if possible. When liver is done, heap onions on top and carry all to table. Serve hot from the skillet.

Remove heart from oven, and slice onto heated platter. Pour juices over it.

This liver-and-heart dinner really does justice to the occasion. Try toasting your success in the hunt with a good dry sherry just before dinner.

Now for the ground meat, of which there is always a lot. When your deer is being cut up tell the butcher to put everything that he feels will not be tender into ground meat. There is no use trying to tenderize a lesser cut when there are so many delectable things to do with ground venison.

Last year my husband's deer was a fat young buck—just the kind for the pot. When cut up the buck turned into: 6 roasts (3 pounds each), 4 packages chops (8 per package), 14 large steaks (wrapped 2 to a package for our family of 4), 2 packages stew meat, and 11 packages (1½ pounds each) of ground venison, in addition to liver and heart.

Do not let the butcher add ground pork to your ground deer meat. Many people suggest this, to add fat and tenderize the meat, but I think that pork only adds to the problems. If I want sausage, I want plain sausage. If I want venison, I want unadulterated venison.

Everything that pork is supposed to do for venison can be done by adding lemon juice (for tenderizing and flavor) and butter or margarine (for fat, which is also what makes meat tender).

The crowning glory of ground deer meat is Meat Loaf. The follow-ing recipe serves 4 to 6 people.

Mix into 1½ pounds ground deer meat the juice of ½ lemon, 2 tablespoons soft margarine, 1 cup cracker crumbs, 1 teaspoon salt, ¼ teaspoon pepper, 1 small finely chopped onion, 1 beaten egg, ¼ cup milk, 1 small celery stick and a few tender celery leaves (very finely chopped or ground). If you have a blender, put everything from the salt to the celery into it and puree. When using a blender you don't need to beat the egg first and you just cut the onion into quarters and the celery into 2-inch sections.

When all ingredients are mixed together well, shape them into a loaf. Place loaf in a buttered pan. Pour ½ cup water into pan. Pour an 8-ounce can of tomato sauce or a can of undiluted tomato soup over loaf. Bake, uncovered, for 1½ hours in a 325° oven, adding water from time to time if meat begins getting dry. Don't pour the water over the loaf, for that will spoil the tomato coating. Just add water to the pan about ½ cup at a time and only if needed. Slip some baking potatoes into the oven just ahead of the meat loaf, and at serving time pour the pan juices either over the meat-loaf slices or onto the potatoes.

If you go on experimenting with ground venison, I'm willing to bet that before long you will come up with a specialty that will make you famous in your circle. Just be sure to add the lemon juice to your meat (if the recipe doesn't call for anything else that is sour) before you add any other ingredient and mix well. And don't forget to add 2 tablespoons of butter or margarine for each 1½ pounds of ground meat.

Last, but by no means least, among my recipes is Venison Stew. Daniel Boone himself could not have thought up a better stew, I'm sure. And you won't have so much trouble cooking it as he would have had.

In the bottom of a 6-quart pressure cooker brown 1½ pounds stew meat or cubed roast in 2 tablespoons margarine. Add 1 cup chopped onion, ¼ teaspoon garlic powder, 1 teaspoon salt, ¼ teaspoon pepper, 1 tablespoon sugar, 1 tablespoon vinegar, ⅛ teaspoon nutmeg, ½ cup water, 4 potatoes (peeled and quartered), 4 carrots (cut into pieces).

At this point it is best to follow the directions for your own pressure cooker; those for mine say to cook stew for 20 minutes at 15 pounds pressure and then to cool the cooker at once by placing it in cold water.

If you don't have a pressure cooker, you can use a heavy, covered saucepan or covered skillet, but then you must cook the stew for about 2 hours after the vegetables are added. A pressure cooker assures more-tender meat.

How about it? Have you been missing out on the fun of eating what our pilgrim fathers considered the food of kings way back before beef became a respectable meat? If so, cook up one of these delectable meals. Let the aroma drift out to your family. And then watch out for the stampede!

Making Old-fashioned Jerky

Walter Haussamen

Photos by Walter Haussamen Jr.

If you happen to know an outdoorsman who isn't excited about dehydrated foods, it may be that he's an old-timer who knows the secret of preparing old-fashioned jerky.

Though it won't stand up to freeze-dried meat in a flavor test, jerky has many advantages. It is easy to prepare and store, and is inexpensive. It never spoils, and is an ideal food when traveling light. And it is just plain good eating.

Almost any meat except pork can be jerked. The fact the meat may have been frozen for several months won't make any difference. Just thaw it out and follow the instructions given here. Any cut may be used, but the round is preferred because of flavor, texture, and it is easy to cut long strips from.

Select lean round steaks about half an inch thick and carefully trim away all fat. This is an important step because the fat does not dry well; this gives the jerky a rancid taste. Slice the meat into long strips about half to three quarters of an inch wide, making the cuts

This chapter originally appeared in the February 1964 issue of *Outdoor Life* under the title "How to Make Old-Fashioned Jerky."

across the grain. Sprinkle the strips liberally with salt and pepper. Instead of black pepper, we sometimes use red chili powder, which offers a delicious variation. Then, with a meat hammer or the rim of a heavy cup, pound the meat well. Turn the strips over and repeat the process. Next, dip each strip into very hot water which has been generously salted and peppered. Dip long enough to slightly blanch the meat; about ten or fifteen seconds should be enough.

You are now ready to hang the meat to dry. Use S-shaped wires. Cover the meat with cheesecloth, if you desire. If the weather is warm and dry, and there is plenty of sunshine, the meat should dry in four or five days. Keep a piece of plastic sheeting to cover meat if it rains.

The meat dries a rich black color and is hard in texture, but it chews easily. If you like venison you're sure to like jerky. Store the meat in coffee cans, and tape shut to exclude moisture. Kept in this manner, it will never spoil and you will always have a ready supply of trail food.

On trips we carry our jerky in plastic bags. Several pieces and some water gives a real pickup to a tired back-packer. For a light meal, we sometimes boil a double handful in enough water to cover it, and we thicken the water with a little flour. This makes a good meat-and-gravy dish. Jerky also goes well in dehydrated stews that have no meat.

Drying meat is one of the oldest and most practical ways of preserving it. The fact that it turns out to be fine eating is just a bonus.

First, cut away all fat from the venison. Completely fat-free meat will occasion the best results.

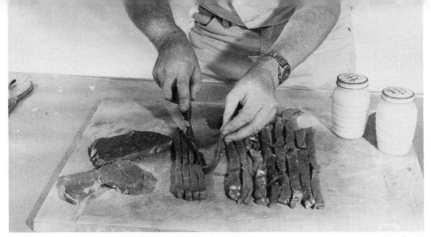

Cut each of the strips about an inch wide. To ensure against stringy, hard-to-chew venison at the dinner table, cut across the grain.

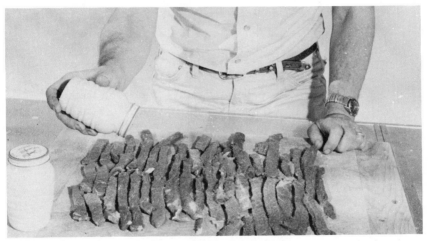

Lay all strips on a board, and then sprinkle them with salt and pepper. Ample doses spell better flavor in the end.

Next, pound the strips with a meat hammer or a heavy cup. Then turn the strips over and repeat the process. (Continued on next page.)

Dip each strip for ten or fifteen seconds in a pan of hot water that has been salted and peppered also.

Using small S-shaped wires, hang the meat strips to dry in the sun. Allow about five days drying time—or until the strips become brittle.

The Authors

The following biographical sketches are arranged in the order each author initially appears in the book.

Erwin A. Bauer, a noted writer-photographer, now coedits (with wife Peggy) the rec-vehicle column in *Outdoor Life* and regularly contributes other articles as well. Prior to becoming a full-time freelancer in 1955, Bauer served as an Ohio game warden. He also edited the *Ohio Conservation Bulletin* and an outdoor newspaper column. Bauer has published ten outdoor books and more than 1,300 magazine articles, most of them illustrated with his own photos. He has over 120 cover photos to his credit. He makes Jackson, Wyoming, his home base.

Jack O'Connor began hunting in Arizona as soon as he was old enough to cock an air rifle. He received an M.A. in journalism from the University of Missouri in 1927, had a novel published in 1930, and became professor of journalism at the University of Arizona in 1934—a post which he held for eleven years. O'Connor began writing exclusively for *Outdoor Life* in 1936. As the magazine's shooting editor from 1941 through 1972, he hunted world-wide. O'Connor has fifteen books to his credit. Of these two are novels; one is an account of O'Connor's youth; and the others address guns, hunting, animals and kindred subjects. O'Connor resides with wife Eleanor in Lewiston, Idaho.

Archibald Rutledge, author of "A Plantation Hunt to Remember" and known to *Outdoor Life* readers for more than fifty years, died at Hampton Plantation, near McClellanville, South Carolina, on September 16, 1973. He was ninety years old. In the latest of his *Outdoor Life* articles, Rutledge noted that in seventy-eight years of hunting he had bagged 299 bucks and 339 gobblers. He was an authority on bird dogs and on rattlesnakes, with which he had many close-call encounters. Rutledge, poet laureate of South Carolina since 1934, authored more than eighty books.

Ben East has been a field editor with *Outdoor Life* since 1946. Prior to joining the magazine's staff, East was for twenty years the outdoor editor of Booth Newspapers of Michigan. Born in 1898, East began hunting as soon as he was old enough to hold a gun. He has hunted in all parts of North America and is recognized as a leading authority on hunting, conservation and game management. He has received eight major awards for his work in conservation. During the 1950's, East gave up to fifty lectures a year, showing his own films to audiences nationwide. He has authored a novel and five outdoor books. He lives in Holly, Michigan.

Norm Nelson Jr., author of the chapters on trail-watching and drives, is resources information manager for Wyerhaeuser Company in Tacoma, Washington. He was editor of *Minnesota* from 1948 to 1965. Nelson's articles on hunting and firearms have appeared in many major magazines. During the 1950's Nelson assisted in planning several Minnesota wetlands restoration projects. Memberships include various local sportsmen's clubs, Ducks Unlimited, the NRA, and the Outdoor Writers Association. Nelson's eldest son Peter is also an outdoor writer.

Byron W. Dalrymple, author of two chapters in this volume, became a full-time writer in the early 1940's. Dalrymple has produced over 2,500 magazine articles, a dozen books, and more than thirty television films. He has hunted in virtually every part of the United States and Canada for all popular game birds and animals. He is also a professional photographer and shoots the photos for his articles, books and films. At his ranch in Kerrville, Texas, Dalrymple also tests fishing and hunting equipment for leading manufacturers.

William Curtis, author of "Hunting the California Blacktail," is a freelance writer who lives near Arbuckle in north-central California. Formerly a U.S. Fish and Wildlife employee, Curtis has hunted, fished, and studied wildlife throughout the West for thirty years. He is a member of the NRA and is a state advisor for the Deer Sportsman Association. He has written for every major outdoor publication.

Ken Crandall, author of "Day of Stealth and Grappling," is executive director of the Okanogan County Agricultural Stabilization and Conservation Committee in Washington state. He is a long-time member of the NRA and the Okanogan Wildlife Council. Four of Crandall's articles have appeared in *Outdoor Life*, which he has read avidly since age nine. Special interests include flying, fishing, outdoor photography, and hunting trophy-class deer. In recent years, Crandall has studied coyote habitats and movement patterns, especially as they relate to predations on winter deer herds.

Charles Elliott, who authored the Mississippi and Wyoming hunt chapters here, has retired as the Southeastern field editor of *Outdoor Life* — a post he took up in 1950 — but still contributes regularly to the magazine. In his long career in the outdoor field, Elliott has also served as director of the Georgia Fish and Game Commission, forester with the National Park Service, president of the Southeastern Association of Game and Fish Commissions, and outdoor editor for the *Atlanta Constitution*. Elliott has eleven books on outdoor subjects to his credit. He resides near Covington, Georgia.

Horace R. Hinkley, author of "Maine's Biggest Buck," lives with wife Olive in Embden, Maine. He retired as a road supervisor from the State Highway Commission in 1962. For some years he was a Maine Guide and a lumber trader. He is a past member of the Canoe City Fish and Game Association of Old Town and ranks hunting, fishing, and gardening as his chief hobbies. As of this printing, the 355-pound buck (dressed weight) featured in Hinkley's story is recognized by Maine's Department of Inland Fisheries and Game as the heaviest on record.

Ray Beck, author of "Finding Wounded Deer," owns three farms near Knox, Pennsylvania, open to public hunting. He laments that "it's harder to get a permit to improve land for wildlife than to destroy it." A retired machinist, Beck runs a trapline each winter and remains active in outdoor associations. Beck is a charter member of the Pennsylvania Trappers Association and has served as its director. His writing has appeared in farm and garden as well as in fiction and outdoor magazines. After trapping, hunting and fishing, Beck rates writing and locating bee trees as chief hobbies.

Clyde Ormond's "Field-dressing and Care" is one of hundreds of pieces Ormond has done for national publications since he resigned from a high school principal's post in 1938 to write full-time. Traveling from Rigby, Idaho, where he lives on land his father once homesteaded, Ormond has hunted and fished over most of North America and has guided others into wilderness regions. From these trips he has returned with many trophies and with action photographs and dramatic stories. Ormond has patented several inventions and has authored eight books on outdoor subjects.

Wm. H. Nesbitt, author of "Measuring and Scoring Trophies," is manager of the Hunting Activities Department of the National Rifle Association (NRA), headquartered in Washington. He is also coordinator of the North American Big Game Awards Program, now a cooperative effort of the NRA and the Boone and Crockett Club. He has taught and conducted wildlife research at Clemson University and at Southern Illinois University, and has worked extensively for the National Wildlife Refuge System. Nesbitt's writing has appeared primarily in scientific journals.

Robert S. Davidson, author of "Butchering the Easy Way," is a retired military pilot—turned freelance photojournalist—who specializes in outdoor, adventure, flying, and prospecting stories. He lives in Bellingham, Washington. Davidson is still an active flier with over 10,000 hours in 133 types of aircraft. Other special interests include fly-tying and handloading. He spent his fifty-sixth birthday on a mountain at 8,000 feet slogging through 30-foot-deep snow to stake gold claims. If he had more interests, says Davidson, he'd have to be six people.

Edna Wagner Piersol, author of "Cooking Venison," is an artist and writer. She is president of the Pittsburgh Watercolor Society and a member of Associated Artists of Pittsburgh and of the National

League of Penwomen. Mrs. Piersol's wildlife art is well-known around Pennsylvania. Her most noted study—of a bald eagle—is kept in a vault with an Andrew Wyeth and a Winslow Homer and other notables at the Butler Institute of American Art in Youngstown, Ohio. In addition to varied freelance writing, she has authored a series of four craft books. Her hobbies include cooking, boating, and "watching with pride as my sons grow into outdoorsmen."

Walter Haussamen, author of "Making Old-fashioned Jerky," is a life insurance agent in Albuquerque, New Mexico. He also does freelance writing and photography. As a photojournalist, he is published in numerous national and Southwestern magazines. Club memberships include Trout Unlimited, the New Mexico Wildlife Conservation Association, and the Albuquerque Wildlife Federation. Haussamen is an active volunteer with conservation and outdoor groups. His hobbies include fly-tying and fly fishing. And with wife Frances, he enjoys hiking and backpacking.

Index